X Y

EUROPEAN PERSPECTIVES

EUROPEAN PERSPECTIVES

A Series in Social Thought and Cultural Criticism
Lawrence D. Kritzman, Editor

European Perspectives presents English translations of books by
leading European thinkers. With both classic and
outstanding contemporary works, the series aims to shape the major
intellectual controversies of our day and to facilitate the
tasks of historical understanding.

XY

ON MASCULINE IDENTITY

Elisabeth Badinter

Translated by Lydia Davis

COLUMBIA UNIVERSITY PRESS

NEW YORK

Columbia University Press
wishes to express its
appreciation of assistance
given by the government of France
through Le Ministère
de la Culture
in the preparation of
this translation.
Columbia University Press
New York Chichester, West Sussex
XY: De l'identité masculine
© 1992 by Editions Odile Jacob
Translation © 1995
by Columbia University Press
All rights reserved

Library of Congress
Cataloging-in-Publication Data
Badinter, Elisabeth.
[X Y, de l'identité masculine. English]
XY, on masculine identity/Elisabeth Badinter.
    p. cm..
Includes bibliographical references and index.
ISBN 0-231-08434-X
1. Men—Psychology. 2. Masculinity (Psychology) 3. Identity
(Psychology) 4. Sex role. I. Title.
HQ 1090.B33 1995
155.3′32—dc20   94–41016
                                    CIP

Casebound editions of
Columbia University Press books
are printed on
permanent and durable
acid-free paper.
Printed in the
United States of America
c
10 9 8 7 6 5 4 3 2 1

For my son Benjamin,
who gave me the gift of this book's title

CONTENTS

CONTENTS

PREFACE TO THE AMERICAN EDITION

Three years have elapsed between the writing of this book and its publication in the United States. In this case, I'm pleased about the delay because it allows me to correct my discussion of genetics by taking into account a recent fundamental discovery that nullifies a certain hypothesis I had shared with some biologists.

The situation may be outlined as follows: In 1984 Jean Weissenbach and Marc Fellous of the Pasteur Institute, seeking the causes of "sex inversions," hypothesized the existence of a gene of masculinity. In July 1990 the Englishman Peter Goodfellow located this gene on the Y chromosome and called it SRY. In November of the same year the Frenchman Philippe Berta showed that it is indeed SRY that permits the development of masculine sex organs (by inhibiting the canals of Müller); he demonstrated also that if this gene mutates, masculinity becomes impossible. In such a case the sex organs of an XY child are feminized to a greater or lesser degree. Because at the time there had been no discovery of a parallel gene of "feminization" in the female embryo, we concluded—a little too quickly—that development into a male implied a labor of differentiation spared female embryos.

The discovery in August 1994 by the Italian-American team of Giovanna Camerino of the DSS gene of feminization (most probably responsible for the inhibition of the development of testicles) put an end to the hypothesis of the masculine genetic exception. One can no longer say that the basic embryonic program is oriented toward producing females. On the other hand, the parallelism revealed between the development of the male embryo and that of the female embryo strikingly confirms the thesis of human bisexuality to which I have made constant reference in order to account for the resemblance between the sexes and, de facto, their equality.[1]

But if the two sexes are so alike, why in the world would one devote a book to the difficulties of achieving masculine identity? Because an essential difference remains between male and female that no genetic discovery can eliminate: the male fetus, unlike the female fetus, develops in the womb of the opposite sex. Its place of origin is female. The fetus, and later the newborn suckling his mother, lives in symbiosis with a person of the other sex, with whom he will have to break his ties in a radical way in order to become a man. My book attempts to explain the problems that arise from this situation.

Another reason I am glad to have the three-year lag between the French and American publication is that during this interval other foreign editions have appeared, notably in most of the European countries. Because of this, I have traveled widely in Europe and have thus had numerous occasions to observe, listen, and learn. Contrary to what some Americans believe, Europe is not a single entity. Masculine identity in Europe depends primarily on the state of relations between men and women; it is much more conditioned by the degree of maternal control and the religious traditions of each country than by any supposed divide between a Protestant and egalitarian northern Europe and a Catholic and patriarchal Mediterranean Europe.

During my travels I often thought about the United States, with which I am acquainted to a certain degree from having lived there when I was a student, and whose immense intellectual production has always fed my thinking. Because the United States and Europe are two continents with the same Judeo-

1. See Elisabeth Badinter, *Mother Love: Myth and Reality* (New York: Macmillan, 1981) and *The Unopposite Sex: Motherhood in Modern History* (Harper & Row, 1989).

Christian origin, both industrialized and democratic, our ambitions and our ideals are similar and permit comparisons and borrowings. I took full advantage of this in my book. Since I could find no real exposition of the problems of masculine identity in France, Germany, or Italy, for instance, I turned to the works of the English and the Americans—which have been proliferating on this subject since the 1980s. At the same time it was important to keep in mind that the American male does not have the same relationship with women as does the French, Spanish, or Swedish male, and that there is no true equivalent of the "mama's boy" in Europe. Still, the total absence of any "men's studies" in France and in most European countries is not without significance.

Aristotle was correct in stressing that thought is always inspired by the need to resolve a problem. The more urgent and painful the problem, the sooner reflection begins, both publicly and polemically. If the United States is taking the lead in debating masculine identity, this is because the issue is more pressing there than it is in France. This is not to say that European women have no complaints to make about men or that the latter are not suffering the effects of formidable change that is taking place almost despite them. I am convinced, however, that the conflicts are, on the whole, less exacerbated in Europe than in America. Nevertheless, even if this is not the forum in which to conduct a comparative study of the American male and the male of the different European countries, I cannot help pointing out certain resemblances between the discourse of German and American feminists, as well as between the behaviors of the males of these two countries, by contrast to the situation in France. Here, the importance we have always given to seduction, as well as our relationship to our bodies, our almost total ignorance of puritanism, our representation of the role of the mother, and perhaps our social and political traditions, has resulted in the absence of any war between the sexes in France such as exists in Germany or in America. Certain of my American feminist friends who know France well think that we are evolving too slowly, while others say that we are evolving more gently, but perhaps more surely. The debate is open, and it is hard for me to make a decision about it.

Whatever the differences between our countries, our goal is the same: to achieve equality between the sexes and warmer relations between men and women. I sincerely hope that this book will, in its own modest way, contribute to this end.

Elisabeth Badinter

PREFACE

XY is the chromosome formula for a man.[1] Providing there are no accidents along the way, these two chromosomes will set in motion all the mechanisms of sexual differentiation that cause a man to be a man instead of a woman. Definitively identified in 1956,[2] the sexual chromosomes define the male genetic sex and symbolize the origin of a man's history. But although xy is certainly the primary condition of the male human being, it does not suffice to characterize him. There are physically normal xy people who disregard their male identity and others who acquire that identity despite genetic anomalies. The development of masculinity involves psychological, social, and cultural factors that have nothing to do with genetics but play a role that is no less determinative and may be more so. From the xy chromosome to the sense of male identity, which marks the culmination of a man's development, the road is long and rife with pitfalls. A little longer and a little more difficult than the road to female identity, contrary to what was believed for so long.

Not long ago, woman was still the dark continent of humanity, whereas no one dreamed of questioning man. Masculinity appeared to be self-evident: luminous, natural, and the opposite of femininity. The past three decades have shattered these age-old certainties. Because women have undertaken to redefine themselves, they have forced men to do the same. XY is still the constant, but male identity is no longer what it was—proof that it was never written in stone.

Questioning one's most deep-seated convictions is always long and painful. We have only to read the novels written by men in the last few years to convince ourselves of that. But this work of deconstruction never occurs by chance. It takes place when the dominant model has revealed its limitations. Such is the case with the traditional model of masculinity, out of phase with the evolution of women and the source of a veritable mutilation of which men are beginning to become aware. The old conception of man is dying, giving rise to a new, different conception of man being born before our eyes and whose shape we can as yet barely see. This book is situated in the period between the two, when nothing is very clear any longer and one must sometimes make up for the absence of knowledge by using one's imagination. The female author talking about men is fully aware of her limitations.

ACKNOWLEDGMENTS

This book is the result of six seminars held at the Ecole Poly-technique. Its beginnings were difficult. I sometimes felt I was guilty of questioning masculinity's traditional criteria without being able to propose new ones. I would like to thank my students for their patience, especially those who helped me gain further insight into the subject.

In addition to the complexity of the subject, I was confronted with a problem of documentation that I would not have been able to solve without the friendly help of many people. My gratitude goes first to Mariette Job, whose encyclopedic knowledge pointed me toward certain novels that illuminated the masculine condition. I am grateful to Claude Durand for the same reason. In addition, I would like to thank those friends in the United States whom I pestered to send me valuable English and American documentation. They include Arno Mayer, Marilyn Yalom, Muriel Jolivet, Tom Bishop, and in particular Nicolas Rachline, to whom I have turned for help so often. Last, I am profoundly indebted to Michèle Bleustein-Blanchet, Merete Gerlach-Nielsen, and Pierre Barillet, who read and reread the manuscript with tireless patience and gave me valuable advice. To all of them, and to Guy Taïeb, Michèle Réservat, and Isabelle Simon, my fervent thanks.

X Y

What Is a Man?

What is the essence of the human male? Spontaneously, we give credence to the eternal masculine without concerning ourselves very much about Rousseau's remark: "The male is male only at certain moments, the female is female all her life, or at least all her youth."[1] Little inclined to ask ourselves questions about an inconstant reality, we wish to believe in a universal and permanent principle of masculinity (maleness) that defies time, space, and the ages of life. We find this principle in the natural order that exhibits the difference between the sexes. As soon as the child is born, the sex is assigned. And if any doubt remains, genetics will make up for anatomy's deficiency.

However, these constantly recalled pieces of evidence do not manage to put an end to all questioning. Our everyday language betrays our doubts, even our worry, in speaking of masculinity as an objective and a duty. Being a man is expressed more readily in the imperative than in the indicative. The order so often heard—"Be a man"—implies that it does not go without saying and that manliness may not be as natural as one would like to think. At the very least, the exhortation signifies that the possession of a y chromosome or male sex organs is not enough to define the human male. Being a man implies a labor, an effort that does not seem to be demanded of a woman. It is rare to hear the words "Be a woman" as a call to order, whereas the exhortation to the little boy, the male adolescent, or even the male adult is common in most societies.[2] Without being fully aware of it, we behave as though femininity were natural, therefore unavoidable, whereas masculinity must be acquired, and at a high price. The man himself and those who surround him are so unsure of his sexual identity that proofs of his manliness are required. "Prove you're a man" is the constant challenge confronting a male person. Yet the display of proofs requires trials that a woman does not have to undergo. The day of her first period comes naturally, without effort if not without pain, and now the little girl is declared a woman forever. There is nothing like this, nowadays, for a little boy belonging to Western civilization. Not that the age-old need to prove his manhood has disappeared. But there has never been such a great contradiction between the need to display what he is and the absence of certain and definitive proofs.

The confusion reaches its height in the phrase *a real man*, so commonly used in ordinary speech to designate a virile man. Does it imply that certain human beings only appear to be men, are false men? Some people complain today about the absence of femininity among women, but the latter rarely express doubts about their identity. On the other hand, it is quite often men themselves who distinguish among themselves by adding the quality label *real*. And it is they, too, who secretly question themselves to find out if they deserve that endorsement.

Duty, proofs, trials—these words indicate that there is a real task to be accomplished to become a man. Manhood is not bestowed at the outset; it must be constructed, or let us say "manufactured." A man is therefore a sort of *artifact*, and as such he always runs the risk of being found defective. There may be a defect in the manufacture, a breakdown in the machinery of virility, in short, a failed man. The enterprise is so uncertain that success deserves to be noticed. As Pierre Bourdieu says: "To praise a man, one has only to say of him, 'he's a man.'"[3] This is the formula for the *illusio* of manhood. Bourdieu goes on to stress the pathetic effort to be equal to the idea of a man and the suffering caused by not being equal to it.

To this suffering another is added. Today, the guidelines have disappeared and man at the end of the twentieth century no longer knows how to define himself. To the question "What is a man?" Günter Grass answers: "A place of wretched suffering . . . a plaything of fortune . . . a theater of anguish and despair."[4] This remark was made, in fact, in the 1970s, a time when men were beginning to question themselves about their identity. Taking their example from the feminists, who spoke up loud and clear against the traditional roles assigned to them, some said they wanted to liberate themselves from the constraints of the *illusio* of manhood. It was the theoreticians in the humanities in the United States who initiated this questioning of the ideal male role, a source of alienation for men and of misunderstandings with women. The first scientific works on masculinity,[5] which appeared in the 1970s, have the passionate tone that accompanies any denunciation. There is a sort of furious joy to be had in challenging the norm and revealing all the contradictions with which it has burdened the male human. But pleasure in denunciation and in the destruction of the model was followed, in the 1980s, by an intensely anguished period of uncertainty. More than ever, man was a problem to solve and not a given. The Australian Lynne Segal[6] and the American Catharine Stimpson,[7] two shrewd experts in the subject of men, noted the same finding: "Man has become a real mystery." What constituted his essence, his manliness, also saw its unity challenged. Class, age, race, and sexual orientation became factors of masculine differentiation, and the English and Americans now spoke of masculinity only in the plural.

If French researchers have remained circumspect regarding these questions,[8] many novelists, on the other hand, are acutely sensitive to them and express their distress in simple words. Philippe Djian is one. In *Lent dehors*, which tells a man's story from childhood to maturity, the hero declares: "For many years I imagined that woman was the absolute mystery. Now I, a man, am the one I have trouble understanding. . . . I think I can understand what a woman is good for, but a man—just what is he good for? What does it mean to say, I am a man?" For Djian, man is the dark continent. He is finding his way without a compass.[9]

Such talk was unthinkable even thirty years ago. Men knew so well what they were that no man dreamed of questioning himself about his male identity. What has happened to bring us to this point? Many accuse the feminism of the 1960s of having "destabilized the well-ordered oppositions and thrown into confusion the stable guidelines."[10] In truth, Western feminism is less to blame for having confused the guidelines than for having shown that the emperor was naked. By putting an end to the distinction between roles and systematically gaining a foothold in all the domains once reserved for men,[11] women have eliminated the universal male characteristic: the superiority of men over women. Since the birth of the patriarchy, man has always defined himself as a privileged human being, endowed with something *more*, unknown to women. He believes he has *more* strength, is *more* intelligent, *more* courageous, *more* responsible, *more* creative, or *more* rational. And this *more* justifies his hierarchical relationship to women, or at least to his own woman. Bourdieu points out that "to be a man is immediately to be established in a position that implies certain powers."[12] He concludes quite rightly that "the *illusio* of manhood is the basis of the *libido dominandi*." But we can also invert the remark and say that the *libido dominandi* is the basis of manhood, even if it be illusory. And even if "the dominant being is dominated by his own domination," this latter quality is the ultimate criterion of male identity. With its gradual disappearance, we confront an empty spot where a definition used to be. Cause enough for bewilderment on the part of all those young men who are trying to navigate a safe passage between two dangers: not being masculine enough and being too masculine.

The urgency of the need to rethink masculinity was perceived by the Americans more quickly than others. They were the ones who instigated "men's studies," which flourish as much in England as in the United States, as well as in Australia and, to a lesser degree, in Scandinavia.[13] If these new questionings come essentially from the English-speaking countries, it is probably because these societies have always been obsessed with virility, as is evident in their history, art, and culture. The men in these countries have had to confront women different from those confronted by Frenchmen. They have had to come face to face with a feminism far more radical and more powerful, whose historical and psychological causes remain to be discovered. American feminists often reproach Frenchwomen for their collusion with men. It is true that beyond the polemics and the criticisms that have pitted men and women against each other, the Frenchwoman has never completely broken off her dialogue with her accomplice. The solidarity between the sexes has survived everything, including the periods of sharpest questioning. Virility is less contested on this side of the Atlantic; the men here are not as violent, they have less fear of women, and vice versa. As a result, the problem of masculinity is less acute in France than elsewhere, though that does not stop it from plaguing all of us, men and women.

When Men Were Men

The French language, not only in the past but also today, employs the same word to designate a male and a human being. In order to make ourselves understood, we must often specify that we are writing it with a capital letter or a lowercase. In doing this, as he has ever since Greek antiquity, the Frenchman only confirms the tendency to compare the two significations. Man (*vir*) sees himself as universal (*homo*). He considers himself to be the most perfect representative of humanity—its criterion of reference. Western thought is divided between two apparently different approaches to the duality of the sexes.[14] Either the model of resemblance is emphasized or that of opposition is preferred. But in both cases, what is asserted is the man's superiority, which justifies his domination over the woman.

According to Thomas Laqueur, until the beginning of the eighteenth century our thinking was dominated by the *one-sex model*. After this, though the model reappeared here and there (notably in Freud), the model of the two opposed sexes predominated in the nineteenth and twentieth centuries until quite recently.

What does the *one-sex model* mean, and how can we still talk about the duality of the sexes? For a very long time, it was a commonplace to think that women had the same genital organs as men, with the sole difference that theirs were on the inside of their bodies instead of on the outside.[15] In the middle of the eighteenth century, Diderot was still able to write: "A woman has all the parts of a man, and the only difference that exists is that between a purse hanging outside, and an inside-out purse contained within."[16] For close to two thousand years, language has ratified this point of view. The ovary, which at the beginning of the nineteenth century was to be the metonymy for a woman, did not have its own name before the end of the seventeenth century.[17]

As Thomas Laqueur points out, before the Enlightenment one's sex or one's body was understood to be an epiphenomenon, whereas one's type, which we consider to be a cultural category, was the first and primordial given. To be a man or a woman was above all a rank, a place in society, a cultural role, and not one form of being biologically opposed to the other. But this model of sexual oneness engenders a qualitative dualism of which man is the luminous pole. That the differences between the sexes are of degree and not of nature does not prevent the hierarchy from remaining. Woman is measured by the yardstick of masculine perfection. Being the opposite of man, she is less perfect.

By the end of the eighteenth century, thinkers with different outlooks insisted upon the radical distinction between the sexes, which they based on the new discoveries in biology. From difference of degree, they shifted to difference of nature. Thus, in 1803, Jacques-Louis Moreau disputed forcefully against Galen. Not only were the sexes different, they were different in every aspect of body and soul, thus physically and morally.[18] This was a triumph of radical dimorphism. In an inversion of the preceding model, the body now appeared as real and its cultural significations as epiphenomena. Biology became the epistemological foundation for social prescriptions. The uterus and the ovaries which defined the woman consecrated her maternal function and made of her a creature in every way the opposite of her companion.[19] The heterogeneity of the sexes compelled different destinies and different rights. Men and women evolved in two distinct worlds and scarcely encountered each other—except during reproduction. Strong in her generative power, the woman reigned as mistress of her home, presided over the education of her children, and incontestably embodied the moral law that determined good manners. To the man was allotted the rest of the world. He was in charge of production, creation, and politics, and so the public sphere was his natural element.

Some chose to see in this dichotomy of the masculine and feminine worlds the realization of an ideal: the complementarity of the sexes, guarantor of harmony between man and woman. In current terms, one would speak of "equality within difference." The advocates of this model, in the large majority in the nineteenth century, argued that one could no longer talk about inequality between the sexes since they were not comparable. Since difference precluded term-by-term comparison, man lost his status as referent. This handsome ideological discourse, so reassuring to men since it prohibited women from joining them on their own territory, masks a reality that is less democratic. Despite his disclaimers, man remains the criterion by which woman is measured. He is *the One*, readable, transparent, familiar; woman is *the Other*, alien and incomprehensible.[20] In the end, whatever model may be envisaged for thinking of the sexes—resemblance or difference—man still presents himself as the most perfect example of humanity, the absolute by which woman is situated.

The new element introduced by men's studies, following after women's studies, resides precisely in the avowed desire to break with this age-old schema. As Harry Brod writes: "Traditional scholarship's treatment of generic man as the human norm in fact systematically excludes from consideration what is unique to men *qua* men."[21] Sociologist Michael Kimmel has highlighted the traditional "invisibility" of the masculine species which has contributed to its identification with the human. Too often, he says, "we treat men as if they had no gender, as if only their public personae were of interest to us . . . as if their interior experience of gender was of no significance."[22] Kimmel says he became aware of this when he witnessed a discussion between a white woman and a black woman on the question of whether sexual resemblance was more important than racial differences. The white woman asserted that the fact that they were women gave them a solidarity beyond their difference in color. But the black woman did not agree.

> "When you wake up in the morning and look in the mirror, what do you see?" she asked.
> "I see a woman," replied the white woman.
> "That's precisely the issue," replied the black woman. "I see a black woman. For me, race is visible every day, because it is how I am not privileged in this culture. Race is invisible to you, which is why our alliance will always seem somewhat false to me."[23]

Kimmel realized, then, that when he looked at himself in the mirror in the morning, he saw "a human being: universally generalizable. The generic person." What was hidden—namely, that he had both a gender and a race—had become strikingly *visible*. The sociological explanation for such blindness

8

resides, says Kimmel, in the fact that our privileges are very often invisible to us.

For most of us today, a man is no longer Man. The male is an aspect of humanity, and masculinity is a relational concept since one defines it only with respect to femininity. The English and Americans insist on this idea, that there is no virility[24] as such: "Masculinity and femininity are relational constructs. . . . Although 'male' and 'female' may have some universal characteristics . . . one cannot understand the social construction of either masculinity or femininity without reference to the other."[25] Far from being conceived of as an absolute, masculinity, the quality of a man, is at once relative and reactive. So that when femininity changes—generally when women try to redefine their identity—masculinity is destabilized.

The history of patriarchal societies proves that it is always women who begin to question things, not men. This is easily enough explained by men's special status in this type of society. But the great crises in masculinity do not only involve power. Psychology, as we shall see, supplies an explanation essential to understanding men. Contrary to the ideology of the patriarchy, it is not men who are the primary referents of humanity, but women. It is in relation to women and in opposition to women that men define themselves. At least, this has been true until now. But men may be assured that the present crisis is not without precedent.

Earlier Crises in Masculinity

Those earlier crises, whose repercussions we are still feeling today, share certain traits. They occurred in countries with refined societies where women enjoyed greater freedom than elsewhere. They expressed a need for a change in the dominant values and followed ideological, economic, or social upheavals. They had repercussions in the organization of the family, of work, or of both. But what distinguished the two preceding

9

crises from the one we are experiencing today was their socially limited nature. The first, in the seventeenth and eighteenth
centuries, involved only the dominant classes—the aristocracy
and the urban bourgeoisie.[26] Both more extensive and more
profound, the second period of masculine malaise, at the close
of the nineteenth century, was to find successive outlets in the
two great world wars.

THE CRISIS OF MASCULINITY IN THE SEVENTEENTH AND
EIGHTEENTH CENTURIES IN FRANCE AND ENGLAND

It was the French *précieuses* (ladies "refined" in sentiment and
language) who were responsible for the first questioning of the
role of men and masculine identity. The harsh violence of the
gibes directed against them were equaled only by the anxiety
they aroused with their own demands, which were judged to be
"mad." French preciosity reached its height between 1650 and
1660, born in response to the crudeness of the men of Henri
IV's court and the men of the Fronde (1648–1653). This was the
first expression of feminism in France and in its neighbor
across the Channel. True, these two countries were known for
being the most liberal in Europe where women were concerned. Unlike their Mediterranean sisters, French women and
English women had complete freedom to come and go as they
pleased and to have dealings with the world. Both, if they
belonged to the dominant classes, benefited from an advantage
exceptional to the time, that of not being burdened with the
duties of motherhood.[27]

The *précieuse* was an emancipated woman who proposed
feminist solutions to her desire for freedom and completely
inverted traditional social values. She militated for a new
ideal of womanhood which took into account the possibility
of her social ascension and her right to dignity. She demanded
the right to education and attacked the linchpin of phallocrat-
ic society: marriage. Against the authoritarianism of father
and husband, the *précieuses* were resolutely hostile to
arranged marriage and maternity.[28] They advocated trial mar-

riage and the severance of such marriage after the birth of an heir, who would be entrusted to his father's care. Unwilling to give up freedom of any kind, on the one hand, or love, on the other, they advocated a tender and platonic sentiment. "I want," said Mademoiselle de Scudéry, "a lover without a husband, and I want a lover who, contenting himself with the possession of my heart, will love me until death." In other words, a situation that would be the reverse of the customary bonds between men and women, who married each other without love. In the eyes of the *précieuses*, love meant first and foremost the love of a man for a woman, rather than the opposite. By demanding of a man in love a limitless submission which bordered on masochism, they reversed the dominant model of masculinity, that of the brutal and demanding man, or the vulgar husband who believed everything was permitted to him.

Only a few men, the *précieux*, accepted the new rules. Their number was negligible but their influence was insidious. They adopted a feminine and refined style—long wigs, extravagant feathers, band collars, chin tufts, perfume, rouge—which was copied. Men who aspired to be distinguished now made it a point of honor to appear civilized, courteous, and delicate. They refrained from showing their jealousy and playing the domestic tyrant. Imperceptibly, feminine values were to progress in "good society," to the point of appearing dominant in the following century. We now know that the *précieuses* were not a ridiculous microcosm. The resistance and the mockery they encountered were the very signs of their influence.

Strangely enough, the debate over masculine identity was more explicit in England than in France, as though already the obsession with virility was a more pressing question than it was for the French. True, English feminists had different demands from the French. In addition to their freedom, they demanded total sexual equality—in other words, the right to orgasm[29] and the right not to be abandoned when they became pregnant. Kimmel, who has studied the history of masculinity in England, believes that Great Britain experienced a true crisis in masculinity between 1688 and 1714 (the period of the English Restoration), and notes efforts to renegotiate the roles of men and women in marriage, the family, and sexuality.[30]

The signification of masculinity was the subject of debates. Women were not content with asserting the equality of desires and rights; they also said they wanted men to be gentler, more feminine. To which the pamphleteers responded that the thing was as good as done and that the inversion of roles had begun. The portrait of the "feminized" man who adopted behavior similar to that of women aroused a fear of homosexuality that we do not see in France among those who so despised the *précieux*. The "new man" of the English Restoration looks like a pervert, as vain, petty, and bewitching as a woman. Women were pitied for having been abandoned by men,[31] and the development of rampant refinement was attacked. In the city, a center for vice of all kinds, women were less closely watched than in the country and were the object of all sorts of temptations. And the English read this as the pernicious influence of French fashion on English customs. Certain pamphlets very soon saw a connection between the feminization of masculinity and betrayal, between traditional masculinity and patriotism.[32]

It is true that the feminization of customs and of men did not excite the same reactions in France. The Enlightenment represents a first rupture in the history of virility. It was the most feminist period of France's history before the present day. On the one hand, manly values were fading, or at least were no longer attracting a great deal of attention. War no longer had the importance and the status it once had. Hunting had become an amusement. Young noblemen spent more time in salons or in ladies' boudoirs than training in garrisons. On the other hand, feminine values were becoming influential in the world of the aristocracy and the haute bourgeoisie. Delicacy of speech and attitudes was gaining more importance than the traditional characteristics of virility. It is safe to say that in the

dominant classes, unisexism was winning out over the oppositional dualism that usually characterized the patriarchy.

The French Revolution of 1789 put an end to this development. When women publicly demanded their rights as citizens, the Convention with a single vote refused them this.[33]
The deputies, who had not known the delights of the Ancien
Régime, reaffirmed forcefully the separation of the sexes and
radical differentialism. Proximity, similitude, and confrontation horrified them and provoked authoritarian, even threatening, reactions. Outside the home, women were considered dangerous to the public order. They were called upon not to min-
gle with men, and they were forbidden even the smallest
position outside those of housewife and mother. Reinforced by
the Napoleonic Code and ratified by the ideology of the nineteenth century, oppositional dualism endured for close to a
hundred years, until the appearance of a new crisis of masculinity even more pervasive than the preceding one.

THE CRISIS OF MASCULINITY AT THE TURN OF THE NINETEENTH AND TWENTIETH CENTURIES

This crisis involved Europe as well as the United States. These
countries all experienced similar economic and social upheavals due to the new demands of industrialization and democracy. Men's lives changed, and feminist demands were heard
again; masculine anxiety was aroused. But depending on which
country one looks at, whether France, Austria, or the United
States, this anxiety took markedly different forms in keeping
with the different history and culture of each country.

Annelise Maugue was the first to study the identity crisis
tormenting Frenchmen a century ago.[34] In the space of a few
generations, from 1871 to 1914, a new type of woman appeared
who threatened the imposed sexual frontiers. Thanks to the
republican ideology, education for girls had become a reality.
The university had made room for them. They had become pro-
fessors, doctors, lawyers, and journalists. They expected to
earn their living outside the home, demanded their rights as

full citizens, and were already saying: "Equal pay for equal work." Most men reacted with hostility to the women's emancipation movement—not only men in the traditional Catholic sector or those in the labor movement, which feared the competition of female labor, but also republicans as dedicated as Anatole France and Emile Zola: all these men "had the feeling they were witnessing not just a simple evolution, but a veritable mutation."[35] In all segments of society, they felt their identities threatened by this new creature who wanted to do what they did, be like them—so threatened that they wondered if they were not going to be obliged to "perform feminine tasks, in short, supreme horror, be women"!

The anxiety of the men when faced with the resemblance between the sexes had no equivalent among women. Men sensed that women were "a fatal trap"[36] which would lead to the dissolution of their specificity. As Maugue correctly notes, the men were afraid. Barbey d'Aurevilly, their spokesman, prophesied gloomily: "One day, Marie d'Agoult will be in the Académie des Sciences Morales et Politiques, George Sand in the Académie Française, Rosa Bonheur in the Académie des Beaux Arts, and we men will be the ones making the jam and the pickles."[37] The same uneasiness was visible in Albert Cim and Octave Mirbeau, who were afraid not only of making jam but of "nursing the brats."[38] Man felt threatened in his powers, his identity, and his daily life. His fears were in fact baseless, since the women of the time did not reject either the family, or motherhood, or the devotion that goes along with them. But "nothing helped, neither the behavior nor the (reassuring) speeches of the women soothed masculine anxiety and an incredible dialogue of the deaf developed between the two sexes until 1914."[39]

Men's anxiety confronting the "New Eve" was fueled by other sources too. As more and more men worked in factories at mechanical and repetitive tasks, or in administrative positions with monotonous daily routines, they no longer found that their work made the most of their traditional qualities.

Strength, initiative, and imagination were no longer necessary for earning their living. Maurice Barrès mocked the civil servants, those "half-males" who aspired only to security, like women, and he contrasted them to men of earlier times who lived "with rifle in hand," in "a virile hand-to-hand combat with nature."[40] The crisis of masculinity was at its height. It was World War I, unfortunately, that would temporarily put an end to men's anxiety. Reentering their traditional roles as warriors, the poor young recruits would leave for the front with a flower in their rifle, as though they rejoiced in the opportunity given them to be men at last—real men . . . However, the crisis of masculine identity was less acute in France than in other countries. Even the most misogynist French writers never committed the excesses of writers like Schopenhauer, Nietzsche, or Otto Weininger.

Jacques Le Rider emphasizes the fact that in Vienna, at the beginning of the twentieth century, the crisis of masculinity was taking place in a context of generalized crisis.[41] In addition to the disintegration of the Hapsburg empire and the self-reflexiveness of the Viennese intellectuals, there was also the explosion of the individual consciousness into component parts:[42] one now spoke of *id*, *ego*, and *superego*. The male Austrian citizen experienced "a permanent identity crisis,"[43] magnificently illustrated by *The Man Without Qualities*,[44] whose male protagonist rejects hasty identifications and puts himself in a position of waiting—an extremely uncomfortable situation since, in a period of "deconstruction," attainments are questioned again, reference points dissolve, and one no longer knows how to define oneself.

It was not so much the dissolution of the traditional family unit in proletarian circles that worried the Viennese intellectual as the emancipation (very gradual) of the middle-class woman. Independent, active, and demanding, she was at the farthest extreme from the gentle and passive woman they dreamed of. As Robert Musil notes, not without irony, "What does 'longing for the mother's breast' mean in a civilization in which woman has been radically masculinized and femininity no longer in any way represents a refuge for man?"[45] The emancipated woman, whom one suspects of being feminist, is "a man in a female body, a virago"[46]—one monstrosity that engenders another: the feminized man, the decadent par excellence. Weininger, an obsessional misogynist, makes this sad statement: "There are periods . . . in which more masculine women and more feminine men are born. This is precisely what is happening today. . . . The increase in both 'dandyism' and homosexuality over the past few years can only be explained by a general feminization."[47] For his part, Karl Kraus denounces the modern cult of the androgyne, that is, of fuzziness, confusion, and "intermediate forms."[48] The concept of bisexuality, introduced by Freud and taken up by Weininger, forces both men and women to recognize their irreducible share of femininity. This is disturbing to a large part of the masculine intelligentsia, who realize that virility is never definitively acquired.

If one of the dominant themes of German literature is certainly fear in the face of woman, there is no doubt that Weininger attained a paroxysm of misogyny. He is aware that the femininity that constantly threatens the virile ideal is lodged in himself. But he was not the only one to cry out in horror at woman and to manifest an uneasiness as to his identity. The end of the nineteenth century, Le Rider remarks, was characterized by a recrudescence of works defamatory toward the female sex.[49] Not only philosophers[50] but also psychologists and biologists, as well as historians and anthropologists, evinced an extremely violent antifeminism. All set out to demonstrate, with success, woman's ontological inferiority.[51] Woman is close to the animals and the Negroes;[52] she is impelled by her primitive instincts—jealousy, vanity, cruelty. But since she has a childish soul and since nature has endowed her with the maternal instinct (which she shares, in any case, with all female mammals), her only true vocation is motherhood. As a consequence, all women who call themselves emancipated are bad mothers—extreme neurotics in degenerate bodies.

The remedies proposed varied widely. Most men declared, like Nietzsche and Weininger, that they favored a return to the healthy polarity of the sexual roles. For men to regain their virility, it was first necessary for women to return to their natural place. Only the reestablishment of the sexual boundaries would free men from their anxiety over their identity. Then the massive repression of their original bisexuality would do the rest. This was the meaning of Alfred Adler's famous phrase "virile protestation." At the opposite extreme, certain marginal figures[53] called upon men to rid themselves of an artificial, oppressive virility, and to rediscover as quickly as they could their primary femininity. These voices were barely heard. As for the women who expressed themselves publicly on the subject, they had no influence on the men's anxiety. In vain did Lou Andreas-Salomé enact "unilateral disarmament" and "wear the ravishing mask of the Eternal Feminine, to reassure men's perpetual doubts about their masculinity":[54] it did not help. Even less effective was the insightful discourse of the Viennese feminist Rosa Mayreder, who argued for a synthesis of the masculine and the feminine for individuals freed of their sexual characteristics.[55] This argument for a true androgyny could only increase men's fears.

Stronger than in France, the anxiety of Austrian and German men over their identity was not unrelated to the rise of Nazism and more generally to European fascism. Hitler's accession to power resonated unconsciously with the promise that manliness would be restored. Klaus Theweleit has shown very clearly that the hypervirility of the heroes of Nazism concealed a fragile ego and considerable sexual problems.[56] Such was not exactly the case with the French. If France was not spared the virus of fascism, its history was different from that of Italy or Germany, and Frenchmen were "haunted by rejection and secession."[57] Unlike the English-speaking countries, which opted for the separation of the sexes and a hypervirile masculine ideal, they chose negotiation and behavior that was apparently less macho.

The United States, in turn, was experiencing a widespread crisis of masculinity. Certain American historians date its appearance from the 1880s,[58] others from the 1890s.[59] All note the clearly expressed fear at that time of the "Europeanization" of America, synonymous with the feminization of the culture and thus of the American man. Now the latter tended at that time to pride himself on having avoided the spinelessness of European civilization.[60] Up to the beginning of the twentieth century, American virility had had numerous occasions for manifesting itself. Geographical expansion—the conquest of the West, the "pacification" of local populations and urban development—combined with a rapid economic growth and the development of the industrial infrastructure encouraged a virile optimism concerning rises in the social scale.[61] Before the Civil War (1861–1865), 88 percent of men were farmers, craftsmen, or independent tradesmen. By 1910, less than a third of American men still lived in this way.[62] Industrialization had very quickly imposed its constraints—mechanical, routine, and compartmentalized tasks—and workers were dispossessed of all control over the organization and the results of their work.

As in Europe, this economic change was accompanied by an upheaval of family life and values that overstimulated men's anxiety. Obliged to work farther and farther from home, they had to leave the upbringing of their children entirely in the hands of their wives. Fatherhood became a Sunday institution,[63] and the new form of virility was identified with the success symbolized by money. The crisis of masculinity burst out into the open when women, as in Europe, claimed the right to fulfill roles other than those of mother and housewife. More noisily than in Europe,[64] they expressed their weariness with these tasks and rebelled against conventions. Frustrated, depressed, they took the offensive by creating women's clubs, by sending their daughters to college,[65] and by working outside the home. The American woman, who chose to be independent, demanded the power to remain single or to marry for love as she wished. If she married, she had fewer children and had no intention of giving up her freedom by submitting to her husband's authority. She demanded the right to divorce, greater participation in public life, and, of course, the right to vote. As in Europe, men demonstrated their hostility to this ideal of womanhood. They attacked the egotism of the New Woman, who was degrading her sex, abandoning her home, and endangering her family. She was dubbed the "third sex" or a "mannish lesbian."[66] The increase in the number of divorces—seven thousand in 1860, fifty-six thousand in 1900, and one hundred thousand in 1914—and the decline in the birthrate[67] provoked thousands of articles on the dissolution of the family. In 1903 Theodore Roosevelt announced that the American race was committing suicide. Even Democratic supporters of women's suffrage felt these feminists were going too far. In fact, the more loudly and clearly women expressed their demands, the more men's vulnerability was exposed: with his masculine role uncertain, with his panicky fear of feminization,[68] the average American man of the 1900s no longer knew how to be a man worthy of the name.

Unlike many Europeans, American men did not blame women as much as they did the feminization of the culture.[69] Parents were alerted against the danger of coddling their boys, and lectures were delivered to mothers who sapped their sons' virility—in other words, their vitality. Separation of the sexes was advocated, along with that of occupations. Football—a particularly violent sport—and baseball became very popular, probably because, as a journalist noted in 1909, "[The football field] is the only place where masculine supremacy is incontestable."[70] The Boy Scouts was founded with the same end in mind, its objectives being to "redeem boys from the rot of urban civilization" and to turn male children into manly men.[71] Theodore Roosevelt, President of the United States from 1901 to 1909, was a hero to American men because he incarnated tra-

ditional manly values. By calling upon American men to rediscover their love of hard work and courage, by extolling the old
distinction between the sexual roles, and by insisting on American women's sacred mission of motherhood, the president
applied a soothing balm to male wounds. Nevertheless, men's
psychic crisis was not thereby resolved. On the eve of World
War I, they still had no answer to the dilemmas of modern virility. In the form of fantasy sublimations, new heroes appeared in
literature. The Wild West was revived, and the emblematic figure of the cowboy invented, the epitome of the manly man:
"Violent but honorable, fighting evil with a phallic six-shooter,
defending women without being domesticated by them."[72] The
middle classes virtually threw themselves on these new books,
as they did on the series of *Tarzan* books by Edgar Rice Bur-
roughs, which began appearing in 1912, and more than thirty-
six million copies were sold! Despite all this, men did not manage to calm their fears. It was America's entrance into the war
in 1917 that served as an outlet and a "test of manliness" for
many of them. Convinced they were fighting for a good cause,
men could at the same time unleash their contained violence
and prove to themselves, finally, that they were real men.[73]

At last, the crisis of masculinity that was rampant at the
beginning of the century was temporarily resolved by the war.
Desperate ills call for desperate remedies! But the war only
masked the essential problems that no one had been able to
resolve and that are reappearing today in all their intensity.
Ever since the cataclysm of World War II, when hypervirility
displayed itself in all its pathology, war has no longer seemed
the remedy for the deficiencies of masculinity. We are now
once again confronted with the question of man without any
means of evading it in sight. A real polemic, set in motion by
the different trends of feminism, has begun within the sciences
that study "man." The stakes are high for everyone, since,
depending on the point of view that prevails, all of pedagogy,
the relations between the sexes, and therefore politics as well,
will be affected by it.

The Current Polemics: Is Man Overdetermined or Undetermined?

Is masculinity a biological given or an ideological construction? The question pits the proponents of biological determinism against the culturalists, who today call themselves "constructivists" in the United States. Appearances to the contrary, this is not merely the familiar debate of the old against the modern, the traditionalists versus the liberals; it is also one that bitterly opposes two contemporary feminist trends, each of which claims a different basis for equality between the sexes—one the absolute dualism of the two genders, the other the resemblance of the sexes and the infinity of human genders.

THE DIFFERENTIALISTS; OR, THE ETERNAL MASCULINE

The term *differentialists* should be understood to designate all those who believe that the irreducible difference between the sexes is the ultima ratio of their respective destinies and their mutual relations. In the end, it is biology that defines the essences of masculinity and femininity. This point of view was given new life with the founding of sociobiology in 1975 by Edward O. Wilson.[74]

The latter, a specialist in the study of insect behavior, is convinced, as are his disciples, that all human behavior can be explained in terms of genetic heredity and neuronal functioning. The latest heirs of Darwin, they think that our behavior is dictated by evolution and the need to adapt.

The theories of sociobiology, distinctly more popular in English-speaking countries than in France,[75] posit in principle that sex is "an antisocial force." The two sexes are not made to get along but to reproduce. Their opposing strategies concerning reproduction are what ultimately explain their natures. As Jeffrey Weeks humorously puts it, "These differences begin and end, it sometimes seems, with the evolutionary characteristics of the ova and testes."[76] From the number of ova and spermatozoids, one can extrapolate the presumed innate characteristics of men and women. The latter are declared to be by nature timid, difficult, finicky; whereas men are fickle and will sleep with anyone.[77] Another postulate deduces from the number of available eggs in the male and female that competition is inevitable among males for the possession of the limited reproductive potential of a woman! Because of this competition, it is the strongest and most aggressive males who win out. And it is this hereditary masculine aggressivity that furnishes the biological basis for male domination over females, for the hierarchies and the competitiveness among men, and for war.[78] David Barash even undertook to prove that rape was natural to men.[79] Taking his examples from the animal world (bees, earthworms, ducks, and so on) and the plant world (he mentions the rape of female flowers by male flowers!), he argues for the innocence of the rapist, and even sings his praises. He suggests firmly that rapists are only the involuntary instruments of a blind genetic instinct. Rape obeys an unconscious need to reproduce and is therefore, biologically speaking, both advantageous and unavoidable.

One would laugh at these theories if they did not still have a following in England and America. Let us therefore move on from the sociobiologists, who look to the insects and the Stone Age for their authority, and turn to the differentialist feminists, who also refer to biological determinism for their definitions of women and men. Even though their objectives may be at opposite extremes, these two trends of thought share the same belief in the existence of an immutable sexual essence. If the first group sees this as the basis for the eternal superiority of men, the second maintains, on the contrary, that this radical difference is the most direct path to equality between the sexes.

Feminist differentialism came into being at the end of the 1970s as a result of disappointments caused by universalist feminism, largely dominant since the time of Simone de Beauvoir, who advocated a politics of coeducation based on the philosophy of resemblance. It was faulted for not having resolved the most important problems. Noting that women had not gained much from this regime except double workdays, the least remunerative jobs, and sexual pressure from men stronger than ever, certain women concluded that they had taken the wrong path. If equality was only a lure, they said, this was because differences were neither acknowledged nor taken into account. In order to be men's equals, women had had to deny their female essence and turn themselves into pale imitations of their masters. In losing their identity, they experienced the worst of alienations and gave male imperialism, without knowing it, its ultimate victory.[80]

The differentialists, also called maximalist[81] or nationalist[82] feminists, have stressed bodily differences again—and more recently the specifically female unconscious—in order to redis- cover the essence of womanhood. The vulva is the metonymy for the woman,[83] as the ovary once was in the eyes of the doc- tors and philosophers of the nineteenth century. Quite natu- rally, motherhood is restored to a place of honor. Even if Luce Irigaray proclaims the right to virginity,[84] one sees a return in force to a celebration of sublime motherhood. This is the true destiny of women, the condition of their power, of their happi- ness, and the promise of the regeneration of the world, so ill treated by men. Differentialist feminists advocate the sep- aration of the sexes and encourage women to give a special place to relations among themselves. Adrienne Rich, as early as 1976,[85] and Luce Irigaray, too, see mother/daughter as the quintessential human couple, the foundation of strength and of friendship among women, and a first response to the patriarchy that is dominating the world.[86] Taking her logic to its extreme, Rich, while not impugning heterosexuality, does encourage women to recognize their latent homosexuality.[87]

Rich was widely read but not closely followed in that par- ticular area. The maternalist and gynecentric ideology, on the other hand, is having some success. Not only does it justify the moral superiority of women over men, but it lays a basis for a number of their prerogatives. If women are naturally "mater-

23

nal," that is, gentle, peaceful, and warm, one can immediately conclude that they are the radiant future of humanity. Maternity—up to then conceived to be a deprived relationship—should be thought of as a model for the public sphere.[88] It will lay the foundations for an entirely new notion of power and citizenship. The citizen will be a loving human being, devoted to the protection of human life, which is so vulnerable.[89] In other words, the world can be saved only by mothers.

This theme was taken up and developed by the "ecofeminists."[90] For them, woman incarnated nature and life, whereas man was flung back toward culture and death. This dichotomy had a certain vogue in France,[91] even before there was talk of fertilization in vitro. It was revived by women's fear of seeing themselves deprived of their function as procreators. Women referred to the power of the male medical corps over the woman's belly and the specter of the artificial mothering machine, the ultimate ruse of the male tyrant to eliminate his enemy. Anxious to submit to nature, certain of these feminists, old militants for contraception and abortion, are now questioning their legitimacy. Opposed to everything that threatens life, the ecofeminists say they are concerned about the environment and about the entire chain of being. Hostile to the seventeenth-century theory of the animal-machine, they perceive the human being as one animal among others. Many go beyond simply proclaiming their sympathy with suffering animal life, insisting on the bonds between women and animals[92]—against men. One of them suggests that the sympathy that many women feel for animals is due to the fact that they are both victims of men.[93] As a consequence, if one wishes to dissolve the patriarchy (exploiter of nature), one must "become aware of the suffering of non-humans"[94] along with all the minorities oppressed by men. Which amounts to breaking the chain of being at the level of man, an animal so perverted that he no longer belongs to the natural world. The difference between woman and animal is only one of degree, whereas the difference between woman and man is one of kind. We see the same discourse, here, as that of the sociobiologists, who can compare a bee and a woman, but not a man and a woman.

Because they each rely on the principle of biological determinism, sociobiology and differentialist feminism arrive at a similar result: one sex is always valorized at the expense of the other. According to this point of view, men and women no longer have to encounter each other except at the time of insemination. Essentialism necessarily ends in separation and worse: oppression. It can offer only a limited perspective on nature and human potentialities. Everything is written in advance, without any possibility of change or creation. Prisoners of a predetermined and even overdetermined schema, men and women find themselves condemned perpetually to play the same roles, eternally beginning the same war over again.

THE CONSTRUCTIVISTS; OR, MASCULINITY EXPLODED

Currently, specialists in men's studies agree in rejecting the idea of a single masculinity. Trained in the humanities, they challenge the primary role of biology and work at demonstrating human plasticity. Well versed in the works of social and cultural anthropology, in all the new historical and sociological research on masculinity (and femininity), they conclude that there is no universal masculine model, valid in every time and in every place. In their eyes, masculinity is not an essence but an ideology that tends to justify male domination. Its forms change (what do the medieval warrior and the family breadwinner of the 1960s have in common?), and all that has survived is the power of men over women. But now that this power is crumbling before our eyes, what is left of masculinity?

Almost half a century ago the American anthropologist Margaret Mead introduced the idea of multiple forms of masculinity. Studying seven tribes of the South Seas, she demonstrated the extreme variability not only of male and female roles and stereotypes but also of relations between men and women.[95] What is there in common between the male Arapesh, an art lover who prefers to let himself be brutalized rather

25

than fight, and the Mundugumor warrior, quick-tempered and aggressive, who talks and laughs as he eats his captured enemy?[96] How can one compare the sexual boldness of the Iatmul boys with the shyness of the Tchambuli?

More recent work shows that diverse forms of masculinity still endure all over the world despite rapid Westernization. Anthropologist David Gilmore reports a multiplicity of models from the Mediterranean south to the Samburu tribes of East Africa, from the New Guinea tribes to the Tahitians, on to American Jews, and many others.[97] In one place we find very tough men anxious about their manliness, stressing the smallest difference between themselves and women;[98] in another place, tender, gentle men who seem feminine by our traditional criteria, living at peace with the commingling of the sexes.[99] What becomes of the myth of men's natural aggressiveness when one studies the little Semai society of Central Malaysia, one of the most peaceful populations in the world?[100] One can't help asking oneself about the "nature" and origin of masculinity. Which is more virile—Rambo, the hero of young American boys, or the little Semai man? Which is more normal, or closer to nature? Which has been subjected to the greatest pressure from his environment and upbringing? Which has most severely repressed a part of himself?

But there is no need to travel around the world to observe a multiplicity of models of masculinity. Our own society is a good place in which to make note of this diversity. Masculinity varies according to the historical period but also according to a man's social class,[101] race,[102] and age.[103]

By now it will be clear that Simone de Beauvoir's famous remark applies to men as well: One is not born a man, one becomes a man. And this truth appears to be demonstrated by the contrasting example of the "wild children" of the nineteenth century, Victor de l'Aveyron and Gaspar Hauser, who grew up without any human contact. True, those observing these children had no interest in problems of sexual identity. But these problems appear clearly in their reports. Gaspar

Hauser wanted to wear girl's clothes because he felt they were prettier: He was told he must become a man: he denied it absolutely.[104] Victor, whom Doctor Itard described as possessed by strong sexual drives, showed no preference for one sex over the other. His desire was undifferentiated, which ought not to be surprising, said the good doctor in 1801, in a creature who had not been taught by his upbringing to distinguish a man from a woman.[105]

If masculinity is learned and constructed, there is no question that it can also change. In the eighteenth century, a man worthy of the name could cry in public and have dizzy spells; by the end of the nineteenth, he no longer could (unless he was willing thereby to sacrifice his masculine dignity). What has been constructed can therefore be deconstructed in order to be reconstructed anew. But the most radical of the "constructivists," inspired by Jacques Derrida, apply themselves only to deconstruction. Their aim is definitively to explode the dualism of genders[106] and even of the sexes,[107] which are merely ideological oppositions whose purpose is always the oppression of one by the other. They believe that in this indirect manner they can rid themselves once and for all of the problems of sexual identity—including those of transsexuals[108]—and establish a regime of complete freedom.

The two positions are therefore irreconcilable. When we contemplate the advocates of biological determinism, who paint a picture of eternal masculinity, and their opponents, who calmly declare that "the masculine gender does not exist,"[109] we have the feeling that the enigma of masculinity is more mysterious than ever. Is a man a question without an answer? A signifier without a signified? Yet we know very well that there are two sexes and that a man is not a woman. Apart from a few exceptions, we can always distinguish one from the other. If diversity of behaviors belies the preeminence of the biological, the multiplicity of forms of masculinity nevertheless does not rule out the existence of shared characteristics, even secret collusions. It is in search of these that we now proceed.

PART ONE

CONSTRUCTING A MALE (Y)

MASCULINE IDENTITY

The Problematics of Sexual Identity

Concern about sexual identity is relatively new. Until the nineteenth century, when a case of intersexuality[1] occurred it was thought that the subject could change sexual identity without great inner turmoil. The case of Herculine Barbin, a false male hermaphrodite, gave the lie tragically to this exclusively social apprehension of sexual identity.[2]

Since the work of Erik Erikson, we know that the acquisition of an identity (social or psychological) is an extremely complex process that involves a positive relation of inclusion and a negative relation of exclusion.[3] One defines oneself by one's resemblances to some people and one's differences from others.[4] One's sense of sexual identity also undergoes these processes.[5]

Freud already believed that identification was the key to the concept of identity, multiple by definition.[6] To this notion Erikson added the concept of differentiation. Today, all psychologists recognize the importance of this second principle, hardly understood only thirty years ago. We know that a young child can distinguish his sexual identity through differentiation with members of the opposite sex, at least as much as through identification with those of the same sex.[7] John Money and Anke A. Ehrhardt insist on the importance of the negative code. Not only is it not "empty," it actually serves as a model both of what one should not do and of what one can expect of the other

sex. Even if cultural differences between the sexes are relatively few, enough still remain for the double coding to survive.
This proves the importance of the recognition of the "dualism
of genders" if the child is to have a clear sense of identity.

The Difficulties of Masculine Identity

Money has stressed that it is easier to "make" a woman than
a man.[8] The evolution of manhood is truly the rockier path.[9]
The road that starts with the conception of an xy and leads to
the manhood of an adult is strewn with obstacles. Spinoza's
remark, that "all determination is negation,"[10] applies more to
men than to women. As early as 1959, the American psychologist Ruth Hartley realized that a little boy defines himself
primarily negatively, that males generally learn what they
must not be in order to be masculine, before learning what
they can be, that many boys define masculinity simply as
what is not feminine.[11] The observation is so true that one
could say that, starting from conception, the male embryo
"struggles" not to be female. Born of a woman, cradled in a
female belly, the male child, unlike the female child, is condemned to differentiation during a large part of his life. He
cannot exist except by opposing himself to his mother, to her
femininity, to his condition as passive baby. Three times, in
order to signify his male identity, he will have to convince
himself and others: that he is not a woman, not a baby, not a
homosexual. Whence the despair of those who do not succeed
in achieving this threefold negation (denegation?), as is well
illustrated by the autobiographical novels of Edmund White.[12]
The hero, who has spent his whole youth hating his homosexuality, would so much like to be an adult, a man, and a heterosexual[13]—synonyms, in his eyes, for control, solidity, and
dignity. But he is none of the three and must accept the shame
of wanting to be protected like a child.

The other difficulty inherent in a boy's masculinity is that it is less stable and less precocious than a girl's femininity. For a long time, it was believed that masculinity was a primary and natural state. In fact, it is secondary, difficult to acquire, and fragile. This is why there is widespread agreement, now, in recognizing the truth of Helen Hacker's remark to the effect that, in general, masculinity is more important to men than femininity is to women.[14]

Now that the difficulties of male identity have been revealed, no one continues to maintain that man is the stronger sex. On the contrary, he is defined as the weaker sex,[15] troubled with numerous kinds of fragility, both physical and psychic. Starting with his life inside the womb, the male has more difficulty surviving: "It seems that the male embryo, then the male fetus, are more fragile than the female. This fragility persists during the first year of life and the higher mortality rate that penalizes males can be observed throughout their lives."[16] In France today, women live, on the average, eight years longer than men. One of the reasons for men's physical vulnerability may come from their psychic fragility, which has been more clearly perceived in the last twenty or so years. The distribution by sex of psychiatric disturbances shows an overrepresentation of males up to adolescence.[17] Boys represent close to two-thirds of outpatients seeking help, both in France and abroad.[18] After adolescence, this overrepresentation diminishes and even reverses, depending on the mental disorder.

Several hypotheses have been advanced by Leon Eisenberg to explain this predominance of males suffering from the psychiatric conditions most common among children. First of all, there is a genetic vulnerability: since man possesses only one x chromosome, the latter accentuates all the harmful effects of every pathological allele[19] on this chromosome. Furthermore, because of the y chromosome, only the male fetus is exposed to the secretion of a masculinizing substance of the ducts and to testosterone. In addition, as psychoanalysts well know, perversion is essentially found among men. Fetishism, transvestism, or transsexualism affect vastly more men than women, as though nature had more difficulty differentiating the identity of the male than that of the female.[20]

The difficulties of masculinity are obvious, especially nowadays, in our countries, where the power that served as man's armor is crumbling on all sides. Without his age-old defenses, man's wounds are exposed, and they are often raw. One has only to read the literature of European and American men of the last fifteen years to grasp the entire range of feelings by which they are assaulted: rage, anxiety, fear of women, impotence, loss of reference points, self-hatred and hatred of others, and so on. One element that is found in all these texts is a man crying.[21]

CHAPTER ONE
Y; or, SEXUAL DUALISM

Evolution has determined the two sexes of the human species by differentiating the twenty-third pair of their chromosomes—xx in the female, xy in the male. The child's sex is defined by the chromosomal formula of the spermatozoon that fertilizes the ovum.[1] It is therefore the male who engenders the male.

Even though the y chromosome has not yet yielded all its mysteries,[2] genetics, and in particular the study of chromosomal anomalies, has already given us a great deal to think about with regard to the masculine difference, its fragility and its in some sense secondary character. Thus, we now know that human beings can be born lacking one chromosome or with an extra chromosome. One can live with a single x (44xo)[3] or with three x's (44xxx)[4]. One also encounters human beings of the male types xyy or xxy.[5] But nature never produces a human being endowed with one or several y's unaccompanied by an x. In Turner's Syndrome (44xo), the single x can be transmitted by either the father or the mother, but in both cases this x seems to represent the basic humanity: that without which no human being is possible. Whereas the y symbolizes the male sexual difference, its presence, necessary to "make" a man, is far from being sufficient to define male identity.

The Prenatal Development of XY: "A Constant Struggle"[6]

The sexual differentiation that turns an XY embryo into a child declared male on his birth certificate proceeds by successive stages that can be represented by the following diagram:

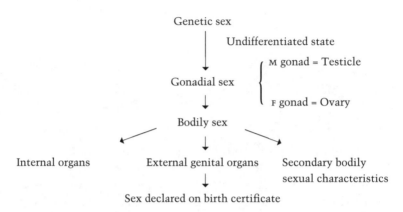

This chain of events, leading to differentiation between the sexes, can be compared to a relay race,[7] to the extent that each stage depends on the proper functioning of the preceding stage. In the XY male embryo, the role of the Y[8] is to deflect the tendency of the undifferentiated embryonic gonad to form an ovary and force it to produce a testicle. The different cells of the testicle begin to perform their specialized functions, the most important of which is the production of a male hormone, testosterone. What is more, if XX fetuses are constantly exposed to injected testosterone, they develop the entire set of male characteristics, including the penis and the genital system, despite the presence of ovaries in place of testicles. On the other hand, if the Y gene determining the testicle is suppressed through mutation, or for lack of testosterone, the XY cells form ovaries instead of testicles and the fetus develops as a female.

During the first weeks, the XX and XY embryos are anatomically identical, endowed with both female and male ducts.[9] They are sexually bipotential. In the male fetus, differentiation begins around the fortieth day, whereas it does not begin in the female fetus until after the second month. There follows a series of "critical phases" of sexual development whose stages cannot be completed either before or after the opportune moment.

All this makes one think there are limits to the alternative model "male or female." Besides the fact that the xx and xy embryos are anatomically similar until the sixth week, that man and woman share the same sexual hormones—only the quantities are different[10]—genetic anomalies produce individuals whose sex and gender are truly difficult to define. These ambivalences or ambiguities open the door to all sorts of interpretations. Proponents of resemblance between the sexes have arguments to prove that what connects the two sexes is much more important than what distinguishes them.[11] The others point to the anomalies that produce male or female pseudo-hermaphrodites in their argument for the theory of the multiplicity of the sexes. But can one base one's argument on an anomaly that occurs every ten thousand to thirty thousand births, as the case may be, and ignore the most general representative case? Certainly, sexual dualism is not absolute and much less radical than one thinks. But even attenuated and relative, it endures as a constant of humanity. Especially since we all have an irresistible tendency to reinforce it starting from the birth of the child.

The Parents' Gaze

In the most probable case, where the assignation of the child's sex at birth is not in doubt, the child, declared to be either a boy or a girl on its birth certificate, is immediately perceived as such by those caring for it, most importantly its parents. The parents' gaze and their conviction as to the sex of their child

are absolutely determinative for the development of the latter's sexual identity and also constitute the most important
factor, as we shall see with respect to intersexual children.
Now it so happens that there is an irrepressible tendency in
human beings to "label" another person sexually, particularly
a baby, and this is accompanied by different behaviors according to the sex assigned to the child.

Zella Luria and Jeffrey Rubin questioned fathers and mothers twenty-four hours after the baby's birth about their impres-
sions of their child.[12] The fathers had seen their baby through
a pane of glass, the mothers had held it in their arms once. The
babies, boys and girls, weighed the same and were the same
size, they were all normal and born at term. The results of the
interviews with the parents were eloquent.

The parents used the word "big" for sons more than for
daughters, and "beautiful," "cute," "sweet" for the latter. The
little girls had "delicate features" and the little boys "strong
features"; the little girls were "small," while the little boys,
who were the same size, were "big." Both parents tended to
stereotype their babies, but all the research has shown that this
tendency is more marked in the father.[13]

All these studies show the extreme importance of the viewpoint of those associating with the baby. As soon as it is born,
we teach the baby through gesture, voice, and choice of play-
things and clothes which sex it belongs to. But we are not truly
aware of the influence of this phenomenon of teaching until
the sex of the child poses problems.

When the external genital organs are ambiguous at birth, the
parents, nowadays, must delay the formal declaration until
more thorough examinations have been carried out.[14] If the
infant is xx, surgical treatment can begin fairly quickly, but if
it is xy, it is necessary to wait.[15] All the examinations required
for the diagnosis may take several months. Doctors earnestly
request that the parents treat their child as though it were
neuter in gender and not give in to the irresistible urge to assign
it a sex, so as not to have to change their behavior in case an

error is discovered. But experience shows that even if parents can, in some countries at least, choose a neuter first name like Pat or Robin, they cannot tolerate uncertainty for very long. Nor can the medical team responsible for the child. In the end, an infant with ambiguous sex will very often be of the sex chosen by its parents.

The body is the source of a primary identity and the sex very soon becomes an area of special emotional investment, being the earliest source of sexual identity. Nevertheless, we see boys acquire a masculine identity despite the absence of a penis,[16] as though other forces (biology and parental behavior) had taken over from the missing organ. In the opposite case, a biologically normal boy (whose four manifestations of sex—genetic, gonadic, bodily, and psychic—conform to one another) may from the earliest age feel that he is a girl. This is the very rare case of transsexualism, which affects boys almost four times as often as girls. Stoller's particular interest is in the cases of very young boys whose feelings of being a girl begin in earliest childhood, at about two or three years of age. All identify with women and have feminine mannerisms, interests, and fantasies. Their progression in transvestism and feminine behavior is limited only by the cooperation of their families, who either do or do not allow the child to behave in a feminine way. These little boys learn feminine attitudes so quickly that they appear almost natural. Certain even show obvious signs of femininity before the age of one. All these children present a very particular parental context.[17]

What, then, induces these little males to maintain, in the face of all anatomical evidence, that they are females? According to Stoller, it is apparently an excessive identification with the mother, due to her incapacity to allow her son to separate himself from her body. Keeping him close to her all day long, she provokes a confusion of the limits of the self between her and her son. This extreme symbiosis, which continues for many years, prevents all the tensions, all the conflicts necessary to psychosexual development, such as castration anxiety,

39

phallic fantasies, or neurotic defense reactions. Psychotic, resistant to all psychoanalytic treatment, or "bizarre mistakes of nature," adult transsexuals demand a sex change in order to be at peace with themselves. The case of the transsexual, rare though it is (there are a few hundred in France), has the merit of posing the question of how sex should be defined. In the case of an anomaly, which of the four manifestations of sex—genetic, gonadic, bodily, or psychic[18]—has priority in defining the human person? These days, the greatest confusion reigns. Aside from the ever-present disagreement among psychoanalysts, psychiatrists, and jurists, the controversy over the genetic test administered to female athletes in the Albertville Olympic Games further adds to the uncertainty. For some geneticists, the discovery of the gene SRY (on the Y chromosome), which controls the formation of testicles in the young embryo, is the ultimate proof of a person's sex. For others, it is not, because of numerous exceptions: the SRY gene is certainly the one that sets in motion the process of masculinization, but from time to time it does not function very well, and then the fetus becomes feminine: the person develops a vagina and a female appearance.[19] The geneticist Axel Kahn prefers, as criterion, the gonadic over the genetic sex: "What causes the difference between a man and a woman, *on the level of competition*, is a male hormone, testosterone. It is this that conditions muscular power and gives the advantage to men, as specialists in doping are well aware."[20]

What remains to be known is whether, outside the domain of competitive sports, the male hormone is really the ultimate criterion for distinguishing between the sexes. Nothing is less sure. In the absence of complete certainty, the spirit of tolerance would dictate that we decide case by case in the best interests of the individual, rather than lay down the law in the name of principles that are challenged on all sides.

It is not enough to be an XY and have a functional penis to feel like a man. Inversely, one can believe one is a man despite various anomalies or dysfunctions. But for the vast

majority, the first fundamental stage of masculine differentiation begins with x y and is completed with the attitude of the
parents. During this phase, the fetus will have "struggled," as
Jost says, in order not to follow the female program of development. This completely biological struggle is a small thing
next to the struggle the male child will have to wage beginning with his birth, and for a long time thereafter, in order to
become a man.

CHAPTER TWO
MASCULINE DIFFERENTIATION

A boy's development is governed by a natural, universal, and necessary given: the fact that he is born of a mother. This particular situation of a boy, that he is nourished physically and psychically by a person of the opposite sex, determines his fate in a more complex and dramatic way than is the case for a girl. All the more so since, within the patriarchal system that has dominated the world for thousands of years, it is the radical difference in roles and sexual identities that has been stressed.

In this schema the male child is one thing and then its opposite, in succession. Feminine originally, he is obliged to abandon his first homeland and adopt another that is opposed to him, even hostile. This uprooting, which is forced on him, is also intensely desired . . . .

The Mother-Son Dyad; or, The Amorous Pair

THE ORIGINAL FUSION

During the nine months of its life inside the womb, the child is one with its mother. We have known for a long time now that the well-being of the fetus depends on that of the mother. Shock, depression, or strong emotions have repercussions on it. But to what extent, exactly, this prehistory determines the life of the individual, we do not yet know. Does the incomplete neurological development allow us to speak of a sort of memory of this period in the cave? Doesn't the nine months spent in the depths of the mother leave an indelible female imprint on the child before it is born?

A number of psychologists have accepted this concept of *imprinting*—a term taken from the science of animal behavior—to describe the influence of the mother on her child, and its attachment to her.[1] In the first weeks following birth, the mother-child symbiosis continues as far as extrauterine life permits. During these very first months, the infant, in absolute dependence on its mother, differentiates itself from her only very slightly.[2] According to Freud, "Here, a love takes root that is the most powerful and complete love it is given to a human being to know." From body-to-body contact to intimate time alone together, the child's relationship with its mother is "unique, incomparable, unchangeable, and it becomes for both sexes the object of the first and the most powerful of loves, prototype of all later loving relationships."[3] The mother, not content with just feeding the child, cares for it and awakens in it numerous physical sensations.

This love of the child for its mother has been celebrated a thousand times, particularly by male writers.[4] If a mother's love can be experienced as a "transport of happiness"[5] by the little boy, it can also be felt as a menace if the mother does not respond in a satisfying way to her child's passion, being either too loving or not loving enough. The right measure of motherly love is all the more crucial when it is addressed to a male child. Too much love would prevent the boy from becoming a male, but not enough could make him ill.

Starting at birth, the male baby is naturally in a state of primary passivity, totally dependent on the one who is feeding him. As Groddeck pointed out early on, "During suckling, the mother is the man who gives; the child, the woman who receives."[6] This very first erotic[7] relationship teaches the infant the nirvana of passive dependence and will leave indelible marks on the adult's psyche.[8] But the consequences of this experience are not the same for the boy and the girl. For the girl, it is the basis of an identification with her own sex, whereas for the boy it is an inversion of later roles. To become a man, he will have to learn to differentiate himself from his mother and repress, within the deepest part of himself, that delicious passivity in which he was entirely and exclusively one with her. The erotic bond between mother and child is not limited to oral satisfactions. It is she who, by the care she gives him, awakens all his sensuality, initiates him to pleasure, and teaches him to love his body. The good mother is naturally incestuous and a pedophile.[9] No one would think of complaining about this, but everyone would prefer to forget it, including the mother and the son. Normally, the child's physical and psychical development gradually allow for a separation. But when the mother's love is too powerful, too gratifying, why would the child ever want to leave this delicious dyad? On the other hand, if this total love has not been reciprocal, the child will spend the rest of his life painfully seeking it.

It is human nature (male or female) to begin one's life in a passive loving relationship and to find in this the pleasure necessary to develop further. Until the present time, we thought it was the mother alone who incarnated the principle of love. If it is unthinkable that she should cease to do so, it is not certain that this exclusive intimacy with her son should be entirely to his advantage.

THE BOY'S EARLY FEMININITY

Steeped in femininity during his entire intrauterine life, then identified with his mother as soon as he is born, the little male can only develop by becoming the opposite of what he is originally. This *protofemininity* of the human baby is looked upon in different ways by the experts. Some believe that it favors the development of the girl and handicaps that of the boy. Others believe it is equally advantageous to both sexes.

The concept of protofemininity in the male child was

referred to for the first time by Stoller in response to Freud's theories about innate masculinity. In so doing, Stoller caused a radical revolution: if Freud was reducing the original bisexuality to the primacy of masculinity (the first two years of life), the American psychiatrist and psychoanalyst is suggesting, on the contrary, that the original bisexuality is reduced to the primacy of femininity.

According to Freud, for whom protofemininity does not exist, the little girl has more obstacles to overcome than the little boy.[10] He believed that masculinity was the original, natural mode of gender identity in the two sexes, and that it resulted from the first relationship with a heterosexual object of the boy with his mother, and from the first relationship with a homosexual object of the girl with her mother.[11] Stoller takes Freud to task for having neglected the very first stage of life, consisting in the fusion that takes place in the mother-baby symbiosis. Because women accept their femininity in a primary, uncontested way, their gender identity is more solidly anchored than that of men. This preverbal identification, which enhances the creation of their femininity, becomes in the boy an obstacle to overcome.

If boy and girl must pass through the same stages of separation and individuation,[12] the male baby encounters difficulties unknown to the other sex. A study of male transsexuals reveals to Stoller the dangers of an excessive symbiosis between son and mother. "The more a mother prolongs this symbiosis—relatively normal in the first weeks or months—the more femininity then risks infiltrating the core gender identity."[13] Since one encounters this process to lesser degrees in most motherhoods, adds Stoller, it is probably here that we may find the origin of the fears of homosexuality which are much more marked among men than among women, as well as "most of the roots of what is called masculinity, namely the preoccupation with being strong, independent, hard, cruel, polygamous, misogynous, and perverse." Only if the boy can separate himself without any problem from his mother's femininity and femaleness will he be able to develop *"that later gender identity that we call masculinity.* It is then that he will see his mother as a separate, heterosexual object which he will be able to desire."[14]

One cannot put it better than this: *masculinity comes second and must "be created."* It may be endangered by the primary and profound union with the mother.[15]

Whereas the homosexual mother-daughter relationship of the first months can only increase the daughter's feeling of identity, the little boy must do his utmost to annihilate his protofeminine impulses. The behavior that societies define as appropriately masculine is formed of defense maneuvers:[16] fear of women, fear of showing any sort of femininity, including tenderness, passivity, and caregiving to others, and of course fear of being desired by a man. From all these fears, Stoller deduces the attitudes of the ordinary man: "To be rough, loud, belligerent; to maltreat and fetishize women; to seek only the friendship of men but also to detest homosexuals; to speak crudely; to denigrate women's occupations. *A man's first duty is: not to be a woman."*[17]

If the early femininity is perceived primarily as a handicap by Stoller, women psychologists perceive it as a great advantage for the boy. Symbiosis with the mother is beneficial to both sexes because it is the origin of nurturing feelings, tenderness, and attachment in the future adult. It is associated with the positive and warm behaviors that constitute the sweetness of later human relations.[18] And if the child is unfortunate enough to have a "cold" mother, he will be incapable, as an adult, of expressing these elementary feelings and will often nourish an inextinguishable hatred of himself and of women.

Margarete Mitscherlich goes farther, maintaining that our society asks the little boy at too early an age to detach himself from his mother and adopt a masculine behavior. It is through this identification with the nurturing person—the mother, as it happens—that children overcome their anxieties and their distress. They interiorize the behaviors of the mother, who comforts and soothes them, and they are able to subdue their hatred for their younger siblings, in relation to whom they will experience themselves partially as a mother.[19] Psychologist Phyllis Chesler speaks of these boys, too quickly torn away from their mothers, as "dematrixed beings."[20] For these authors, the first relationship with the mother is the very condition for the male's human identity. If that relationship is not good or if the identification is not possible, the child will have all sorts of difficulties in becoming a human male.

One of the consequences of the interest taken in the symbiotic relationship between mother and son is the new acknowledgment of the importance of the pre-Oedipal phase. Freud had mentioned it belatedly a propos the specificity of female sexuality: he saw this "mother fixation" as the necessary prehistory for the establishment of the little girl's femininity.[21] Freud says little about this phase in the boy: "It also exists, but is not as long, is less rich in consequences, and more difficult to differentiate from Oedipal love since the object remains the same."[22] It was Melanie Klein and her English and American successors, especially those who studied the development of male identity, who turned their attention to this early period. In 1967 the psychoanalyst Ralph Greenson, who worked with Stoller on transsexuals, attracted some attention, in a paper read before the 25th Congress of Psychoanalysis, to the importance for the young boy of "disidentification" with respect to his mother.[23]

American psychoanalysts see the Oedipal stage as generally less perilous for the small male than the pre-Oedipal phase, since the principal danger for the boy is not so much fear of paternal castration as the ambivalent feeling composed of desire and fear with respect to his mother: an ineradicable desire to return to the symbiosis with his mother and a fear of restoring the early unity.[24] It is on the successful resolution of this conflict that the formation of male identity depends.

THE LITTLE BOY IN THE MOTHER'S WORLD
The duration of the mother-son symbiosis varies enormously from one era to another and, nowadays, from one culture to

another. The longer, the more intimate, and the greater a source of mutual pleasure the symbiosis is, the greater the probability that the boy will become feminine. "This effect will persist if the boy's father does not interrupt the fusion qualitatively and quantitatively."[25]

The lesson is recent and does not concern our contemporary industrial societies. Because women have radically transformed their way of life, symbiosis with their children has been singularly shortened. The constant increase in the number of mothers who work outside the home has meant that their capacity to nurse is limited and along with it the prolongation of their fusional body-to-body contact with their babies. Quite aside from economic necessities, it is less and less evident that they desire this prolongation beyond the first months following the birth. Interest in the baby vies with other professional, cultural, or social interests. Very soon, the small child knows the frustration of separation, a varied diet, and the sight of faces other than that of its mother. For mothers who devote themselves entirely to their children, school comes along to ring in the hour of separation. Even though in France school is not obligatory until the age of six, it is customary to send one's children to school at around three years of age, or even younger—as though by chance, at the close of the pre-Oedipal period!

On the other side of the world, mothers in the numerous warrior tribes of New Guinea behave quite differently with their sons.[26] In the first place, postpartum taboos[27] contribute to reinforcing the mother-child couple. The new Sambian or Baruyan father must avoid the mother and child, first, because one or the other can pollute the infant by the very fact of the mother's contaminants at birth and, second, because the sexual arousal that might be caused by the sight of nursing could lead the father to infringe the taboos and cause the baby to fall ill or die.

Until the time of weaning, the father does not see much of his child. The Sambia tend to think that the baby is an extension of the mother's body during the first nine months. The child has free access to the mother's breast, sometimes even into its third year. It lives in her arms, skin to skin, and sleeps naked with her until the time of weaning. Afterward, boys and girls sleep apart from their mother, but only a foot or two away from her. In time, boys are urged by their parents to sleep a little farther from their mother, but not yet in the "male space" of the house. Despite increasing contact with their father, boys continue to live with their mother and their brothers and sisters until the age of seven to ten.

The tribes of New Guinea, conscious of the danger of feminization of a boy, perform initiation rites that are generally very long and traumatic, depending on the intensity of the mother-son bond that must be loosened. We shall see, farther on, how the ritual separates the child from its mother by force, wresting him from her loving embrace.

To a lesser degree, the American "momism" that appeared in the nineteenth century with the beginnings of industrial society is another sort of prolonged fusion with the mother. The body-to-body period is followed by an intimate association with an all-powerful woman who poses some problems for the son. The fathers being absent, the sons are victims of the "suffocation of a mother's protective love."[28] The absence of male identification is cruelly felt, especially when custom tolerates a mother's dressing her little boy as a girl until the age of six (as was the case, for instance, with Franklin D. Roosevelt), or when she allows him to grow long curls. Certain boys would never recover from this, one being Ernest Hemingway, who suffered all his life from problems with his sexual identity. According to his biographer, Kenneth Lynn, his mother, a forceful personality, authoritarian and domineering, for several years fantasized that he was a little girl.[29] Not only did she dress him, arrange his hair, and treat him as though he were "the twin" of his older sister, she had also established little Ernest in a delicious relationship of dependence beginning with his first cry. For six months he slept in his mother's bed, where she allowed him to pat her face, squeeze up close to her, and feed at will from her opulent breasts. "He is contented to sleep with Mama and lunches all night," she happily recorded in her scrapbook. Although his father was a weak man, without authority and profoundly neurotic,[30] it was probably his interference that saved Hemingway from being more severely disturbed.[31] As a child, Ernest had had real bonds of affection with him: his father, in search of anything that could reinforce his son's virility, took him fishing and hunting, starting at the age of three. But if his father was able to prevent the worst, he was not strong enough to save him completely from the mother's domination, since he himself was his wife's castrated victim. In order to resist his mother, Hemingway had no other recourse than to run away and to hate her; his old friend Dos Passos remarked that "Ernest was the only man he had ever known who really hated his mother." Haunted by her all his life, and by a profound desire for femininity, he was regularly heard to refer to her, in his adult life, as "that bitch."

Cut to the Quick; or, The Necessary Betrayal of the Mother

The attribute of male identity (as opposed to female identity) resides in the stage of differentiation with respect to maternal femininity, the essential condition for the sense of belonging to men as a group. Their resemblance and their solidarity is constructed by putting women at a distance, and first and foremost the first woman, the mother. Some speak of betrayal, others of symbolic murder—so that one may believe that in the primitive horde referred to by Freud, matricide preceded patricide.

As Hermann Burger clearly saw, every man is confronted by the following problem: "On the one hand, to proceed actively against his mother; on the other, to suffer from her passively. . . . We must kill her and die because of her. In so doing, a man must take care that he does not wound his feminine soul."[32]

THE PAIN OF SEPARATION

Rereading Virginia Woolf's *To the Lighthouse,* Pierre Bourdieu speaks of "the metaphor of the knife or the blade that situates the male role in the area of the cut, of violence, of murder, that is, in the area of a cultural order constructed against the original fusion with the maternal nature."[33]

The knife and the blade refer not only to the cutting of the umbilical cord, which involves both sexes, but also to the second separation from maternal femininity represented by circumcision. Performed several days after birth, or when the child is three or four years old, or even in adolescence or later, its object is always to reinforce the boy's masculinity. Because it constitutes a symbolic castration, it has attracted the attention of numerous psychoanalysts. Theodor Reik, Géza Roheim, Herman Numberg, and Bruno Bettelheim have shown that it detaches the boy from his mother and introduces him to the community of men. Further, it marks the importance of the penis.

Bettelheim stresses that for boys, "the display of the glans freed of the foreskin is part of an effort to assert their virility. On this point, the circumcised boy has a distinct superiority: his glans is visible, which is often considered the sign of a more clearly asserted virility."[34] Numberg insists on the fantasy of rebirth that accompanies circumcision: the circumcised child is reborn without a foreskin and thus is a man.[35] In Groddeck's eyes, the circumcision of the Jews is the repression of bisexuality, and this distinguishes them from all other humans: "The foreskin is cut off in order to eliminate every feminine feature from the distinguishing mark of masculinity; because the foreskin is feminine, it is the vagina in which the male glans is tucked away. . . . If the Jews cut off the foreskin . . . they eliminate the man's bisexuality, they remove the feminine characteristic from what is masculine. They thus renounce, in favor of bisexual divinity, their innate divine similitude. Through circumcision, the Jew becomes only a man."[36]

Circumcision, the symbolic renunciation of divine bisexuality, is at one and the same time the mark of human finitude and of masculinity. Performed eight days after the birth in the Jewish tradition, it occurs at the strongest moment of the mother-son symbiosis. Just recently born, the baby is still part of the mother's body. When men come to take her child from her to carry out the circumcision, they signify to the mother that the boy belongs to them and no longer to her. The circumcision wounds the son at the same time as the mother, who feels that a part of herself has been amputated. However painful this separation "by the knife" may be, it is not merely a sign that fusion with the mother must come to an end; it is also the symbolic recovery of the son by the father, the first act of sexual differentiation.

The three years that follow the birth of the boy constitute the time needed by the son to separate psychologically from his mother. For this he must strengthen the boundaries between her and him, put an end to their first love and to their sense of an empathetic bond.[37] The boy must develop a masculine identity in the absence of a narrow and continuous relationship with his father parallel to that which a daughter experiences with her mother. Nancy Chodorow notes that in the absence of a strong personal identification with a man, "boys in father-absent and normally father-remote families [characteristic of contemporary families] develop a sense of what it is to be masculine through identification with cultural images of masculinity and men chosen as masculine models."[38] The great difficulty for them consists in bringing about a disidentification, with all its accompanying negation and rejection of femininity, without the effective support of a positive model of identification. This is the origin of a masculine identity more negative than positive, which stresses differentiation, distance from others, and a denial of the affective relationship. Whereas the processes of feminine identification are relational, those of masculine identification are oppositional.

Lillian Rubin, inspired by Chodorow's work, has deduced consequences from it for the adult man. She thinks that male aggressivity toward women can be interpreted as a reaction to that premature loss and to the feeling of betrayal that accompanies it, that a scornful attitude toward women comes from the inner rupture demanded by the separation. This scorn, according to her, comes from fear and not arrogance, the fear experienced by the child who finds himself obliged to reject the all-powerful presence of his mother.[39]

Even thoroughly repressed, the maternal symbiosis haunts the male unconscious. Because men have been raised for thousands of years solely by women, they must expend an infinite amount of energy guarding the boundaries. Keeping women at a distance is the only means of saving their manhood. Rousseau was already aware of this when he called upon men and women "to live separately ordinarily. . . . Men are affected as much as and more than women by their too intimate commerce. Women will thereby lose only their morals, and we will thereby lose both our customs and *our constitution*. No longer wishing to endure separation, and unable to turn themselves into men, *women turn us into women*."[40]

MASCULINITY: A REACTION, A PROTESTATION

The manly man is the embodiment of activity. But this activity is in truth only a reaction against the passivity and impotence of the newborn. The monopoly on activity by males does not come from a social necessity. The interiorization of the norms of masculinity requires a surplus repression of desires for passivity, notably the desire to be mothered. The masculinity that is formed unconsciously in the very first years of life is strengthened as the years go by before exploding literally in adolescence. This is the moment at which suffering and the fear of femininity and passivity begin to become evident. Most young men fight against this inner suffering by strengthening the ramparts of masculinity even more.

This reaction is a long struggle that creates a formidable ambivalence. The fear of passivity and femininity is especially strong because these are a man's most powerful and deeply repressed desires. The incessant struggle is never definitively won, for how can a man repudiate once and for all his recollection of Eden? If in real life men resist more or less successfully the rarely articulated desire for regression, the latter can appear openly in novels.

Many novelists have described the yearning for the mother's womb. *Le Rêve du singe fou* compares adult men to small Peter Pans who refuse to grow up. More explicitly, the author describes "the stubborn adult who persists in wishing to pass through a small door by which, as a child, he entered . . . that orifice (the mother's sex) which one travels only once, in only one direction."[41] The same desire is expressed in Günter Grass's superb panorama, *The Flounder*. Men are only babies dreaming of a three-breasted mother. "Three times a day we get suckled. Even doddering old men can count on it. We feel contented and sheltered. . . . We never have to decide for or against anything. We live . . . without responsibility."[42] The same desire again, though this time repressed, appears in *La Mère artificielle*: "To hell with the eternal whining of baby-men afflicted with mamamnesis . . . who would like to scramble back into their mother's bellies. It's high time to begin talking about papamnesis!"[43]

Philip Roth went even farther: his hero, David Kepesh, has metamorphosed into an enormous female breast. Unable to deal any longer with his virility and the incredible self-control it requires, he sinks into a delirium that allows him to taste all the pleasures of total helplessness.[44] Here is the desire to return to the mother's breast or to the state of a baby at the breast—those first hours of life when the baby *is* the breast. Beyond this romantic delirium, every work by Roth recounts the merciless war waged by the adult against the helpless, dependent baby: "a kind of psychological civil war that had broken out between the dreamy, needy, and helpless child I had been, and the independent, robust manly adult I wanted to be."[45]

In order to abandon oneself to these regressive fantasies, one must already have acquired some distance from one's anxieties. Perhaps, too, the current questioning of masculinity and femininity is loosening the knot of repression which, only twenty years ago, was strangling men. But not all of them are capable of such lucidity about themselves. The most fragile, the most pained also, can only sustain their masculinity and fight the nostalgic desire for the mother's womb by hating the female sex. Remember Baudelaire's disgust: "a pouch . . . full of pus." An adolescent making love for the first time with a teacher older than he who reminds him of his mother experiences the same disgust for a woman's sex: "a warm, gluey conduit . . . want to throw up . . . feel I'm being sucked from inside . . . feel bad."[46] These sensations are shared by many adolescents when they discover the sexual act, and normally fade with the strengthening of masculinity.

The fact is that from infancy until adulthood, and sometimes throughout life, masculinity is more a reaction than a positive choice. The little boy positions himself by opposing: I am not my mother, I am not a baby, I am not a girl, his unconscious proclaims. As Alfred Adler puts it, the advent of masculinity occurs through a *protestation of manhood*. The word "protestation" indicates clearly that doubts have been raised. One protests one's innocence when there is suspicion of guilt. We proclaim it loud and clear in order to convince others that we are not what they suspect us of being. In the same way, the little boy (and later, the man) protests his manhood because there remains a suspicion of femininity. But this time the doubt comes less from others than from himself. He must convince himself of his innocence—that is, of his masculine authenticity.

This protestation is primarily addressed to the mother. It consists of three propositions: I am not her. I am not like her. I am against her.

THE BETRAYAL AND MURDER OF THE MOTHER
The separation from the mother moves back and forth between two complementary themes: the betrayal of the loved mother

(the good mother), which haunts a writer like Philip Roth, and liberation from the oppressive mother (the bad, frustrating, and overpowering mother), which obsesses most notably contemporary writers writing in German.[47] Depending upon which image of the mother predominates (though they always go hand in hand), either guilt or aggressivity is more strongly aroused. Freud attributed man with a "normal scorn" of woman due to her lack of a penis, but Janine Chasseguet-Smirgel, subtler than the master, detects "behind the pronounced scorn . . . an imago of the mother that is powerful, envied, and terrifying."[48] It is terrifying because it symbolizes death, a return backward, being sucked in by a greedy uterus.[49]

Psychologists have often discussed the theme of the betrayal of the mother. The adult man is said to distrust women in memory of his mother, who supposedly betrayed his love by abandoning him gradually to the world of men. But there is another sort of betrayal that appears implicitly throughout Roth's work: that of the mother by the son. This, for him, is the real scandal, much more than the male's phallocentrism.[50] One cannot be a man without betraying one's mother, "cutting one's childhood bonds of love."[51] Manhood, says Roth, is: "Saying no to one's mother, in order to be able to say no to other women." Or, again: "To be at all is to be her Philip, but . . . my history still takes its spin from beginning as [his father's] Roth."[52] Portnoy consults a psychoanalyst, seeking manly strength from him: "Make me strong, make me complete."[53] In other words, help me betray my mother. He feels too guilty toward her to dare to leave her orbit, her body, and become a man. As an adolescent, he is always treated by her like her baby, and at his slightest inclination toward autonomy, she weeps. To betray her is surely to cause tears in her and, in him, guilt, terror, and anxiety. Portnoy's drama resides perhaps less in the omnipotence of his mother and the helplessness of his father than in the fact that she considers him "her lover" and he knows it. But he cannot hope to preserve this title except as long as he remains her baby.

Result: at the age of four, he scarcely knew which sex he belonged to.[54] He remembers that in his ninth year, when one of his testicles had not descended, he was seized by a terrible anguish: "And what if I began to grow breasts too? And what if my penis became dry and fragile, and broke off one day in my hand while I was peeing? Then I would change into a girl."[55] Girl or baby: such are the obstacles that the boy must remove in order to become a man. In both cases, it is a matter of breaking with the mother at that point. But how can he manage this when she threatens to take her love away from him, and even to castrate him?[56] She who taught him to pee standing up "by tickling his bottom . . . her hand on my dick quite probably represents my future!"[57]

Culpability is succeeded by aggressivity and hatred. Roth does not escape this either. He struggles furiously against the omnipotence of the mother that prevents him from growing up. Because he has not fought, he has lost his balls. As an adult, he submits to all the women he loves: powerless, masochistic,[58] he "knuckle[s] under like a defenseless little boy."[59] He has become "an egomaniacal baby,"[60] who knows only one defense: to reduce all women "to the state of masturbatory sexual objects." Other writers express more brutally their hatred and their need to kill their mother. *The Flounder* says it directly: the manly act par excellence is to murder the mother.[61] Without this initiatory act, which allows a man to emerge from the obscure prehistory of the mother's breast, death will be more powerful than life.

Literature is rich in denunciations of the mother. One cries out louder than the next. Michaël Krüger illustrates contemporary man's mother complex. The man-baby is sick from an infernal symbiosis. He feels he is nothing, a rag without identity, devoured by an all-powerful mother and women torturers.[62] Peter Rosei describes with horror the frightened man as a child in the presence of the woman-goddess, self-sufficient and cruel. Unable to kill her, he fetishizes her, takes a part of her and rejects the whole woman.[63] The woman-goddess casts spells: she prevents her son from growing up and makes him impotent.[64] No one has drawn a better portrait of the all-powerful mother and her son as eternal nursing baby than the Nordic Portnoy, the writer Knut Faldbakken, in *The Bad Boy* (the English title of the Norwegian original): powerless, apathetic, shorn of identity, masochistic, passive, he despises himself because he is afraid of everything, even his own shadow. The heroes of Faldbakken's novels weep like infants over their impotence and they experience homosexual episodes. Only the body of another man can reassure the infant-man, prey to a deep depression.

Novels written by men, from north to south and from east to west, have made the castrating and death-dealing mother one of the most widespread themes in contemporary literature. One is louder than the next in denouncing these women, "thieves of solicitude"[65] who engender doll-men.[66] Fathers, when they are not dead, are described as shadows with substance: emotionally absent, pitiable, humiliated, scorned, incapable of tearing their sons from the amorous claws of the mother. Result: the different heroes of these novels have great trouble extricating themselves. We have mentioned impotence, depression, homosexual episodes, suicides or madness, but the aggressiveness of the castrated man can also be directed toward the outside world. He treats women like disposable objects, becomes sadistic or murderous. The hero of *Fausse note*, invaded by his mother's symbiotic, sensuous love, turns into a woman-killer.[67] A blond young god of uncertain sexuality, childish and feminine, he will in the end be killed by his mother, who with this gesture will be offering the ultimate protection (against justice) and taking the ultimate "anthropophagous" maternal possession. There are also those who dream of killing their mother in order to rid themselves of all their accumulated hatred,[68] and there are those who actually kill her.[69] Ludovic Janvier's fascinating murderous son is a caricature of the abortive male: without courage, irascible, meek, flabby, loving his excrement, he has always merely pretended to exist. He speaks of himself in the feminine and in fact resembles a woman, with breasts and hips. By killing his mother, he hopes to free himself of his fear of existing. But the act imprisons him. He refers to "the glue of love" and plays with the idea of the pregnant man who would offer a male baby a "manly environment."

In truth, once the opportune moment is past, the break with the mother is impossible without the help of therapy. And even in this case, the prolonged symbiosis results in serious aftereffects. Failures of separation give rise to the worst disorders, ranging from transsexualism to psychosis (there is neither prohibition of incest nor paternal castration) and including multiple identity and behavioral disturbances: hegemonic masculinity,[70] scorn of women, unchanneled aggressiveness, hunger for the father,[71] and so forth.

All this seems to gives grounds for saying that the tribes of New Guinea, who fear the fatal influence of mothers on their sons, are quite correct: that because the mothers prevent their sons from growing up and becoming men, the adult males must tear the sons away from them in the cruelest fashion.

The Vital Need for Differentiation

The difference between the sexes is extremely variable from one society to another. Whether strongly emphasized or scarcely perceptible to a foreign observer (in our societies, it is sometimes difficult these days to distinguish a young man from a young woman), whether late in emerging (Tahiti) or early (Western societies before the 1900s, for instance), sexual differentiation is a universal given. It is true that society evolves slowly and that the most popular media continue to propagate traditional male and female stereotypes. But it is time we recognized that the social explanation is not enough. Resistances are also psychological, and as such, not aleatory. The need to differentiate oneself from the other sex is not the effect of conditioning but an age-old necessity. "Most societies use sex and gender as the main cognitive schema for understanding their environment. People, objects, ideas, are commonly classified as male or female."[72] Children use it not only to understand the world but above all to understand themselves. The act of knowing begins with distinction and classification, and first of all with dualism. The child learns to classify people and objects into two groups, one like him, the other opposed.

Another given characteristic of early childhood is the tendency to define what one *is* by what one *does*. To the question, "What is a man?" or "What is a woman?" the child responds by articulating roles and functions, generally stereotyped and oppositional. This is why criticism of the theory of sexual roles in the United States,[73] legitimate where adult men and women are concerned, should be softened with respect to children. If it is quite normal to teach the same things to children of both sexes, it is just as necessary to allow each the possibility of expressing his or her distinction and opposition. Although mom and dad may both be officeworkers or doctors and share household and family tasks, a young child will always feel the need to find a criterion for distinguishing between them (even an imaginary one) that will help her differentiate herself from one and identify herself with the other.

THE UNIVERSAL SEXUAL SEGREGATION OF CHILDREN

In all human societies there inevitably comes the time when male and female children are separated to form unisex groups. Even in Tahiti, where sexual differentiation is one of the least marked in the world, boys and girls cease to play together around preadolescence.[74] They begin to separate at the age of ten or twelve, and until they are fifteen or sixteen the boys' group no longer associates with the girls'. This is the age of "homosexual" friendships, so important for consolidating sexual identity. In Western society, the separation of the sexes occurs much earlier and lasts much longer.

In a recent article, Eleanor Maccoby, supported by her

research and by the current literature on the subject, has confirmed that "from nursery school to puberty, children group themselves essentially by sex."[75] In their longitudinal study, Maccoby and Jacklin (1987) note that at four-and-a-half, children in nursery school would spend three times as long playing with children of the same sex as with children of the opposite sex. At the age of six-and-a-half, the ratio was eleven to one.

Segregation is even more distinct in situations that are not structured by adults. What is more, if the latter go too far in their attempts to bring the two sexes together, the children put up resistance. Between six and twelve years of age, boys and girls avoid mixed groups. Barry Thorne has also stressed the intensity of the mockery inflicted by other children on those who show any interest in a child of the opposite sex. According to Maccoby, this desire to avoid the other sex does not result from pressure by adults. Whatever efforts the school makes to increase coed activities, the effect is only temporary: the children always revert to the model of segregation.

The tendency to prefer playmates of the same sex begins very early. Maccoby notes a study done in 1984 in a large Canadian day-care center on children from one to six years of age. Around the age of two the girls begin to turn to other girls, while the boys do not actively seek partners of the same sex until around three years of age. At the age of five, they outstrip the girls in their preference for companions of the same sex. Maccoby and Jacklin (1987) have observed in addition that the level of interaction was much higher in nonmixed pairs: boys are more active socially when they play with another boy than with a girl. Starting at thirty-three months, their style of play becomes different and the children get along better with children of the same sex, for although girls' play is not passive, it is not rough and physical like boys' play.[76]

According to Maccoby and Jacklin, the bases of sexual segregation are already present before the children enter school. They appear as soon as the children are able to classify others as well as themselves correctly according to sex. The differences observed between groups of boys and groups of girls are related to three main factors: the *socialization* of the child according to its sex, starting at birth (but this differs greatly from one parent to another, from one family to another); *biological factors*;[77] and last, *cognitive factors* that are as yet not very well known: children can distinguish boys from girls well before they are familiar with genital differences.[78]

This phenomenon, observable at all times and in all places, ought to inspire prudence in those contemptuous of sexual dualism. If it is true that it has been used by the patriarchy as a formidable weapon against women, it is no less true that it is a basic given of the child's consciousness of identity. To deny it would be to run the risk of a sexual confusion that has never been favorable to peace between men and women. To acknowledge its status as a necessary stage is perhaps the only means of subsequently recognizing a common bisexuality—in other words, the resemblance of the sexes.

The Devastating Myth of the Maternal Instinct

I have already demonstrated elsewhere that the theory of the maternal instinct has been belied by the history of behavior.[79] Alienating and guilt-inducing for women, the myth of the maternal instinct turns out to be devastating for children, particularly for sons.

The theory of the maternal instinct postulates that the mother *alone* is capable of concerning herself with the infant and the child because she is biologically determined for this. The mother-child couple supposedly forms an ideal unit that nothing can or should disturb. By promoting the idea of an exclusive attachment of the child for its mother,[80] and of a natural predisposition on her part to concern herself with him, one legitimizes the exclusion of the father and thereby reinforces it, furthering even more the mother-son symbiosis. Which is as much as to say that one prolongs the boy's protofemininity to the detriment of an identification with the father. English psychoanalysts have been fervent defenders of this theory. They have painted the portrait of an ideal mother totally devoted to her little one, her own interests identical to those of her child.[81] Whereas Margaret Mahler had described the normal "autistic" phase of the infant, D. W. Winnicott developed the idea of a symmetrical state in the mother, a "normal illness" in a new mother consisting of a psychiatric state of withdrawal, dissassociation, something like a schizoid episode.[82] In fact, concedes Winnicott, an adoptive mother or any other woman can be capable of experiencing this good "illness," which is the maternal instinct. As though it were enough to be born a woman to be maternal![83]

In fact, only one category of human beings is judged to be incapable of experiencing the primary maternal feeling: men, and in particular, fathers. Not only does Winnicott accept the idea that certain fathers are never interested in their babies,[84] but he pushes the contingency of paternal love so far that he adds, coolly, that if the father is present and wants to know his child, the child is lucky.[85] In general, for most classical psychoanalysts, the father cannot and should not be substituted for the mother. He should not even share the mothering. He should remain the possible overspill area for the child's hatred,[86] the embodiment of the reality principle,[87] and leave to the mother the privilege and duty of incarnating the pleasure principle. Representing the law, the father should know how to keep his distance. Not very long ago in France, in fact, one could turn on the radio and hear Françoise Dolto issuing this solemn warning: "Above all, fathers should be well aware that it is not through physical contact, but through their words that they may cause their children to love and respect them."[88] What better way could there be to say that the father is advised not to mother or fondle the toddler, or he will lose his status as maintainer of equilibrium for the child? Fatherly love should have this particular quality, that it be expressed only from a distance. Between him and his child, reason is the necessary intermediary that will in fact allow him to keep his distance.[89] Before the infant is one year old, the father should have a very small role to play with respect to his child. This concept of fatherhood, in every way conforming to the patriarchal tradition, results in strengthening the mother-child dyad, particularly the mother-son dyad. As the mother was always thought to be endowed with an admirable instinct, it was believed that she knew how to modulate it to give each stage of the child's development the necessary "dose" of love. Once the time came, she should encourage her little boy to leave the symbiosis and detach himself from her. In fact, motherly love was thought to be like mother's milk: it would adapt quite naturally to the child's evolving needs.

The truth is altogether different. Motherly love is infinitely complex and imperfect. Far from being an instinct, it is conditioned by so many factors independent of the mother's "good nature" or "good will" that in fact a minor miracle would be needed for this love to exist in the way it is described to us. It depends not only on the personal history of each woman (there can be generation after generation of bad or mediocre mothers), the timeliness of the pregnancy, her desire for the child, and her relationship with the father but also on many other factors—social, cultural, professional, and so on.

Of course there exist here and there admirable mothers who give their child what he needs to be happy without holding him prisoner, who spare him excesses of frustration and guilt, hindrances to his development. But these "gifted" women, like great artists, are miraculous exceptions that confirm the rule that the reality is difficult, unclear, and most often unsatisfying. If men and women are questioned about their mothers, they almost always define them using the words "too" or "not enough." *Too* present or *too* absent; *too* warm or *too* cold; *too* loving or *too* indifferent; *too* devoted or *too* selfish, and so forth; *too* much a mother for many sons or *not enough* of a mother for daughters who complain about it (Freud noted) on the psychoanalyst's couch. Good motherhood is an almost impossible mission that proves—if there were still any need to—that there is no such thing as an instinct in these matters. The secret that can't be taught is the "good distance" described by Lévi-Strauss in order to avoid racism and war. Neither too close, nor too distant, the good mother preserves the inner peace of her children and in particular her son. For him, "the good distance" from his mother conditions his feeling of masculine identity and his subsequent relationships with women.

The more mothers bear down on their sons, the more the latter fear women, flee them, or oppress them. But rather than accuse "castrating" mothers of engendering sexist sons (implying that women are the ones responsible for women's misfortunes),[90] it is time to put an end to exclusive mothering by the mother in order to break the vicious circle.

We now know that men can mother just as well as women when circumstances demand it.[91] A father is just as sensitive, affectionate, and competent as a mother, when he mobilizes his femininity.[92] It is only necessary that the mother, relieved of a mythical instinct, agree to share her condition with the father (or any man who embodies the image of the father), and that the latter cease to be afraid of his maternal femininity. As we shall see later, the absence of the father has graver consequences for his son when the son is under five years of age than it will later—and yet another of our beliefs is thus contradicted.

CHAPTER THREE

"IT IS MAN WHO ENGENDERS MAN"

This remark of Aristotle's[1] concerned the reproduction of the human species. It meant that it was man—the male—who transmitted to the child the principle of humanity. One can extend it today to the development of the male gender.

We now know that the male sex, characterized by the chromosome Y, is transmitted by the father. It is he, the sire, or any other man (even a group of men) incarnating the image of the father, who must complete the process of masculine differentiation. The child must still be helped to change his primary feminine identity into a secondary masculine identity. Within the patriarchal system, men have used different methods to succeed in turning the young boy into a man in his turn, a "real" man. Whether we are talking about initiation rites, homosexual pedagogy, or confrontation with his peers, these institutions all prove that masculine identity is *acquired* at the price of great difficulties. Furthermore, they have three points in common.

The first is the idea of a critical threshold to be crossed. At some point during his preadolescence the boy has the duty to leave behind his undifferentiated childhood. In most societies, becoming an adult man is problematic. By contrast to "the woman who *is*, the man must be *made*. In other words, menstruation, which gives the adolescent girl the possibility of having children, lays the basis for her feminine identity; it is a *natural* initiation that causes her to pass from girlhood to womanhood; on the other hand, in a man the *educative* process must take over from nature."[2] To put it another way, becoming a man is a willed fabrication, and one may wonder, with Jungian psychoanalyst Guy Corneau, if the son's masculinity would ever awaken if it were not forced to, at a given moment in its development.

The second point shared by the different pedagogies of manhood is the necessity for tests. Masculinity is won at the end of a combat (against oneself) that often involves physical or psychic pain. As Nicole Loraux points out with respect to the beginnings of the Roman Republic, "Virility can be read on the body like an open book."[3] The warrior's scars bear witness to the wounds and the spilled blood that prove the valor of the man and the citizen. "Pain is primarily the business of women. . . . A man owes it to himself to scorn it if he does not wish to find himself stripped of his manhood, and reduced to the level of the female condition."[4] Stoicism, both moral and physical, is learned through the passage of time and from the endurance of trials. In order to learn it, the young boy is often confronted with situations of an extreme cruelty. Even if we tend, nowadays, to perceive only their sadistic and negative aspect, it is important to stress that these tests always have as their object the strengthening of a masculinity that, without them, would risk being found wanting or never appearing at all.

The third point shared by traditional forms of developing manliness is the father's nonexistent or unobtrusive role. It is mainly older boys or adult men who take responsibility for the masculinization of the younger boys. Initiated by a mentor or a group of elders, the young boy enters the world of men with the help of men other than his own father. It is as though the father were afraid of inflicting suffering upon his son, or of giving him pleasure. Caught between fear of retaliation and dread of homosexual incest, he has for a long time chosen to take no part and keep his distance. Supporting his case on a considerable anthropological apparatus, Theodor Reik maintains the idea that, in his feelings for his son, a father revives his ambivalent feeling for his own father. This is the source of the fear of retaliation so clearly grasped by Otto Rank: "The son who experiences hostile impulses toward his father and who must repress them will be afraid, once he himself becomes a father, of the same attitude on the part of his son, because of the same unconscious complex."[5] One could call this the Isaac complex. Elsewhere, Joseph Pleck stresses the contrast between the traditional masculine role, which involves strong emotional bonds between men (bonds whose ritualized forms limit their intimacy) and the modern masculine role, in which emotional relations between men are weak and often absent.[6] One of the reasons for these differences in attitude probably lies in the fact that a young boy nowadays no longer has an initiator and that his father has not been able to perform this function. Fathers, being homophobes, are afraid of too close a contact with their sons.

Initiation Rites

The objective of all initiation rites is to change the status and identity of the boy so that he may be reborn as a man. In certain societies—such as the Fox tribe in Iowa—to be an authentic man is considered "The Big Impossible."[7] Only a few elite men succeed in this. But in most ritual societies, masculinity is a challenge accepted by all boys through the strength of their elders. For the most part, the trials are undergone, the transmutation takes place: the boys feel they are men. But at what price! A veritable inversion of the primary female state, initiation rites have been referred to as "a radical surgery of resocialization."[8] These trials are comprised of three stages, each more painful than the last: separation from the mother and the female world; transfer into an unknown world; and subjection to dramatic, public trials.

THE THREE STAGES

"The son of the female is the shadow of the male."[9] This observation of Shakespeare's is acutely felt by most ritual patriarchal societies. The contamination of males by females, and in particular of sons by mothers, is an old obsession that one finds in cultures and institutions as different as Rousseau's eighteenth century, the American Marines, and the tribes of New Guinea: prevailing everywhere is the idea that if one does not remove sons from their mothers, they will never be able to become adult men. Whether we are talking about the Samburu or the Kikuyu of eastern Africa, or the Baruya or the Sambia of New Guinea, among many others, the first act of male initiation is the wresting of the boys (generally between the ages of seven and ten) from their mothers.

Among the Sambia of New Guinea, the sound of flutes signals the beginning of the boys' initiation. Torn from their mothers by surprise, they are taken into the forest. Here, for three days, they are whipped until they bleed, in order to open their skin and stimulate their growth. They are beaten with nettles and made to bleed from the nose in order to rid them of the feminine liquids that prevent them from developing. On the third day, they are told the secret of the flutes, which they must never reveal to the women under pain of death. Young initiates subsequently questioned by the American anthropologist Gilbert Herdt have described to him the trauma they experienced upon separating from their mothers, their feeling of abandonment and despair.[10] One aim of male initiation is, in fact, brutally and radically to break the mothers' loving embrace.

After this separation, the boys, under threat of the worst punishments, will no longer speak to their mothers, nor touch them, nor look at them until they have attained their full status as men—that is, when they in turn have become fathers. Only then will they be able to lift the maternal taboo, offer her game, speak to her, and eat in her presence. "The first woman a Baruya leaves, in his life, is his mother, and she is also the last whom he finds again."[11]

The second stage marks the transition between the female world he must resolve to leave and the world of men he must adopt if he wishes to avoid being quite nonexistent. This social and psychological change of identity resembles immigration from one country to another, the adopted country having a language, customs, and a political system in every way opposite to those of the country of origin. In order to effect a transfer from one to the other, a long detour is necessary. It may last five, ten, or fifteen years, punctuated by great ceremonies marking these intermediate stages. Among the Baruya, ten years of sexual segregation are required, as well as four great ceremonies several years apart, in order to separate a boy from his mother, detach him from the female world, and prepare him to confront women again at the time of his marriage.

Even before proceeding to the first ceremony, the novices who have just been taken by force from their mothers are first isolated in an unknown place for several days (among the Baruya) or weeks (among the Hopi). Left there with nothing, without eating or drinking, often stripped of their clothes, the boys in a state of shock go through a necessary liminal phase in which they are no longer anything at all. Neither the children of their mothers, nor those of their fathers, these boys are "betwixt and between,"[12] literally between the two: in a cyclical and necessary state of nonidentity[13] that shows that the feminine child of the mother must die so that the male child can be born.

The third stage of male initiation rites is the endurance of harsh, often dramatic, and always public trials. Rituals include scarifications, circumcision of the preadolescent, subincision of the penis[14] (especially among the Australian aborigines), flagellation until blood is drawn, or the infliction of various wounds on different parts of the body. Even the gentle, androgynous Tahitians practice a sort of circumcision as a rite of passage for young boys. Unlike most of the rituals, the operation takes place in private, in an undramatic manner. Nevertheless, it remains true that in order to become an adult man, here, too, blood must flow. Psychoanalysts have often analyzed these "symbolic wounds" as being the representation of men's desire for the power of procreation possessed by women. But what is of interest here is less the spilled blood than the dramatic aspect of the trial and the scar that results from it. The anthropologist David Gilmore, who has recorded the different manhood tests among warrior peoples (for example, the Samburu of East Africa or the tribes of New Guinea) or peaceful peoples (Masai or Boshiman of Africa) notes that these trials are a species of confrontations enacted on the public stage.[15] They give the young boy an opportunity to display before everyone his courage when faced with pain,[16] sometimes his impassivity, and always his scorn of death. Confrontation with death, represented by physical pain and a sense of aloneness, marks the end of the state of childhood or possession by the mother and entry into the antithetical world of men. The scars left on the body are the indelible proofs of this change of state achieved once and for all within sight and in the knowledge of the men of the tribe.

Initiation rites continue to exist in many human societies, with differing degrees of cruelty and dramatization. Those that exist among the warrior tribes of New Guinea are certainly among the longest and most traumatic that a boy can experience. But they are proportionate to the survival demands of the society and especially proportionate to the exceptional bond that joins the boy to his mother. Whether it be the tribe of the Baruya, the Sambia, the Busama, or others, what is at issue is the transformation of sweet little boys into terrible warriors, and the purgation from the child of all the fluids, essences, and powers of women that prevent him from growing up. But the rites of the Bimin-Kuskusmin are among the most terrible and the most exemplary.[17]

The Bimin-Kuskusmin devote an extraordinary amount of time and energy to male ritual activities. These involve no less than ten stages lasting ten to fifteen years. Once removed from their mothers, the boys (seven to ten years old) listen to the song of the initiators, which designates them as soiled beings polluted by feminine substances.[18] The boys, terrorized, are undressed, their clothes burned, and they are washed by female initiators who coat their bodies with a yellow funerary mud, all the while making unkind remarks about their sex. This humiliating experience is followed by a speech of the initiators that announces to them that they are going to be killed because they have been weakened and polluted by their mothers. The children, extremely distraught, begin to cry, and their cries redouble when they are made to bleed from the head. They are shown one last time to their mothers, who also cry and go into mourning.

The boys are taken farther into the forest and beaten by surprise with sticks until their bodies are covered with stripes. During the following four days, they are humiliated and maltreated almost uninterruptedly. Constantly addressing them as "polluted" and describing them as puny, the initiators alternately flagellate them with stinging nettles, which makes their bodies bleed, and feed them emetics, in order to purge them of all the femininity that has accumulated in them since their birth. In order to force them to vomit, they are made to swallow the blood and urine of pigs. The trauma of the pain, and the stink of the incessant vomiting, the filth, the weeping and the terror experienced—all these put the children into a physical and psychic state of extreme misery. Scarcely is this first trial ended than they are forced to eat forbidden "female" food that increases their panic and provokes renewed vomiting. After a respite of several hours, the initiators make incisions in the boys' navels (in order to destroy the menstrual residues), and in their earlobes, and burn their forearms. The blood collected is then applied to their penises. They are told that this blood (female) will dissolve their penises and they are made to feel humiliated when their penises retract at the contact with the blood.

In the view of the anthropologist observing these ceremonies, the children are by now in an indescribable state of shock. Many of them, their bodies bloody, faint or become totally hysterical. This is the moment chosen by the initiators to announce to them that they are dying . . . Then they are tended and given a masculine name, all the while continuing to have regular incisions made on their temples. Despite the early attentions of the older men, the novices remain prostrate, in a state of distress and fear. These are the principal events that punctuate the very first stage of the initiation rites, which include yet many others.

F. J. Porter Pode questioned novices and initiators about their personal feelings during these trials. Having noted the extreme trauma of the children, who collapsed into hysteria or lost consciousness, he asked the older men if they were not moved by such torture. Many told them they regretted the suffering, but felt it was necessary for the boys. In their eyes, there was no alternative to this suffering. This was the price to be paid for passing from a state of female vulnerability to that of a powerful male. Questioned after these first trials, the novices confided to him their profound despair, which involved feelings of rage, of having been betrayed by their mothers, who did not protect them, and of hostility for their fathers, who went along with the torturers. But most of the novices also expressed their pride at having gone through this and at having survived. Those most pampered by their mothers, the most feminine, are those who have the most trouble enduring these trials. They say that something inside them broke. They have cut the umbilical cord and feel a new masculine solidarity, formed of an uncontested power and of separation from the danger of the feminine.

THE LESSONS OF THESE RITES

The first lesson taught by these rites is that masculinity is achieved only through a detour all the longer and more painful the more prolonged the mother-son symbiosis was. In order to bring about the radical resocialization described by Herdt, the little boy must "rattle the very gates of life and death."[19] The Sambia novices, like all those of the Eastern Highlands of New

74

Guinea, say clearly that they fear being killed at the time of the bleedings.

It should be pointed out that these rites concern only boys. Girls are subjected only to much shorter and infinitely less painful ceremonies. So much so that Maurice Godelier even wonders if one can speak of "a real initiation" for women.[20] How can one compare ten years of sexual segregation and four great ceremonies to separate the boy from his mother with the two weeks necessary for turning an adolescent girl into a young woman ready to marry? Adolescent girls spend only a few days in an exclusively female world before returning to the same everyday family life. They simply begin increasing their visits and services to the family of their future parents-in-law.

These rites, which may appear as strange as they are barbarous to a reader from an industrial society, are one of the possible responses to a need universally felt by the male child: to be recognized as a man; to be one who has broken with the weakness and dependence of childhood. Today, in our societies in which rituals have lost their meaning, the transition is more problematic, for it is not sanctioned by glaring proofs. In the United States, people are very concerned about those young men who refuse to grow up and become responsible men. Some speak of the Peter Pan complex,[21] others of the culture of the playboy who, in the manner of the adolescent, rejects all emotional ties with women.[22] This is one reason why many American men say they are nostalgic for the old initiation rites.

Our preindustrial societies also practiced them, as we can see from Georges Duby's description of the education of a knight's son in the Middle Ages.[23] This male initiation outside the paternal house survived in France in other forms. Beginning in the seventeenth century, residence in boarding schools took over from those parents who could afford it, and this continued until the nineteenth century, which established the fashion of education by parents. In Anglo-American countries, more obsessed with virility, masculinization rites survived longer. In modern England, the children of the "gentry," like the boys of East Africa or New Guinea, continued to be taken by force from their mothers and their homes at a tender age. Sent to the celebrated public boarding schools, they were subjected to an extremely cruel ragging on the part of the older boys, which included physical violence, terror, and humiliation. In the eyes of their parents, this was the only means of turning them into men worthy of leading the British empire. The regime of the English schools was well known for its extreme severity, including obligatory team sports, an entirely military discipline and training, and little food—in short, Spartan conditions. According to Christine Heward, the harshness of these schools peaked before the First World War and began to decline after 1920.[24] Autobiographies by men of that time give us a glimpse of the feelings of pain and destruction that persisted in them as adults.[25] The English writer Gerald Brennan confessed that in the worst moments of the First World War he comforted himself by thinking that at least he was no longer at Radley School. War was easier than school! Even in Victorian England, a civilization that was not characterized by excess, masculinity "was an artificial product coaxed by austere training and testing."[26]

Today there still remain vestiges of these male initiation rites in certain military units. In France, the training of the Foreign Legion has the reputation of being one of the harshest. In the United States, it is the Marines who claim to be the most "manly." Recruits undergo a regime that many, these days, feel is inhuman: iron discipline, extreme conformism, exhausting physical training, mockery and humiliation of new recruits, who can barely sleep or eat. Perpetually called "fags" and "queers," they must submit to a great deal of ragging without flinching. These are the conditions for the birth of a new man, a real man, free of all female contamination.[27] Homophobia and misogyny are included in the philosophy of the American Marines, who say openly that if one wants to create a bunch of killers, one should kill the woman in them.[28] Pat Conroy, in *The Great Santini*, describes in detail a boy's terrifying education by his father, a tyrannical Marine, who treats his son like one of his recruits.[29] Between physical and verbal acts of violence, one perceives the father's obsession—that his son does not conform to the manly model of the soldier. He teaches him scorn of women (good for screwing), exaltation of his private parts, horror of anything remotely resembling femininity, tenderness, or respect for another. On the boy's eighteenth birthday, the father makes him drink and smoke (signs of virility) until he is sick. He constantly reproaches him for his lack of manliness: he is too much his mother's son and not enough his father's.

Homosexual Pedagogy

The expression "homosexual pedagogy" may invite confusion. Here it does not mean some sort of proselytizing aimed at turning young men into exclusive homosexuals, and still less is its aim the transmission of an erotic art. Homosexual pedagogy as it was practiced in other times and is practiced today in other cultures is the teaching of virility by the indirect path of homosexuality. This idea, strange though it may seem to many of us, nevertheless contains a hidden soundness.

Homosexual pedagogy, much older than is often believed,[30] appears in societies in which virility has the status of an absolute moral value. As John Boswell notes, among ancient peoples it was often understood that men who loved other men were more masculine than their heterosexual counterparts. The logical argument behind this (one about which there is room for skepticism) was that men who loved men would try to equal them and be like them, whereas men who loved women would become like them, that is, "effeminate."[31]

In fact, numerous Roman emperors practiced homosexuality officially. Antinoüs, favorite of the wise emperor Hadrian, was even the object of an official cult after his premature death.[32] Even seven centuries earlier, homosexuality was considered an activity so noble that Solon forbid slaves to practice it. As Michel Foucault wrote: "To love boys was a 'free' practice . . . not only permitted by the law (except in particular circumstances), it was accepted by opinion. Moreover, it found solid support in different (military or educational) institutions. . . . It was a cultural practice that enjoyed the prestige of a whole literature . . . that vouched for its excellence."[33]

In other, very different societies in which virility has, if not a moral value, at least a vital significance, homosexual pedagogy is the secret of the transformation of boys into men. Such is the case with the Sambia and Baruya warrior tribes, obsessed by masculinity, considered a primary condition for their survival. Living in a very difficult geographic and human environment, these small societies of one or two thousand persons, formerly in a perpetual state of war, have survived owing only to the toughness of the men. In other words, for them homosexuality is not tied to femininity. On the contrary, it is an unavoidable stage on the way to heterosexual masculinity.

VIRILITY: A KNOWLEDGE TRANSMITTED THROUGH
INTIMATE CONTACTS

We have already stressed the advantage the little girl derives from acquiring her sense of feminine identity from repeated contact with her mother's body. This contact is not neutral, as Rousseau thought. What is good for the little girl must also be good for the boy. A close relationship with an adult man must strengthen his identity and cancel out the bad habits of his body-to-body contact with his mother. As Guy Corneau points out, "To see other men . . . to touch them, to talk to them, confirms each one in his masculine identity."[34]

But virility is not only a sense of identity; it is also a knowledge transmitted through an initiatory relationship (in ancient Greece) and an intimate relationship; further, it is a biological reality. The Sambia believe that the body of a young male does not produce sperm naturally the way adolescent girls begin to menstruate. Only fellatio by young men can activate the boys' sperm production. The Greeks and the Sambia, the Romans and the Medieval Scandinavians, the Japanese samurai and the Baruya—all have believed that true virility is achieved through a close relationship between two men.

According to Foucault, it is through sex that one has access to one's own intelligibility. Now, "in Greece, truth and sex were linked in the form of pedagogy, through the transmission from one body to another of a precious knowledge; sex served as a support for the initiations of knowledge."[35] From the training of the warrior for the sacred batallion of ancient Thebes[36] to that of the honest Athenian man, all masculine education makes great allowances for initiatory and pedagogical homosexuality, which has the value of an institution.[37] "In Sparta, the boys, beginning at the age of seven, were drilled in brawling by their elders. At twelve, those who had a good renown found lovers who attached themselves to them; the older boys, for their part, looked out for them more, often went to the gymnasiums and watched their fights and the exchanges of mockery which they addressed to one another. And, far from exerting only a superficial control, they all regarded themselves in some manner as the fathers, the overseers, and the leaders of all the young boys."[38]

It is therefore within the framework of a pedagogical process that the boys take a lover. The aim of the liaison is explicit: "to make the child as good as possible." Such is the task of the lover, the *eraste*, who is the master of the *eromene*. In Athens, where pederasty became widespread and where war was no longer the reason for it, the pedagogical nature of homosexuality survived. For lack of specialized educators, "once the educative function passes from a consanguineous member of the family to a stranger or to a member of the family by marriage, it is completed with an erotic dimension, whether assumed sexually or not."[39] Even the conservative Aristophanes, who celebrates the modest customs of ancient Athens, is moved by this erotic atmosphere: "In the home of the gymnastics teacher, when they were resting, the children had to put their

79

legs out in front of them in order not to show anything shocking to strangers. In that time a boy would never have rubbed
himself with oil lower than his navel: and what a fresh down
on their organs—velvet, a vapor, as on a peach!"[40]

According to Bernard Sergent, the great principle of education is that an adult male, a citizen worthy of his station, transmits to a pupil, close to civic maturity, his *arete*—that is, his
virtue, his merit, his courage, his intelligence, and his honor.
And this transmission of qualities from the eraste to the young
eromene was for a long time achieved through carnal contact.
Even if Socrates advocated the love of the soul rather than that
of the body, the amorous relationship between men was to
remain the key to male pedagogy in Greece.

In the Baruya and Sambia tribes, the great secret of masculinity—which no woman must know—is that "the sperm
gives men the power to cause boys to be reborn outside their
mother's bellies, in the world of men and through them alone.
This secret, the most sacred, is that the young initiates are fed
the sperm of their elders and that this ingestion is repeated for
many years with the aim of making them grow larger than the
women and capable of dominating them."[41] By virtue of the
analogy between blood and sperm, it is probable that the ritual
of the African Kikuyu has a similar function. The elders of the
tribe perform the role of "male nurses." Each in his turn, with
the same sharp knife, cuts his arm and gives his blood to the
adolescents to drink. It is thus that the latter become men.[42] In
both rituals it is believed that by sucking the mother's milk,
one becomes feminine and by drinking masculine liquids, one
becomes manly. This is an idea very close to a prejudice still
strong in France in the eighteenth century, with regard to the
choice of a wetnurse. People were so convinced that the nursing baby would assume the character of the woman from
whom he nursed that they based their choice of nurse on her
temperament as well, and they showed the greatest reserve
with respect to cows' and goats' milk.

Among the Sambia, the fact that identity is transmitted by

the sperm gives rise to a ritualized homosexual fellatio. The men consider constant insemination to be the only means by which the boys will grow and acquire manly competence. On the third day of the initiation, flutes are held out to them with obscene jokes; they are supposed to put them in their mouths. If a child refuses, the initiator uses force. After this, fellatio and copulation are obligatory within a ritualized framework. The boys practice fellatio only with young bachelors who have not had sexual relations with women, and thus have not risked contamination by them. But the fellatio is not reciprocal. The purveyors of sperm do not receive any. To desire to suck the penis of a prepubescent boy would be considered a perversion. Furthermore, the ritualized homosexuality is rigorously structured by the incest prohibition, which prevents such contacts between related men. In the third stage of the initiation, which corresponds to puberty, the young adolescents in turn become donors of sperm for a new group of initiates. During this period, all contacts with women are forbidden, and the strongest social pressures are exerted on the boys so that they will conform to their roles in the fellatio.

The flute ritual permits the transfer of the boys' attachment to their mothers to the bachelors. The flute is a substitute for both the breast and the phallus, the secret that unites fathers and sons against the mother. For Herdt, the flute ritual confirms that an imaginary isomorphism is created between the flute player and the mother figure, and also between the sucker of the flute and the image of the child. In this system of the fantastical, an association is formed between the experience of the mother's breast and that of the initiator's penis.[43] The flute is considered a means of defense against the anguish of the loss of the mother.

To convert little boys too attached to their mothers into manly and aggressive warriors is no small task. But to create a male identity that changes men who were first erotically excited by boys into heterosexuals and lovers of women is an even more monumental challenge.

THE CONDITIONS OF HOMOSEXUAL PEDAGOGY

Homosexual pedagogy is very strictly regulated. The age and status of the initiate, as well as the practices and objectives of the initiation, are the object of multiple injunctions.

This privileged relationship implies first of all a difference in age between the partners, and with it a distinction of status. One, still quite young, is not yet fully formed; the other is considered an adult. Indications as to the real age of the partners are often vague in the texts of ancient Greece.[44] But the decisive moment, which varies from one adolescent to another, is the appearance of the beard. Ancient tradition confers upon it the signification of the emergence of virility. Furthermore, the eraste—like the Sambia or Baruya bachelor—is himself a young man. In the eyes of the legislator, the "normal" Athenian no longer desires young boys once he is past the age of forty.[45] As a general rule, the eraste is not much older than his eromene.

Sexuality, says Foucault, is a particularly dense point of passage for relations of power.[46] It is even more so when it is given a pedagogical finality. The relationship between the eraste and his eromene is not that of equal to equal. No more is that of the Sambia bachelor with the young novice. If the secret of the flutes heralds male hegemony, it is first the symbol of hierarchy among men. This sexual and psychological subordination is a necessary stage for arriving at the status of dominator, which is the essence of the male sense of identity. One expects from the Greek preadolescent the timidity and discretion that go along with the status of child (*pais*). Inequality in age goes hand in hand with inequality in feelings. If the eraste has real desires, the eromene, on the other hand, feels only a friendship (*philia*) free of sexual connotation.[47] And if he has a taste for the sexual relationship, he is a pervert. To the sexual attraction of the eraste, the eromene responds with a feeling of admiration and gratitude toward his elder.

The roles of the two partners are fixed by the practices. The eraste is in a position of initiative, which gives him rights and obligations.[48] Unlike the forced fellatio of the boys of New

Guinea, it was customary, in Athens, to respect the young man's freedom. One could not exert upon him—as long as he was not of servile birth—any statutory power. One had to be able to persuade him. On the other hand, in earlier times boys were the objects of rapes, and the erastes, compared to hunters, considered their eromene to be their prey. But whether voluntary or not, homosexual pedagogy always pursues the same end: apprenticeship into the male role. Whether it be willingly or by force, the adult man teaches the younger man the mastery of self that defines manliness. He is a substitute for the father (natural fathers have other things to do)[49] or an older brother, or even a stepfather. But he has the advantage—unlike these three family figures—of having access to the boy's body and of proceeding to transmit knowledge by this route.

One last condition of pedagogical and initiatory homosexuality is that it can only be temporary. Whatever the eraste's passion may be, it must evolve into friendship upon the appearance of the first hairs of the eromene's beard. Many Greek texts criticize bad erastes, who cause the erotic liaison to persist beyond what is necessary and permitted. Love between two adults no longer has anything to do with the initiation and will readily be the object of criticism or irony. The reason for this is the suspicion of a passivity that is always frowned upon in a free man and particularly serious when it is a question of an adult. The tribes of New Guinea, much stricter than ancient Greece, absolutely forbid adult homosexuality, which they consider an aberration.

HOMOSEXUALITY: ONE STAGE ON THE WAY
TO HETEROSEXUALITY

Homosexuality is a transitory practice but necessary for achieving one's heterosexual masculinity. This may appear paradoxical to us, but in other civilizations it is not. The Greek texts are categorical: there are not two different sorts of desires, homosexual and heterosexual, but a single sort which can attach itself to a beautiful object.[50] The same man may become infatuated, as he likes, with a courtesan or an adolescent boy.[51] There is no opposition between two exclusive choices. Michel Foucault sees this as the proof of a certain bisexuality among the Greeks that did not imply, for them, "a dual, ambivalent, and "bisexual" structure of desire."[52] Preference for boys or girls was "a matter of taste," not a matter of typology involving the very nature of the individual; there were simply, rather, two manners of taking "one's pleasure." In other words, this was a bisexuality without implications to do with identity. Furthermore, Zeno, founder of stoicism, recommended that one not choose his sexual partners according to their gender, but according to their personal qualities.[53]

Robert Stoller and Gilbert Herdt, who worked together on the signification of the Sambia rites, believe that these homosexual practices have a value as an introduction to eroticism. Observing the flute ceremony during two different initiations, Herdt confesses to having been intuitively struck by something unsaid: the initiators revealed "the erotic components of the mouth and the penis—penile erection, sexual impulses, semen, homosexual activities in particular, and genital eroticism more broadly."[54] The rigid structure of ritualized masculinity allows "the Sambia males to be excited first by boys as sexual objects and subsequently by women whose mouths, vaginas, and bodies are exciting, dangerous, fetishized."[55] Even if the ritual cult puts a momentary restraint on the development of heterosexuality by means of three mechanisms (institutionalized fellatio, the taboo of avoiding women, and the fear of reduction of sperm), its function is to create fierce warriors to defend the community but also heterosexual men to assure its reproduction. The two go together, like homosexuality and heterosexuality. This established fact, drawn from observations of societies foreign to ours, is beginning to be taken into account by certain specialists. For instance, E. James Anthony notes that a long practice of homosexuality in childhood and adolescence does not significantly affect adaptation to adult heterosexuality.[56]

This introduction of homosexuality in the formation of the boy is perhaps one of the reasons for the unobtrusive role of the father. Beyond the rationalizations that one finds in Plato's *Laches*, or among present-day fathers who confess they are too busy to raise their sons, is hidden the fear of paternal homosexuality, increased by a horror of incest. Whereas the mother is not afraid of any such thing with her daughter,[57] the pedophile father belongs in the record book of the great perverts. Perhaps it is also to avoid temptation that certain societies have resorted to initiators who are strangers to the family. The latter take over from the mother and substitute for the unthinkable pedophile father. Often, the initiator is a plural person. Baruya and Sambia novices have homosexual relations with several bachelors without "belonging" to any one. Other societies that do not practice these initiation rites also think that a single father is not enough for the son. Suzanne Lallemand, an Africanist ethnologist who has worked among the rural Mossi of the Upper Volta, observes that each child has ten or so available fathers in his or her family environment. In the extended family that lives in the large Mossi dwelling, all the men, whether close or less close, serve as fathers to the children and very often the biological father is not the boy's favorite.[58]

If our industrial societies are moving farther and farther away from African or ritual solutions—as is evidenced by the very sharp increase in single-parent families and the failure of attempts at communes—certain American psychoanalysts are calling for a return to the old institution of the male mentor,[59] the wise counselor who guides the boy and gives him the benefit of his experience. Robert Bly, best-selling author of a book about the formation of the male identity,[60] sees this as the only solution to the many problems that young American males are confronting today. Less mystical and mythical than the very Jungian Bly, Samuel Osherson reaches the same conclusions. He points to several studies proving that young men who have been taken in charge by an older man (say, a college professor or a more experienced man in the workplace) have better success with their lives and are more mature than those who have not had a mentor.[61]

Industrial Societies: Peers Rather Than Fathers

One of history's ironies is the fact that Freud's theory of the identification of the son with the father in the Oedipal relationship appeared at the very same time that fathers in cities left the family home in large numbers to work outside and rituals surrounding separation from the mother began disappearing everywhere. The knight's son now stays at home under his mother's authority. The nuclear family is often reduced to a mother-children duo.

FATHER SICKNESS

Starting in the mid-nineteenth century, the industrial society imprinted new characteristics on the family. Men were obliged to spend all day working outside the home in factories, mines, offices, and so on. Contacts between fathers of urban families with their children were considerably reduced, and the father became a distant personage whose occupations were often mysterious in the eyes of his offspring. This new organization of work engendered de facto a radical separation of sexes and roles. Whereas in the eighteenth century a husband and wife worked side by side on the farm, in the marketplace, or in the shop, helped by their children, fifty years later the world was divided into two heterogeneous spheres that scarcely communicated: the private sphere of the family home, governed by mothers, and the public and professional sphere, the exclusive realm of men. On one side was the woman, mother and housekeeper; on the other, the man, worker and "breadwinner." In accordance with Rousseau's ideals, it was up to the mother to incarnate moral law and the emotions; the father was to incarnate the laws of politics and economy.

As the century advanced, family handbooks[62] referred less

and less to the father's duties and adopted more and more firmly the position that mothers were providentially endowed with
all the qualities necessary for raising children of both sexes. In
Europe as in the United States, fashion favored the good mother devoted body and soul to her children. If it is true that one
insisted more in France on the sacrosanct maternal instinct
whereas puritan America exalted the mother's moral purity, a
mother's responsibilities increased everywhere. In addition to
nurturing the children, she also took responsibility for their
moral and physical education and often their book learning.[63]
Industrial society, by distancing the father from his son, under-
mined the father's power. It put an end to the omnipotent patriarch laying down the law to his wife and children.[64]

If the image of the loving father[65] tended to replace that of
the bogeyman in the avant-garde bourgeoisie, many men were
prevented from being fathers and many others took no interest
in it. Peter Stearns points out that all this goes hand in hand
with a redefinition of traditional masculinity. Physical force
and honor were replaced by success, money, and a valorizing
work that justified the father's distance. He maintains that the
end of the nineteenth century was more traumatic for men
than the twentieth century.[66] In the United States, the 1929
crash was the final humiliation for fathers. The unemployed,
obliged to stay at home for long periods of time, lost confidence
in themselves and felt their manliness assaulted—especially
since American films of the 1930s began to broadcast the
image of the "career woman."

Finally, two images of the father were dominant in the United States and, to a lesser degree, in Europe: the distant, inaccessible father, and the unmanned and scorned father. In effect,
since the end of the nineteenth century, the literature of English-speaking countries has been one long complaint addressed
to the father. Shere Hite's recent investigation confirms that
almost no men (out of seven thousand questioned) say they
have been, or are presently, close to their fathers. Very few even
recall having been held in his arms or caressed by him, whereas

they recall very clearly having been spanked or punished.[67]

From the nineteenth to the twentieth century, the prosecution of American fathers has been pursued by men of different sensibilities and cultures. At the beginning of the twentieth century, Henry James, senior, the father of Henry and William James, complained bitterly of the puritan education given to him by a severe and distant father. The latter, more preoccupied with expanding his commercial empire than with anything else, devoted little time to his numerous offspring, apart from teaching them the Presbyterian rules of good conduct. The son would remember all his life Sundays on which the children were taught not to play, not to dance, not to read storybooks, and not even to review lessons for Monday's classes.[68] The father appeared to his son as an intransigent, inaccessible God, a terrible man of whom the son would later say that he didn't remember his father ever questioning him about what he was doing outside the house, about his companions, or that his father was ever really concerned about school results.[69] This unhappy child of an authoritarian patriarch and a distant mother became an exceptionally affectionate father.[70] Yet his own children judged him harshly because of his complete submission to his wife. According to the biographer of Henry James Jr., the mother enveloped the whole family, including the father, who existed only for her and through her. Retrospectively, Henry James remembered her lap, wide open and yet insidiously enveloping. She was him (Henry James, the father), she was each of them.[71] He saw his parents in an ambiguous and inverted relationship: a strong, manly, and yet weak father, feminine in his tender and accommodating side, who yielded defenselessly to his children; and a mother who was strong, resolute, yet unreasonable and inconsistent. The future novelist accepted his mother's sovereignty and authority, but not his father's dependence.[72] The latter was to produce a son panicked by women, one who abstained from sexual relations all his life. Is this to say that a tender father is even more harmful than one who is distant and authoritarian?

To judge from Ernest Hemingway's biography[73] or those of other famous American men, an all-powerful mother who ceaselessly castrates those around her and a father obsessed by a feeling of incapacity produce boys who are very badly off. Unlike Henry James, who measured his words, Hemingway hid neither his scorn for his father nor his hatred of his mother. Then again, his manic-depressive father was sometimes very hard on him as a boy. Quite different is the father evoked by Philip Roth in his work: a man devoted to his family, dissatisfied, fearful, ignorant, exploited, anonymous. Portnoy unflinchingly depicts a father eternally constipated, with a pitiful physique, and no match for his wife, who is audacious, energetic, perhaps too perfect. To his psychoanalyst Portnoy describes his father as a clot, a moron, a philistine . . . no King Kong, a miserable creature in the eyes of his son, who weeps with rage over it.[74] Even if the indictment is less forceful in Roth's other novels, the father is always described as a gentle, retiring man without prestige or authority.

Too distant or too familiar, too harsh or too tender, too authoritarian or not enough so, the father also seems to have trouble finding the proper distance from his son. Perhaps one has been too quick to accuse the castrating and "voracious"[75] mother, as did English antipsychiatry in the years between 1960 and 1970, of all the father's sins. The systematic attack against women, and particularly the unyielding condemnation of mothers by R. D. Laing and David Cooper, has more to do with a settling of accounts than with an explanation of the obstacles faced by fathers. But whether they prosecute the lost and wounded father or mourn for him,[76] a number of boys no longer see him, in our industrial society, as their role model. They seek this model in literary fiction and even more in the movies. The legendary image of the cowboy, the adventurer, Rambo and other "Terminators," as well as the actors who play them, have become substitute fathers for our sons. But even more than these unreal, supervirile heroes, the best role models for boys are their peers.

89

THE IMPORTANCE OF PEERS

As we have seen, beginning in nursery school boys and girls tend to play with children of the same sex. This tendency toward sexual grouping increases at the age of six or seven, lasts into adolescence, and creates very different subcultures. The American Gary Alan Fine has posed questions about the little boys' love of "dirty play,"[77] by which he means activities that adults consider reprehensible and that range from throwing stones at frogs, as Plutarch observed so long ago, to aggressive jokes, and include endless conversations about sex. For Fine, all this comes not so much from a natural aggressiveness as from a social desire to assert their male identity. "Dirty play" exteriorizes a status, and its aim is less to do harm than to obtain recognition for one's boldness. Male preadolescents' love of noisy activities, dirty games, and obscenity is another way of asserting their virility in opposition to the maternal feminine world in which all this is forbidden. These attitudes persist among many adult men when they find themselves alone together, as in locker rooms.[78]

The company of their peers is more important for boys than for girls, and they readily seek group life and collective activities and sports. The research carried out by Régine Boyer into the activities of highschool boys and girls from fifteen to nineteen shows that, taking all social classes together, boys spend more time with their peers than girls do[79]—one hour a day more, on average. Depending on their social origin, boys like to meet in cafes, on playing fields for sports, or in the evenings at parties, whereas a greater number of girls read and have long telephone conversations[80] and spend more time with family members.

Packs, gangs, teams, and groups of boys of all sorts are less the expression of a gregarious instinct characteristic of their sex than that of a need to break with a feminine familial culture in order to be able to create another, male one. Without the effective presence of a father model of manliness, young males join together under the rule of another male who is slightly older, slightly stronger, or slightly brighter, a sort of older brother, the "leader" who is admired and copied and whose authority is recognized.

At the end of the last century, in the midst of industrial expansion, more and more American men were openly worried about their sons' manliness. Terrorized by feminist speeches, concerned about the feminization of family and school education as well as the dominance of the mother's law, they were afraid that young boys no longer had the opportunity to learn to be men. Gradually they proposed a new masculine ideal that would stress moral and physical self-affirmation. There was a shift from "an earlier idealization of passive traits such as piety, thrift, and industry to an emphasis on vigor, forcefulness, and mastery. . . . Literary masculinization extended beyond mortals like Teddy Roosevelt to Christ who was portrayed as 'the supremely manly man': attractive to women, individualistic, athletic, self-controlled, and aggressive when need be."[81] Furthermore, the distinction between the sexual roles was emphasized and rigidified as rarely before.

All these preoccupations lay at the origin of the founding of the institution of the Boy Scouts in 1907 in England, and in America in 1910. Theodore Roosevelt, having just completed two terms as president of the United States, became its honorary president. Its advertised objective was "to turn little boys into grownup men and fight the forces of feminization." In order to do this, boys of the same age were brought together in troops in the charge of an adult man who was to encourage team spirit and all forms of manliness and tolerate no sort of "effeminacy." Tests, challenges, discipline, moral rigor, and above all a communal life away from any feminine presence formed the substance of scouting.

For the same reasons, collective sports experienced an exceptional development that has continued right up to the present.[82] Sports that involved competition, aggression, and violence were—and still are in the United States—considered the best initiation to manliness. It is on the playing field that the American preadolescent earns his stripes as a male. Here he publicly displays his scorn of pain, his control over his body, his toughness when knocked about, his desire to win and to crush the opposition. Here, in short, he proves that he is not a baby, a girl, or a homosexual,[83] but a "real tough guy." Sporting fields and locker rooms are still places where coeducation is unthinkable, microcosms of the purest machismo without real equivalents in ordinary life.[84]

Apprenticeship in group sports in the United States has some features in common with the initiation rites described above. Sociologist Michael Messner, who has devoted numerous articles to this subject, has demonstrated the relationship between apprenticeship in sports and the *construction* of masculinity. He tells how he himself, as a boy of eight on a baseball field for the first time, was reprimanded by his coach-father because he threw the ball "like a girl."[85] Reflecting later on the anguish caused by his father's comment and the trouble he went to to discover a motion that would be sufficiently virile, Messner makes two interesting observations. First of all, it was the horrifying fear of being a girl that served as a motive for his learning to play baseball. Then, he noticed that the "feminine" way of throwing the ball was an anatomically natural movement for the arm, whereas the "masculine" way was not and would eventually cause damage to the arms and shoulders. This observation led children's baseball leagues to prohibit such motions. Despite this, pain remains at the center of the teaching of manliness in sports. The sociologist Don Sabo has evaluated the physical harm he suffered from playing football when he was young and the reasons that goaded him to endure the pain starting at the age of eight: "I played for the rewards. To win at sports meant winning friends and creating a place for oneself in the order of males. Success transformed me: I was less myself and more like the older boys and my hero Butkus. . . . As an adolescent, I hoped that sports would make the girls pay attention to me."[86]

As a result, Don Sabo learned to endure everything without

showing his pain, just like the young initiates: the most painful wounds, broken bones, black eyes, a shattered nose: "Pain and wounds are part of the game." In order to become captain of his team, he was "fanatically aggressive and mercilessly competitive." A man, in other words! Or more precisely, according to Sabo, a man within a patriarchal system that includes not only the domination by men of women but an intramale domination in which a minority lays down the law to the majority. In this ideology, a boy is taught that to endure pain is courageous and manly, "that pain is good and pleasure bad, as is clearly shown by the principle repeated by coaches a thousand times: *no pain, no gain.*"[87] He is also encouraged to consider his body as a tool, a machine, and even a weapon used to defeat an "objectified opponent."[88]

Messner points out that such a conception of masculinity—as competitive, hierarchical, and aggressive—does not favor the establishment of intimate and lasting friendships with other men. Nevertheless, despite a proclaimed homophobia, team sports, which give men a way of touching and grabbing one another without being suspected of homosexual intentions, are in fact the occasion for a homoeroticism all the stronger because it is unconscious—the proof being those football and rugby players who take hold of one another around the neck or the waist, embrace and rub one another, and pat one another affectionately on the buttocks in front of millions of television spectators, at every opportunity and without the slightest embarrassment.

American literature, whether autobiographical or not, is rich in stories about the childhood and adolescence of boys who were transformed by manly sports. Sometimes it is the father who serves as initiator, but it is more often the emblematic figure of the coach who embodies manliness and serves as a father substitute. Whether it be football (Thomas Faber or Pat Conroy),[89] or basketball (John Updike),[90] or baseball (Philip Roth or Edmund White),[91] all agree in singing the praises of sports, which was their veritable male initiation rite. Even if today the mythology of sports no longer has the same influence on boys' education, it nevertheless remains powerful, synonymous with virility and success. "Sports," observe Baudelot and Establet, "is one of the components of the modern competitive culture. It unites men of all social classes. Women, by contrast, do not engage in it except when it is divested of its competitive components: they prefer training to competition."[92] This opinion is confirmed by Michel Bozon's research on the leisure activities of young Frenchmen and Frenchwomen.[93]

Today, violent sports as an initiatory trial is argued against by some people who believe that the virility engendered by such practices derives from the old patriarchal model that is no longer theirs. But in these days, at the end of the twentieth century, many men also express their nostalgia for the rituals of earlier times in which a test of manliness strengthened their identity. Alain Finkielkraut, who admits that he no longer knows what masculinity is, regrets not the disappearance of the old power of the male but that of the "manly cogito: I risk myself, therefore I am."[94] In the United States there are more and more men like Ray Raphaël, Robert Bly, Douglas Gillette, Robert Moore[95] and other Jungians proclaiming the need to create new initiation rites. But how can one help fearing that the appearance of the new will merely camouflage the old formulas of the patriarchy which we have had such trouble leaving behind? Those nostalgic for the old rituals should not forget that these still involve a radical opposition to women, sustained by feelings of superiority and contempt that are hard to suppress later. The fact is that we do not desire such relations between men and women. And we will not mourn the passing of the old type of man, who is dying before our eyes.

Robert Bly has carved a solid success for himself among American men by talking once again about the mother-son break and the role of the mentor (his own, perhaps?), without seeing that today's masculinity is already very different from that of earlier times: multiple, subtle, indissolubly linked to the feminine. Tomorrow's masculinity will be less the result of a brutal break from the world of women, arranged by strangers, than it will be a consequence of the involvement—unprece- dented—of the father starting at birth. The new masculinity will bear very little resemblance to the old, but it will exist no less, with all its strength and its fragility.

CHAPTER FOUR

IDENTITY AND SEXUAL ORIENTATION

Today, one of the most obvious characteristics of masculinity is heterosexuality. The definition of gender spontaneously implies sexuality: who does what and with whom? Masculine identity is associated with the fact of possessing, taking, penetrating, dominating, and asserting oneself, if necessary, by force. Feminine identity is associated with the fact of being possessed, docile, passive, submissive. Sexual "normality" and identity are inscribed within the context of the domination of a woman by a man. According to this point of view, homosexuality, which involves the domination of a man by another man, is considered, if not a mental illness, at least a gender identity disorder.

Heterosexuality is the third negative proof of traditional masculinity. After dissociation from the mother (I am not her baby), and radical distinction from the female sex (I am not a girl), the boy must prove (to himself) that he is not homosexual, therefore that he does not wish to desire other men or be desired by them. In our society the idea predominates that one is really a man if one exclusively prefers women—as though possessing a woman reinforced the desired otherness by distancing the specter of identity: to *have* a woman in order not *to be* a woman. In the eyes of some, the very fact of not being homosexual is already an assurance of masculinity. As witness one survey conducted by a men's magazine.[1] To the question: "Would you still consider yourself a man if you had a homosexual experience?" 57 percent of the men questioned answered no.

If heterosexuality seems to us today one of the most obvious features of the masculine identity, to the point of being perceived as a natural given, our ancestors did not always think the same.

Recent Evidence

THE STATUS OF THE SODOMITE BEFORE THE NINETEENTH CENTURY

Sodomy is a "catchall category"[2] that includes sexual contacts—not necessarily anal—between men, men and animals, men and women, that go against the idea of reproduction. Foucault points out that it figures in the list of serious sins alongside debauchery (relations outside of marriage), adultery, abduction, spiritual or carnal incest, and reciprocal caressing. If they are often described as "infamous," sodomites evade all precise classification. Montesquieu, wondering about this strange crime, punished by fire, acknowledges that "it is very often obscure."[3]

Under the Ancien Régime, sodomy was prohibited for religious reasons. It was called the "silent sin" or the "abominable vice," about whose existence it was better to say nothing to the people.[4] To show the uncertainty of the concept of sodomy, Pierre Hahn had the good idea of consulting confessors' handbooks. Thus, the *Traité de sodomie* by Père L. M. Sinistrati d'Ameno (mid-eighteenth century) notes certain subtle distinctions surprising to the twentieth-century reader. For the ecclesiastic scholar, sodomy was indeed defined as carnal relations between two males or two females, yet not all "homosexual" acts constituted a crime. For there to be a crime, there had to be coitus, the introduction of the penis into the anus "in order to distinguish it from simple voluptuousness [defilement, masturbation] obtained mutually between one male and another, or between one woman and another."[5] There was sin when one used the wrong "vessel"! According to certain doctors, "The intromission of the virile member into the posterior vessel had to take place regularly and it was necessary that there be semination in the inside of the arse. This was 'perfect sodomy,' absolution for which could be given the sinners only by the pope or the bishop."[6] On the other hand, if a male copulated in the anus with a woman, this sodomy was "imperfect" and a simple confessor could absolve him.[7]

In the eighteenth century the crime became secular, and the vocabulary changed: the term *sodomite* became less and less common (indicating a rejection of the biblical reference), and the term *pederast* more and more so (especially starting in 1730) along with "infamous ones" (police jargon).[8] According to Maurice Lever, the secularization of the homosexual offense, which became a "philosophical sin" against state, class, and nature (they spoke also of "antiphysical" love), desacralized the vice, which no longer smacked of heresy. The crime was vulgarized and became a simple offense. Whatever the philosophers' opinion might have been, homosexuality was never described as a specific identity. Sodomy was a temporary aberration, a contempt for nature, and nothing more. Even if Rousseau, Voltaire, or Condorcet did not hide the disgust that such a practice inspired in them personally, they never sought to indict "the criminal"—quite the contrary. Voltaire insisted on the idea of a misunderstanding, that young males brought up together, feeling a force that nature was beginning to unleash in them, and not finding an object for their impulse, had recourse to similar young men.[9] This was no reason for stigmatizing a human being his entire life! Voltaire's friend Condorcet, so sensitive to the notion of the Rights of Man, proposed removing the penalty for sodomy when "there was no violence."[10]

The most tolerant of all was unquestionably Diderot. In his writings, most notably in *Entretien*, which followed *Le Rêve de d'Alembert* (1769), not only is there no hint of sin or infamy associated with homosexuality, but it acquires the status of a precious pleasure, of the same sort as masturbation. According to Diderot, who speaks through the persona of the wise doctor Bordeu, abstinence drives one mad.[11] This is the occasion for him eloquently to sing the praises of sexual pleasure. The state of need must be satisfied at all costs. After having legitimized solitary practices,[12] Diderot-Bordeu proclaims to Mademoiselle de Lespinasse, who cannot believe her ears, the superiority of homosexuality in the name of the pleasure principle and the sharing of pleasure.[13] The French Penal Code of 1791, taking legal cognizance of this normalization, would no longer condemn sodomy as such. This tolerance, ratified by the Code of 1810, came to an end with the law of April 28, 1832, which instituted the crime of pedophilia. On the other hand, the Penal Code still closes its eyes to heterosexual relations between an adult and a minor. True, the status of the pederast is in the process of undergoing a radical change, and it will give rise to new questions.

THE NINETEENTH CENTURY: DEFINING IDENTITY BY SEXUAL ORIENTATION

The last thirty years or so of the Victorian century saw the appearance of new conceptions of homosexuality. The sodomite, who was only suffering a temporary aberration, was replaced by the "homosexual," who represented a particular species. With the invention of new words, *homosexual* and *invert*,[14] to designate those who were interested in the same sex, people's conception of them changed.[15] The creation of a word corresponded here to that of an essence, of a psychic malady and a social ailment. The birth of "the homosexual" brought with it a problematic question and an intolerance that have survived to our day.

Hahn gives 1857 as the date of the first investigation into French homosexuals carried out by Doctor Tardieu and some policemen.[16] Now began the hunt for pederasts, who were more and more interesting to the police, the judiciary, and the worlds of law and medicine. According to the great doctor, the vice tended to increase each day . . . and public scandals led to a more severe repression of pederasty, rapes, and indecent assaults on children. But curiously enough, it was the homosexuals themselves who ignited the powder-keg by inventing the problem of identity. They wanted their specificity to be recognized; they demanded what would today be called their right to be different. It was a Hungarian, Doctor Benkert, who in 1869 created the term *homosexuality*[17] and asked the Ministry of Justice to abolish the old Prussian law against it. During the same period, an old magistrate in Hanover, Heinrich Ulrichs, himself a homosexual, analyzed homosexuality from the point of view of a historian, a doctor, and a philosopher. Unfortunately, of the scholarly distinctions he made between pederasts and what he called "uranists," all that survived was the definition of the latter: "a female soul that has dropped into a man's body."[18] Without wishing to, Ulrichs started pederasts down the slippery road of mental pathology. It was this belief in a sort of third sex that led the German psychiatrist Westphal to publish his 1870 study on *The Congenital Inversion of the Sexual Feeling with Morbid Awareness of the Phenomenon* that led Havelock Ellis to define the invert by a congenital anomaly, and that led Hirschfeld to speak of "the intermediate sex."

Gradually, everyone came to regard homosexuals as sick people. In 1882 Magnan and Charcot dubbed them "sexual inverts" and situated them within the framework of degeneration. "At the end of the century, no man could call himself healthy, normal, if he did not assert his sexual identity in every possible way."[19] The birth of pathological homosexuality went hand in hand with that of the "accursed race," to use Marcel Proust's expression, and also with that of heterosexual normality. Sexual identity became a destiny.[20] Because of the decisive influence of Richard Krafft-Ebing's *Psychopathies sexuelles*,[21] the extreme attention paid to the perverse and to abnormality threw a new light on the "normal." "Normal" male sexuality was dependent upon an "instinct" whose natural object was the other sex. The concept of *heterosexuality* was created to describe this normality, which postulated a radical difference between the sexes at the same time that it indissolubly linked gender identity (being a man or a woman) and sexual identity.[22]

When all was said and done, the medical discourse of the nineteenth century transformed sexual behaviors into sexual identities. Perverts replacing libertines gave individuals a new specificity. Whereas the sodomite, notes Foucault, was only the juridical subject of forbidden acts, "the homosexual of the nineteenth century became a personage: a past, a history, and a childhood; a morphology too, with an indiscreet anatomy and perhaps a mysterious physiology. Nothing of what he is as a whole escapes his sexuality. . . . The homosexual is now a species."[23] Following in succession after the platonic soul and Cartesian reason, sex becomes the ultimate truth of being.

The medicalization of homosexuality should have protected it from moral judgments. Nothing of the sort happened. The problematical question of "perversions" allows for all kinds of ambiguities. No distinction is made between disease and vice, between psychic illness and moral illness. By consensus people stigmatize these effeminate men who are incapable of reproducing! In England as in France,[24] antihomosexual attitudes are linked to the fear of the decline of the empire and the nation. There are by now innumerable texts describing with anguish the disastrous consequences of the fall in the birthrate! The homosexual is a threat to the nation and the family. But he is also a traitor to the cause of masculinity.[25] Doctors themselves condemn these effeminate men, who do not fulfill their obligations as men. They accuse them of lacking greatness of soul, courage, and devotion; deplore their vanity, their indiscretions, their gossiping. In short, these are would-be women, incomplete men.[26]

The stigmatization of homosexuals is unquestionably the result of the process of classifying sexualities. It is another of history's ironies that, for the most part, homosexuals themselves, along with reform-minded sexologists, were the ones to consign "deviants" to abnormality. The best example of this skewing of events comes from the sexologist Havelock Ellis. Thinking to strengthen the tolerance of bourgeois society toward homosexuality, he developed the argument of innateness and lack of responsibility: one can do nothing about it, one is born that way. As a result, "The hypothesis of a biologically determined homosexuality prevailed in the medical literature of the twentieth century, giving rise to all sorts of hormonal and surgical attempts to change lesbians and male homosexuals into heterosexuals."[27]

Jeffrey Weeks has brilliantly demonstrated the sexologists' responsibility in forming the homosexual "type." Despite its scientific fervor, sexology was neither neutral nor simply descriptive. It declared what we were supposed to be and what made us normal creatures.[28] The obsession with the norm was to give rise to a considerable effort to account for the abnormal. Etiological explanations multiplied (corruption or degeneration, innateness or trauma in childhood), and complex typologies were produced to distinguish different sorts of homosexualities.

Ellis distinguished the invert from the pervert, Freud the absolute invert from the contingent invert. Clifford Allen defined twelve types including the compulsive, the nervous, the neurotic, the psychotic, the psychopathic, and the alcoholic; Richard Harvey recorded forty-six sorts of homosexuals; and Alfred Kinsey invented the continuum from the heterosexual to the homosexual.[29] Subsequently, as Weeks points out, many sexologists were to understand the danger of these rigid typologies. But it was too late. Once the type of "homosexual" was imposed, it turned out to be impossible to escape it.

Sexual practices had become the descriptive criterion of the person. Is this to say that the sexologists *created* the homosexual, as Michel Foucault and Jonathan Ned Katz believe?[30] Yes and no. Homosexual practices exist everywhere and always have. But until sexology pasted a label on them, homosexuality was only a vague part of the sense of identity. Homosexual identity as we know it is therefore a production of a social classification whose essential aim was regulation and control. To name is to imprison.[31]

The twentieth century has not taken the homosexual out of his prison. A century after Oscar Wilde's trial, a number of our contemporaries continue to regard him as a criminal sexual type, at best a sick man and a deviant. Two reasons may explain these discriminatory attitudes. The first has to do with our ignorance: after a hundred and fifty years of studies, and of polemics, we still cannot define with any precision this fluid and multiform behavior whose origin we cannot identify with any certainty. The multiplicity of explanations has only increased its mystery and thus its strangeness. The other reason is ideological. Given our conception of heterosexual masculinity, homosexuality plays the useful role of foil, and its negative image strengthens by contrast the positive and enviable appearance of heterosexuality.

Homosexuality: A Universal Impulse or the Specific Identity of a Minority?

On one side, we have those who stress the resemblances between homosexuals and heterosexuals and insist on the universality of the homosexual impulse; on the other, those who emphasize the differences and the specificity of the homosexual.

Researchers who have studied homosexuality from a trans-cultural point of view have noted a certain number of constants. Thus, the sociologist Frederick Whitam, after having worked for many years in homosexual communities in countries as different as the United States, Guatemala, Brazil, and the Philippines, suggests six conclusions: (1) homosexual persons appear in all societies, (2) the percentage of homosexuals seems the same in all societies and remains stable over time, (3) social norms neither prevent nor facilitate the emergence of a homosexual orientation, (4) homosexual subcultures appear in all societies that have a sufficient number of persons, (5) homosexuals of different societies tend to resemble one another as to their behavior and their interests, and (6) all societies produce a similar continuum between very masculine and very feminine homosexuals.[32]

All this would lead one to believe that homosexuality is not created by a particular social organization but is rather a fundamental form of human sexuality expressed in all cultures.

If the explicit expression of homosexuality is always confined to a minority, the question is to what extent one can distinguish among the homosexual impulse, act, and orientation.

ADVOCATES OF RESEMBLANCE

Freud was the most tolerant and enlightened of the theoreticians of homosexuality. Because of his theory of original bisexuality, he recognized that all human beings may take as sexual objects persons of the same sex, as of the opposite sex, that they share out their libido either overtly or in a latent manner on objects of both sexes.[33] Through his entire oeuvre, Freud would defend the natural and nonpathological aspect of homosexuality against the sexologists, advocates of a "third sex" or an "intermediate sex,"[34] but also against his own people, the psychoanalysts.

In radical opposition to his time, Freud asserted that heterosexuality was no less problematic than homosexuality.[35] And he was never to waver on this point. In *Leonardo da Vinci and a Memory of His Childhood*, he even went a little farther by asserting not only that we are all capable of making the choice to be homosexual but also that everyone has made it at a given moment in his life, and then either continues to hold to it in his unconscious, or protects himself from it through an energetic contrary attitude.[36]

As to the causes of homosexuality, Freud always remained

very prudent, acknowledging that he had not managed to find the explanation for the inversion. In *Three Essays* he refers to the predominance of age-old dispositional elements and primitive psychic mechanisms, the narcissistic choice of object and the preserved erotic importance of the anal zone,[37] as well as a very strong erotic fixation on the mother. But all these factors do not suffice to distinguish clearly the homosexual from the heterosexual.

The question of homosexuality was so important to Freud that he opted for an extreme tolerance again and again in his life. Although he was so nonmilitant, he agreed to be interviewed in 1903 in the Viennese journal *Die Zeit*, in defense of a man who was being prosecuted for homosexual practices. In 1930 he signed a petition for the revision of the Penal Code and the elimination of the offense of homosexuality between consenting adults. He opposed Ernest Jones, who denied the status of psychoanalyst to a homosexual. Sachs, Abraham, and Eitington sided with Jones. But Freud persisted and continued to refuse to analyze homosexuals unless he found them neurotic, because for him they were normal people. Nothing could be more touching than the letter of consolation he addresses to an American mother who had asked his advice about her son:

> I gather from your letter that your son is homosexual. I was most impressed by the fact that you do not mention this term yourself in your information about him. May I question you why you avoid it? Homosexuality is assuredly no advantage, but it is nothing to be ashamed of, no vice, no degradation; it cannot be classified as an illness; we consider it to be a variation of the sexual function, *produced by a certain arrest of sexual development*.[38]

After the Second World War, the Kinsey report made an essential contribution to the theory of human bisexuality.[39] This famous report, published in 1948, drew attention not only to the heterosexual-homosexual continuum but also to the fluid-ity of sexual desires. Kinsey and his collaborators proved, in effect, that homosexual and heterosexual tendencies exist in the majority of human beings and that their respective proportions vary from an exclusively heterosexual penchant (which Kinsey calls degree 0 on his scale of gradation) to an exclusively homosexual penchant (degree 6 on the scale). Each intermediary degree corresponds to a greater or lesser proportion of homosexual or heterosexual penchant.[40] The new Kinsey report, based on research conducted in 1969 and 1970 on homosexuals in the San Francisco area, confirmed the results of the 1948 report, notably by insisting on the diversity of kinds of homosexuality.[41]

The more recent Shere Hite investigation of seven thousand American men confirms the earlier studies: "Perhaps surprisingly, given most men's emphasis on maintaining physical distance from other men, many boys—most of them 'heterosexual' in later life—had sex with other boys as children or teenagers. Forty-three percent of those who answered had had some form of sex with another boy. . . . There was no correlation between whether a boy had had sexual experience with other boys in his youth and whether he considered himself 'homosexual' or 'heterosexual' in later life. Many 'homosexual' men had never had relations with other boys in youth, and many 'heterosexual' men had had such relationships."[42]

Ought one to conclude, as certain people do, that everyone is both homosexual and heterosexual, that it is inappropriate to speak of homosexuals as a sexual minority, and that there is no more reason to say that everyone is heterosexual than to assert that everyone is homosexual?[43]

ADVOCATES OF SPECIFIC IDENTITY

Robert Stoller and Richard Friedman challenge the idea of a universal homosexuality. According to Stoller, homosexuality is not an illness. It is a sexual preference and not a set of uniform signs and symptoms; but homosexuality belongs only to homosexuals, who are different from others and therefore constitute a minority. In Stoller's eyes, they are no more ill than other minorities (Jews, American blacks, and so on)[44] but it is incorrect to confuse them with heterosexuals.[45]

This is also the opinion of Richard Friedman, who has attempted to show that "most heterosexual men are not predisposed to unconscious homosexuality and, inversely, most exclusively homosexual men are not predisposed to an unconscious heterosexuality. . . . There exists only a minority of bisexual men forced to repress either their homosexual fantasies, or their heterosexual fantasies."[46]

If homosexuality is a characteristic belonging to certain men and not others, where does this specificity come from? Three hypotheses, which have all revealed their limitations, have been proposed: an endocrine anomaly, a genetic anomaly, or psychic factors.

For fifty years, there have been attempts to demonstrate the correlation between male homosexuality and quantities of testosterone—to no end: although sexual hormones have been injected into male homosexuals in the hope of stimulating their desire for women, the opposite result occurred: what was stimulated was their desire for men. Furthermore, most of the hormonal studies show that the vast majority of homosexuals have the same level of testosterone as heterosexuals.[47] Today, most researchers favor the hypothesis of a prenatal endocrine influence on sexual orientation. They think that if there is a hormonal orientation of behavior, it occurs in the life of the embryo at the time when the sexual hormones are "sexualizing" the nervous system at all stages. But it is difficult to go farther than the forming of hypotheses in humans because one cannot give all fetuses systematic doses of hormones. However, the work Dörner has done on rats shows that if the males are temporarily exposed to a lack of androgens during the critical prenatal period of differentiation of the brain, they display distinctly feminine behaviors when they are adults. He concludes from this that an insufficient prenatal androgenization of the central nervous system leads to a partially female differentiation of the brain, and thus to masculine homosexuality, and that an excess of androgens at the same stage is at the origin of female homosexuality.[48] This last point seems to be confirmed by the observation of women exposed in utero to an excess of androgens.[49]

The genetic hypothesis quite regularly captures people's attention. A researcher in one place or another asserts, after examining a few homosexuals, that he has found a genetic anomaly in certain of them. Then it is demonstrated shortly afterward that the experiment was biased and that one can conclude nothing from it.

More interesting are the studies carried out on monozygotic and dizygotic twins. In 1953 F. J. Kallman observed that in all cases of monozygotic twins, when one was homosexual the other was too (a concordance that was not found in fraternal twins).[50] Since Kallman's work, the existence has been demonstrated of a certain number of cases of identical twins having divergent sexual orientations. Here too, indisputable proofs are missing.

There remains the case of the "sissy boys," young boys who are effeminate from earliest childhood. This is a situation that fuels the fires of the essentialist theory. Richard Green, a student of John Money and Robert Stoller, studied sixty-six "sissy boys" and fifty-six masculine boys over a period of fifteen years.[51] The results of his observations tally with those Bieber and his team made in 1962 and those, more recent, of Bernard Zuger (1984). The "sissy boy" is one whose behavior is exaggeratedly feminine from the age of two or three—his poses, gestures, vocal intonations all caricaturing a feminine affectation. He shows a particular interest in feminine clothes (notably those of his mother), talks about them, and enjoys wearing them. He carefully avoids the noisy games of the boys and prefers the girls' games and toys, as well as their companionship. Many of these children even say they would rather be a girl. Most (who come for a consultation because of their parents' concern) become atypical men as adults: transsexuals, cross-dressers, or homosexuals. In Green's sampling, as in that of Zuger,[52] very few—scarcely 5 percent—would in the end become heterosexuals. The case of the "sissy boys," whose feminization was precocious and whose orientation could not be changed, gives us reason to believe that there are "constitutional" factors[53] in this type of homosexuality, especially since our society offers no model for a man loving men. But care must be taken to distinguish homosexual acts from a homosexual orientation, which reveals itself more through sexual fantasies (during masturbation) than through acts and behavior. Here too, caution is necessary, since an adolescent may have homosexual fantasies and yet become a heterosexual adult.[54]

More striking than all these analyses are the accounts by the subjects themselves. The biographical work of Edmund White is rich in information. At a very early age he felt himself to be a "sissy" who could not succeed in talking in a manly way, in seeming manly, in playing baseball like the other boys, and who failed all the tests of virility.[55] Having a hypervirile sister, a totally indifferent, even rejecting father, and a mother who did not concern herself with him at all (contrary to the widespread portrait of the homosexual's mother), he said he hesitated between being a man and having a man.[56] As an adult, having become a very active homosexual, he felt his identity was multiple and not clearly determined ("a fat bear or a supple girl without breasts or a vagina").[57] He wanted to be treated like a woman but sometimes asked himself with anguish if he was being embraced as a woman or if he was a man.[58] At times, he dreamed of having a real woman by his side so that he could rid himself of his fantasy of being a woman and put an end to his feminine affectation, his simpering.

In *Kiss of the Spider Woman*, the Argentine Manuel Puig tells the superb story of love between two men, a heterosexual and a homosexual, who share the same prison cell in a fascistic and macho country.[59] Although this is another culture and another situation, the anguish is the same. The homosexual thinks of himself as a woman and speaks of himself in the feminine. He will tend his very sick lover like a mother and will keep asking himself what manliness is, what a real man is. He seeks the friendship of a man rather than that of queers. He confesses to feeling "like a normal woman who loves men."[60] Whereas the heterosexual does not feel threatened in his virility by this homosexual episode, an act of pure tenderness, the homosexual admits that he does not know if he is a man or a woman. His lover will speak the only words that can console him: "If you like being a woman, you shouldn't feel diminished by that, you don't have to pay for that with something, ask forgiveness. . . . Being a man does not give anyone the right to anything at all."[61]

The exemplary aspect of Puig's novel is this total love between two men whose sexual orientations are so different. Whether by choice or fate, accident or lifestyle, homosexuality is plural. Any proposal aiming to unify and reify it will lead to an impasse. Instinct is certainly universal, but sexual orientation is not.

THE EVOLUTION OF GAY STUDIES

At the end of the 1960s, parallel to the feminist questioning of sexual identities and roles, a number of American homosexuals emerged from their forced silence to put an end to a clandestine existence painfully experienced as pathological. To begin with, they changed their label. In place of the term *homosexual*, which has a medical connotation linked to perversity, they preferred the more neutral term *gay*[62] (in existence since the nineteenth century), which would come to designate a specific, positive culture. This was the birth of the gay movement, whose most notable aim would be to show that heterosexuality was not the only form of normal sexuality. "Gay Studies" includes all the studies—often very remarkable—that have been done on homosexuality, its history, its nature, or its sociology. As Gary Kinsman points out, by rejecting heterosexuality as a psychological and social norm, gays have challenged certain aspects of male institutions and male privilege.[63] In so doing, they have contributed significantly to feminist thought.

The Australian Dennis Altman notes that in the space of one decade, from 1970 to 1980, in the United States and in other parts of the world, we have witnessed the appearance of a new minority, endowed with its own culture, lifestyle, political expression, and claims to legitimacy.[64] This minority, having become visible, has had an impact on global society.[65] In a country like the United States, where people define themselves by reference to race and religion, it is not surprising that homosexuals have come to see themselves as another ethnic group and to demand to be recognized on the basis of that analogy. But in so doing, they have reopened the debate about homosexual identity, which causes the very exclusion they wish so much to avoid.

And indeed, the identity approach has revived the old question of the innateness of homosexuality, and with it the idea that the homosexual is a species apart whose ultimate explanation lies in a genetic and hormonal disorder. When all is said and done, the acknowledgment of homosexuals' status as a minority has had both advantages and disadvantages. Among the former is the development of a feeling of self-confidence and acceptance, beneficial to those who have acknowledged themselves as such. Among the latter: once the idea of a minority is emphasized, it becomes difficult to see that homosexuality, whether explicit or repressed, is an aspect of everyone's sexuality.[66] Another disadvantage is that the more "visible" and demanding homosexuals became, the more one saw the appearance of new forms of hostility toward them—a fact that belies the liberal argument according to which the better known one makes oneself, the more one is accepted. In truth, if a number of homosexuals have changed considerably in the space of a decade (others continuing to live in secrecy), heterosexual society has not evolved in the same manner but has retained a number of negative prejudices and fantasies.

In the 1980s, affected by the emergence of the antifeminist, antihomosexual, antiabortion Moral Majority, advocating as it did a return to "traditional values," homosexuals modified their theory and their tactics. Realizing that homosexuality is a concept much broader than that of sexual identity, gay studies undertook to show that homosexuals were men like other men. Even if homosexuality is a rejection of traditional sexual roles, sexuality does not determine gender. Henceforth, those studying homosexuality take great care to reject all assimilation of sexual "identity" and "orientation." They criticize the essentialist philosophy and hunt down all the terms associated with it.[67] To distinguish between homosexual conduct and the homosexual condition, some propose no longer using the word *homosexual* as a noun, but only as an adjective.[68] Katz goes farther, suggesting that we get rid of the very division between *homo* and *hetero*. In view of the Kinsey continuum and the frequency of rectal coitus among heterosexuals, Katz does not see the necessity of maintaining the dualism of sexual activities.[69] Last, others suggest getting rid of the label *gay*,[70] which reifies sexuality and serves as an identity card. Kenneth Plummer, one of the fiercest opponents of sexual essentialism, rejects even the concept of *orientation* as used by geneticists, clinicians, and other behaviorists, and suggests holding to the idea of a social construction of identity, very much in vogue today in the United States.[71]

Let us pay tribute to Jeffrey Weeks, who has consistently reminded us of the existence of a multiplicity of kinds of homosexuality and refuses to be the prisoner of an extremist alternative. In opposition to the constructivists, he allows that there are differences between homosexuals and heterosexuals. In opposition to the essentialists, he maintains that these real differences do not necessarily engender antagonistic interests and identities.[72] Close to Michel Foucault, who conceived of homosexuality as a "stylistic,"[73] Weeks conceives of identity in terms of choice and struggle: in the end, identity is perhaps nothing more than a game, a stratagem for being able to enjoy certain types of relationships and pleasures.[74]

All things considered, the gay rights movement and its accompanying ideology have experienced the same evolution as the other minorities which have expressed themselves since the end of the 1960s. After a period of noisy claims to the right to be different—constituting a necessary stage, namely, acknowledgment by the majority—minorities have quickly understood the danger of persevering in a path that so often leads to stigmatization and ghettoization, at which point difference is no longer a personal choice but a constraint imposed from the outside. Homosexuals no longer demand the right to be different but the right to indifference. They wish others to regard them, at last, as human beings and citizens like others, without either particular handicaps or particular privileges. But the drama of the homosexual minority is that its fate depends on the way the heterosexual majority views it. Now, in the same way that certain minorities play the unenviable social and political role of scapegoats, homosexuals serve as psychological foils for heterosexual males imprisoned by the patriarchal ideology. Their fate, as well as that of women, depends very much on the death of the patriarchy. But whereas feminists can wage a merciless war on misogyny with the official consent of society as a whole, homosexuals do not have the same mobilizing force against homophobia, nor the same legitimacy in the eyes of this last bastion of the patriarchy.

Homophobia and Patriarchal Masculinity

Most patriarchal societies identify masculinity with heterosexuality. To the extent that we continue to define gender by sexual behavior, and masculinity by opposition to femininity, homophobia, like misogyny, will undeniably play an important role in the male sense of identity. Certain thinkers do not hesitate to say that what we have here are the two most critical forces of socialization in a boy's life.[75] They are directed at different types of victims, but they are two sides of the same coin.

Homophobia is the hatred of feminine qualities in men whereas misogyny is the hatred of feminine qualities in women.

BEING A MAN MEANS NOT BEING A HOMOSEXUAL

We have already mentioned the importance to male identity
of defining oneself "through opposition" to something. No
doubt traditional heterosexual masculinity also includes positive aspects, such as status, success, endurance, independence,
or the social domination of adult men over other men, and
their sexual relations with women.[76] But male identification
remains more largely differential than female identification.
Traditionally, masculinity is defined more often by the avoidance of something than by a desire for something.[77] To be a
man signifies *not* to be feminine, *not* to be homosexual; *not* to
be effeminate in one's physical appearance or manners; *not* to
have sexual or overly intimate relations with other men; *not* to
be impotent with women. Negatives are so typical of masculinity that an American writer achieved a resounding success for himself by publishing a book with the ironic title *Real
Men Don't Eat Quiche!*[78]

Homophobia[79] is an integral part of heterosexual masculinity, so much so that it plays an essential psychological role: it
signifies who is not homosexual and shows who is heterosexual. Emmanuel Reynaud has shown very clearly the roots of
homophobia: "In current speech, a homosexual is not really a
man who has a sexual relationship with another man, but
rather one who is supposedly passive: a homosexual is actually a pansy, a queer, a nancyboy . . . a woman, in short. Whereas, in its active form, homosexuality can be considered by a
man as a means of asserting his power, in its 'passive' form it
is, on the contrary, a symbol of loss. For instance, it would not
occur to anyone to make fun of the *enculeur* [the one doing the
buggering], whereas the term *enculé* [the one who has been
buggered] is undoubtedly one of the most virulent insults in
the French language."[80]

In certain men (particularly in young boys), homosexuality

arouses a fear that has no equivalent in women. This fear is expressed by behaviors of avoidance, aggressivity, or an undisguised disgust. Behavioral studies are very eloquent on this point. Certain of them simply use the placement of a chair, a criterion of social distance, to determine the effects of the perception of a homosexual on interpersonal space.[81] It was observed that when the experimenter wore a "Gay and Proud" badge and introduced himself as a member of the association of gay psychologists, the participants placed their chairs distinctly farther away from that experimenter than from another, a "neutral," who displayed no homosexual characteristics. The men reacted by creating a distance between themselves and the homosexual experimenter that was three times as great as the distance women created when questioned by a female experimenter displaying a "lesbian" badge.

Homophobia involves only a minority of people.[82] It is linked with other fears, notably that of equality between the sexes. Homophobes are conservative, rigid, and favor maintaining traditional sexual roles, even in other cultures.[83] Even research conducted among young people who were better educated and more liberal than the average American shows a real distrust of the homosexual.[84] In fact, homophobia is tied to a secret fear of one's own homosexual desires.[85] To see an effeminate man arouses a dreadful anxiety in many men; it makes them aware of their own feminine characteristics, such as passivity or sensitivity, which they consider to be a sign of weakness. Women, of course, are not afraid of their femininity. This is in part the reason why men are more homophobic than women.[86]

Homophobia reveals what it seeks to hide. And yet it is often displayed and even asserted. In reading the different studies published by the French media, one can see that homophobia is officially admitted, unlike racism or sexism.[87] In the United States, it goes well beyond a simple psychological and moral rejection. A study on violence conducted in New York State in 1988 concluded that of all the minority groups, homosexual men and women were the objects of the greatest hostility. Whereas adolescents seemed reticent about expressing racist opinions, they openly expressed their homophobia.[88] Aside from the habitual insults, physical attacks are common.[89] Generally, the aggressors are boys of twenty-one or younger, who act in a group and attack an isolated man or a couple walking together. These gangs hunt down homosexuals, seeking them and provoking them wherever they are. For them, the gay man symbolizes the stranger. The psychologist Gregory Herek stresses that the attack solidifies the feeling of belonging to the group of attackers and expresses their shared values. But it is also their heterosexuality that they are asserting by treating homosexuals as strangers.[90]

THE ADVANTAGES AND DISADVANTAGES OF HOMOPHOBIA

Homophobia strengthens the fragile heterosexuality of a number of men. It is therefore a psychic defense mechanism, a strategy for avoiding the acknowledgment of an unacceptable part of oneself. To direct one's aggressivity against homosexuals is a way of exteriorizing the conflict and making it tolerable. According to Herek, homophobia can also have a social function: a heterosexual expresses his prejudices against gays in order to win the approval of others and in this way to increase his confidence in himself. Finally, homophobia is an aspect of a more general ideology, such as, for instance, the conservative religious ideology that prescribes strictly defined behaviors for men and women.

Yet homophobia does not merely have "advantages." Aside from the fact that it is scandalously aggressive toward homosexuals—without mentioning the homosexuals who have themselves interiorized this homophobia[91]—male heterosexuals pay dearly for it. Not only does it make them martyrs to the male role, as Joseph Pleck writes,[92] but it is a major obstacle in the way of friendship between men. The Hite report is eloquent. To the question "Describe the man you are/were closest to in your life," many men answered that they had no "best friend" at the time of the study.[93] Ever since Freud, we have known that male friendship originates in the sublimation of homosexual desire,[94] and that, furthermore, men feel a great resistance to expressing their passivity with other men. This is the reason that many of them avoid intimacy with men. In his study on friendship, sociologist Robert Bell notes the radical difference between the sexes on this subject. Whereas women cultivate intimacy among themselves, men see one another in groups more often than individually. In so doing, they keep the temptation of homosexuality at a distance, make personal communication difficult, and provide one another with a mutual confirmation of their masculinity. What is more, Bell says he is struck by the number of times men confide that their best friend is their wife,[95] another way of avoiding these fears. Homophobia limits choices of friendship and deprives men of enriching experiences and the kinds of knowledge one can acquire only by being close to another person.[96]

Guy Corneau astutely suggests that homophobia—whose primary function is to strengthen heterosexuality—may in fact be one of the roots of homosexuality. The fear of being homosexual "poisons every possibility of male eroticism and prevents many fathers from touching their sons."[97] When fathers hand over to the mother the only direct access to the child's body, "sons cannot develop positively in relation to the father's body, but rather negatively in opposition to the mother's body."[98]

Still, we cannot break the vicious circle (the transmission of homophobia from father to son) by waving a magic wand. No rational or ideological decision is enough to put an end to this fear. But a generation of feminism has already exploded the model of masculinity and caused us to ask hard questions about the traditional role of the father. Here and there, new parental behaviors are appearing which ought to quiet these fears.

PART TWO

BEING A MAN (XY)

The patriarchal system gave birth to a mutilated man incapable of reconciling x and y, his paternal and maternal heritage. The construction of masculinity merged with the process of differentiation. One was recognized as a man worthy of the name once one had cut all one's ties with maternal femininity—in other words, with one's original soil. No one dreamed, then, of gluing back together the "pieces" of one's primary and secondary identities.

Industrial society made the situation worse by withdrawing fathers from their sons. Men no longer produced men. Spectral fathers with "symbolic" status were often poor models for identification. Sons abandoned to their mothers had still more difficulty differentiating themselves from her and strengthening their sense of identity. More recently, after the feminist rejection of the patriarchy and of the male type it engenders, some people have thought that one could dispense with differentiation. For them, *virility* and *masculinity* were words without content, even dangerous, synonyms for a crumbling oppression. The human being identified with the feminine ignored the masculine, and with it human bisexuality. The results were scarcely more brilliant. The antipatriarchal reaction—certainly very limited in time and space—engendered a man just as mutilated as the first, but one who is, this time, ignorant of the paternal heritage.

Many men today are sick from this fragmentation of self.

The painful consciousness of a truncated identity may favor
the rebuilding of a masculine landscape that would at last take
cognizance of the twofold heritage.

Man Cut in Half

For some fifteen years now, men's studies have noted the close
relationship between masculinity and the large-scale repression
of a part of oneself. A denial of bisexuality is the condition for
the establishment of frontiers. But the result is a man distorted,
fragmented, who will have experienced completeness only in
the very first period of his life with his mother.[1] The extreme
case of the man cut in half is that of the male fascist under
Hitler as described by Klaus Theweleit: "Men were at that time
torn between an interior (female) and an exterior (male), mortal
enemies. . . . What fascism promised men was the reintegration
of their hostile components in a tolerable way, namely, by a
domination of the 'hostile female' element."[2]

But as everyone knows, this is not a way to get rid of what
is repressed. Excessive repression leads to repressed self-hatred
projected outside and objectified in the figure of a woman if
one is a misogynist, in that of a Jew if one is an anti-Semite,
and even in that of a man if one rejects his manliness. Otto
Weininger was one of those men consumed by self-hatred.
Originally from a Jewish family that had converted to Protes-
tantism, Weininger felt a hatred of Jews that was equaled only
by his hatred of women. In his eyes, Jews, like women, were
the embodiment of immorality, degeneration, and the negative, in contrast to Aryan men. Weininger set about showing
everything that the feminine had in common with the Jewish
spirit[3]—two components of his person—in order to include
both in the same rejection. Along with remarks that are completely delirious, *Sexe et caractère* offers an explanation for
anti-Semitism that can be applied at every point to that for
misogyny: "*In the same way that one LOVES in the other*

what one would like to be, one HATES what one would not like to be. One hates only that to which one is close, and the other is in this case only a revealer. He who hates the Jewish soul hates it first and foremost in himself: if he hunts it down in another, it is only in order to give himself the illusion that he is free of it."[4]

The analogy between woman and Jew, the coinciding of misogyny and anti-Semitism (to which homophobia should be added) can be found in a number of twentieth-century writers.

Examining contemporaries from Weininger[5] to Henry Miller,[6] and from D. H. Lawrence[7] to Ernest Hemingway,[8] we see that one is rarely without the other. It is Freud, once again, who provides us with an explanation for this double hatred by revealing its origin: "The castration complex is the deepest unconscious root of anti-Semitism, for even in the nursery, the little boy hears that something has been cut off the penis of the Jew—he thinks: a piece of the penis—which gives him the right to despise the Jew. And there is no deeper root to the feeling of superiority over women."[9]

Even rarer in patriarchal societies is male self-hatred. In contrast to Otto Weininger, his contemporary Otto Gross calls for the advent of the matriarchy and the abolition of the law of the father. Addicted to drugs, confined a number of times (some considered him to be suffering from dementia praecox), the brilliant Otto Gross was just as fragile as Weininger. His entire life consisted of a settling of accounts against his father and a hatred of manliness; his entire body of work, a criticism of the patriarchy and of traditional male values. In quite a different context, the essay of the American feminist John Stoltenberg, *Refusing to Be a Man*, which calls for an end to masculinity, also arises from self-hatred.[10] Identifying male identity with rape, he asserts that the male sex requires injustice in order to exist. His watchword is: for a new ethic, refuse to be a man, reject the dualism of the sexes. Basing his thought on Andrea Dworkin's theory (according to which *man* and *woman* are fictions, caricatures, cultural constructions, totalitarian, and inappropriate to human evolution),[11] Stoltenberg agrees with Dworkin's conclusion: "We are, clearly, a multisexed species which has its sexuality spread along a vast continuum where the elements called male and female are not discrete."[12]

Beneath its liberating guise, the idea of a "multisexed species" is, here, a denial of sexual identity and especially of male identity. The obviousness of this self-hatred appears in all its clarity when Stoltenberg adopts as his own Andrea Dworkin's terrifying denigration of the penis: "Nothing is less an instrument of ecstasy and more an instrument of oppression than the penis."[13] The aggressivity of a feminist becomes masochism in a man's writings.

Last, there is the extreme case of total self-hatred, aimed at both femininity and masculinity. Such is the situation of the hero of the beautiful novel by Hermann Ungar, *Les Mutilés*:[14] a man whose mother has died shortly after his birth is raised by a harsh father who beats him and a sadistic and perverse aunt whose body disgusts him. The result is that this sick man, terrorized by sex (his own and the other), who is himself neither man nor woman, will experience an extreme derangement that will fill him with horror.

Within the patriarchal system, female self-hatred, by far the most widespread, quite naturally gives rise to an oppositional sexual dualism. The assertion of difference is a reaction to the loss of identity and to the vagueness that reinforces masculinity. It is believed that by opposing the sexes, by assigning them different functions and spaces, one will distance the specter of inner bisexuality. In truth, one only splits oneself by exteriorizing the part of oneself that has become a stranger, even an enemy.[15]

The Sick Man of the 1980s

The feminist critique of the patriarchal man makes the splitting of the self intolerable. Traditionally forbidden to display his femininity, a man is now also forbidden to express a manliness that is being challenged. The new equation, male = bad, has given rise to a loss of identity for a whole generation of men. Ferdinando Camon recognizes this condition and concludes that "if it is difficult to be a woman . . . it is impossible to be a man."[16] A number of writers are outdoing one another on the subject of the bankruptcy of man, and psychologists unanimously attest to the increase in his psychological distress over the last twenty years. Whether it be in Germany, Canada, or the United States, people are recording the sicknesses of men "at their last gasp."[17] Whereas traditionally women were more subject to depressions, headaches, nervousness, and so on, for the last twenty years all the studies done in the United States show that the difference between the sexes is gradually lessening.[18]

The loss of a sense of sexual identity can lead to the suicide of a Weininger or a Hemingway, or to the madness of an Otto Gross. More common these days, male unwellness as documented in doctors' offices or in Western literature is expressed in terms of impotence, fetishism, or homosexuality as evasion—manifestations of the fear or the rejection of women which accompany masculine fragility. As two experts in male problems propose, since normal sexual activity is considered a proof of masculinity, the treatment of sexual disorders is actually the treatment of issues of gender identity.[19] We must learn to dissociate sexuality from a sense of manliness, in order to break up the identification between sexual performance and masculinity. The latter can be confirmed by something other than an erect penis.

As we await the revision of the ideal image of masculinity, we cannot fail to be struck by the increasing numbers of fictional characters who, bewailing their defective virility, seek refuge in alcohol, drugs, and wandering,[20] or flee to homosexuality as the ultimate refuge forbidden to women. Many novels by men describe men aged thirty to forty who lack identities, are impotent with women, and regress to the occasional homosexuality of adolescence.[21]

Men are at a crossroads that often takes the form of an intolerable dilemma: either one's femininity or one's manliness will be mutilated; either a mortal wound will be dealt to one's "feminine soul" or one must stifle in a mother's lap. But in fact, it is not impossible to get out of this painful dilemma: a third path is available.

CHAPTER FIVE

THE MUTILATED MAN

For many, the idea of a mutilated man calls to mind first one who has lost his sex, the symbol of his virility, in, say, an accident or in a war. By extension, the humiliated man is also one who has a sex but cannot manage to use it (who is impotent). This is the man who fails to desire and possess a woman. From this point of view, the homosexual is the very type of the mutilated man. But as soon as one begins questioning the patriarchal norms, one realizes that mutilation involves not so much the sex and sexual orientation as identity. Homosexuals and heterosexuals alike are subject to two sorts of psychological mutilation that can affect them equally. The first is the amputation of a man's femininity, which gives rise to the *tough guy,* the macho man who has never reconciled himself to maternal values. The second concerns the absence of virility noted in many men who were fatherless as children and were brought up by their mothers.

The Scandinavians use a picturesque terminology to characterize these two types of mutilated men: the *knot-man* and the *soft man.*[1] The expression "knot-man" is one that appeared for the first time in the novel *Le* by the Danish writer Herdis Moellehave.[2] It suggests at once the knot in a tie, symbol of the traditional well-dressed man, and a knot of feelings, the male sensibility hampered by conventions and complexes. The knot-man "is a catalogue of the worst male stereotypes: he is obsessed by competition, attached to his intellectual and sexual performance, handicapped emotionally, pleased with and sure of himself, aggressive, alcoholic, incapable of committing himself to other people. . . . This man with hair on his chest, centered on power and objectivity, has been rejected by the feminists and by a great number of women in general." We will call him the *tough guy*, as opposed to the soft man who has succeeded him.[3] The *soft man* is one who of his own accord renounces male privileges, gives up the power, the preeminence of the male traditionally conferred on him by the patriarchal order. He overcomes his own tendency toward aggressivity and abdicates ambition and career to the extent that they might prevent him from devoting himself to his life and children. He favors equality of men and women in all domains. The couple that consists of a feminist and a soft man share all household tasks and organize "a scrupulously exacting democracy, to such a degree must the division of tasks be fair." Merete Gerlach-Nielsen points out that adaptation to the role of the soft man is not easy: it is often the feminist spouse who imposes this new behavior on her partner, though it may be profoundly alien to him. The man feels his masculinity is being attacked, his identity becomes uncertain, and most often the couple separate.

The Norwegian novelist Knut Faldbakken has provided a perfect illustration of these two types of men, tough and soft, in his *Journal d'Adam*, which tells the story of three men tied to the same woman. The hard man, the *thief*, takes and gives nothing. He seeks only to protect himself emotionally and refuses to commit himself. His apparent graciousness masks indifference. One vulnerable spot: he needs alcohol in order to become erect. Unlike him, the soft man, the *eternal student*, is dependent on the woman to the point of existing only through her, like a baby with its mother. What is more, she considers him a child. She has trained him to do whatever she wants. "Pitiful creature, just barely human, groping, nebulous,"[4] his pleasant nature and submissiveness are unlimited. In a complete inversion of the traditional roles and identities, he is the one "possessed by her," incarnating the female sensibility and she, the trainer, is the indifferent dominator. An advocate of sexual equality, he wants to remain unemployed in order to look after the house while she works to earn their living. After a few months, she no longer respects him and he himself becomes "a miserable dog."[5] To these two types of men, Faldbakken adds a third, characteristic of our time: the *father-mother*, who takes care of his little girl by himself because the mother is not able to take charge of her. Having discovered "the strange joy that a man finds in the responsibility for a child,"[6] he refuses to give his daughter up to her mother and indulges in serious acts of violence against the latter. Imprisoned for a long time, he proclaims his hatred of women and takes refuge in homosexuality.

This negative reckoning of the male condition in our time, at the end of the millennium, however excessive and exaggerated it may be, has the merit of pointing to masculinity's impasses, all of which are direct or indirect consequences of the patriarchal system.

The Tough Guy

According to Norman Mailer, being a man is an endless struggle that lasts an entire lifetime.[7] Man wages war perpetually against himself in order never to yield to the weakness and passivity that are always lying in wait for him. The Mailerian man exhausts himself in a struggle that is never won. Homophobic and misogynistic, he is the "dematricized" creature Phyllis Chesler[8] and Margarete Mitscherlich[9] talk about, ravaged by an ideal of masculinity that ends by causing him to die before he should—and, statistically, at an earlier age than women.

THE MASCULINE IDEAL
Still fully alive today, this model of masculinity has changed very little over hundreds of years. Two American academics

have earned renown by articulating the four imperatives of masculinity in the form of popular slogans.[10]

First and foremost is: *no sissy stuff* (nothing effeminate). Even though we now know that men have the same emotional needs as women, the stereotyped male role requires that a man make certain sacrifices and mutilate a part of his humanity. Since a man—a real man—is one who is pure of all femininity, he is being asked to abandon a whole part of himself.

Next, the real male is *a big wheel* (a bigshot, an important person). He must be superior to others. Masculinity is measured by success, power, and the admiration he wins.

The third imperative—that he must be *a sturdy oak*—means that he must be independent and rely on himself alone. This one has been superbly illustrated by Kipling's famous poem *If–*,[11] which sings the praises of male impassivity: a man must never show emotion or attachment, signs of feminine weakness.

The last imperative—*Give 'em hell*—insists on a man's obligation to be stronger than others, even violent, if necessary. He must put on a display of boldness, even aggressivity, and show that he is ready to run all risks, even when reason and fear would suggest that he should not.

The man who obeys these four imperatives is the supermale who for a long time has been the idol of the crowds. He is wonderfully illustrated by the image associated with Marlboro cigarettes ("the Marlboro man"), whose poster has crossed the world. This is the hard man, solitary because he needs no one, impassive, as virile as anyone could wish. All men, at one time, dream of being this: a sexual animal with women, but one who does not become attached to any one woman; a creature who meets his male counterparts only in competition, war, or sports. In short, the toughest of the tough, "emotionally mutilated,"[12] more suited to dying than to marrying and mothering.

Most cultures have adhered to this masculine ideal and created their own models, but it is America, without cultural rival, which has imposed its images of virility on the whole world: from the cowboy to the Terminator by way of Rambo, as incarnated by cult actors (John Wayne, Sylvester Stallone, Arnold Schwarzenegger), these heroes of the big screen have served as outlets and still incite millions of men to daydream. Even though these three representations of hypervirility conform to the four imperatives mentioned above, it will not have escaped anyone's notice that in progressing from the cowboy to the Terminator, we have gone from a flesh-and-blood man to a machine.

The mythical figure of the cowboy, much older than its two successors, has given rise to numerous analyses.[13] The psychoanalyst Lydia Flem has scrutinized the different aspects of the masculinity of the solitary horseman come out of nowhere, of the administrator of justice above the law, "of this pure creature who knows neither transformations nor adulterations . . . and who has not reached the stage of subtleties."[14] The cowboy embodies all masculine stereotypes, and the western always tells the same story, of an incessant pursuit on the part of men in search of their virility. Gun, liquor, and horse are the obligatory accessories for this, and women play only secondary roles.

The cowboy's relationship with women is a silent one. For some, this does not signify an absence of feelings, but a difficulty in expressing them directly for fear of losing his virility.[15] Others see it as proof of an emotional impotence.[16] Frozen in action, the manly hero ceaselessly confronts other men. Flem speaks of the men's joy at meeting each other on common, properly masculine ground, that of combat. The confrontation does not prevent virile feelings. Furthermore, friendship among men—with latent homosexual overtones—strengthens masculinity, which is threatened by the love of a woman. In the case of conflict between the two feelings, it is almost always the duty of masculine solidarity that wins out: the cowboy goes off again toward new adventures. Even though impassive and silent, the hero of the western allows the spectator to divine his humanity: his conflicts, his feelings, therefore his "weakness." For the space of a glance, he shows a temptation, or a regret; he shows that he has, in short, a heart. One suspects him of loving his horse, a male friend, or a woman. This is the great difference between him and Rambo or Terminator, who no longer have even these weaknesses. Endowed with "super-human" strength, they have emptied themselves of all feeling. Rambo, in his armor of muscles, does not encumber himself with horse, friend, or woman.[17] His only companion is an immense, sharp dagger that serves him as a "lucky charm," a phallic reinforcement of a virility that is still human and there-fore defective. No such thing remains to threaten Terminator, the all-powerful machine. The male in the pure state no longer has anything human about him, not even a sex, which is the most fragile part of a man and the part he is least able to con-trol. For the space of a film, male spectators can enjoy an iden-tification with absolute power. Terminator is free "of the con-straints of morality,"[18] of fear, pain, and death, as well as of all emotional attachment.[19] The virile machine is incomparably less vulnerable than the strongest of males. To do exactly what one wants to do when one wants to: this is the hidden dream of all the little boys who slumber inside many men. This explains the worldwide success of a film with undeniable tech-nical feats but with an inconsistent script, whose greatest merit is to offer two hours of a hypervirility that does not exist in real life.

Without going as far as the fantastic excesses of the virile machine, the masculine ideal as defined by David and Bran-non's four imperatives remains inaccessible to most men: too hard, too constraining[20] because it is too obviously contrary to the original bisexuality of every human being. To turn a little boy with his mommy into the "pitiless monster"[21] in keeping with this model smacks of a cruel exploit. Sooner or later, most men realize that they are struggling with a male type which they will not succeed in achieving. The result is a cer-tain tension between the collective ideal and real life. And yet this "myth of masculinity" survives thanks to the complicity of the very ones it oppresses. Australian sociologist Robert

Connell wondered about the reasons for this complicity.[22] Beyond the fantasy satisfactions offered by the images of a Bogart[23] or a Sylvester Stallone, the masculine ideal they embody expresses the superiority of men and their ascendancy over women, an asymmetry between the two sexes that reinforces the boundaries.

The disadvantages of the masculine ideal remain no less considerable for most men, who are in fact deviants from the mythical norm of success, power, control, and strength. The promotion of this inaccessible image of virility leads to a painful realization: that one is an incomplete man. In order to fight a permanent feeling of insecurity, some men believe the answer is to promote a hypervirility. In fact, they find themselves prisoners, once again, of an obsessional and compulsive masculinity that never leaves them in peace. On the contrary, it is a source of self-destruction and aggressivity against all those who threaten to cause the mask to fall.

For most Americans of the 1950s, Ernest Hemingway was the man who incarnated, in his life and his work, the "true virility," the "tough guy." At the beginning of the 1970s, John Updike was able to write: "An entire generation of American men learned to speak in the accents of [his] stoicism."[24] His action books and his life—boxing, hunting, fishing, drinking, always in pursuit of manly activities—were two ways of illustrating North American masculinity. In devoting his life and his work to the legend of his own virility, "Papa" Hemingway, as he preferred to be called (starting at the age of twenty-seven), also showed its tragic risks.[25]

His biographer Kenneth Lynn insists at length on this inner conflict between the quest for a virility free of all femininity and Hemingway's desires for a feminine passivity, a neurotic contradiction which appears very clearly in his posthumous work *The Garden of Eden*, extracted from an interminable manuscript that the author spent fifteen years writing. Here, his desires for sexual passivity and his transsexual fantasies are expressed quite frankly.[26]

But these moments of abandon are exceptional in Hemingway's life. As a general rule, he transforms this desire for a female identification into aggressive and humiliating remarks against his successive wives and incessant accusations of sterility, impotence, and homosexuality[27] against other men, both friends and enemies. Vanquished, in the end, by this illness of masculinity, the writer killed himself with a bullet from a rifle. Perhaps we could apply to him Lynne Segal's reflection about Yukio Mishima's suicide: "His furious quest for masculinity . . . provoked the desire to purge himself of all sensitivity in order to become a fully virile object, a complete man—something that was possible only at the moment of his self-destruction, at the moment of death."[28]

Though it does not always attain this paroxysm of destruction, obsessional masculinity is always a source of conflict and tension. It forces a man to wear the mask of an exhausting omnipotence and independence. Should the mask fall, says anthropologist David Gilmore, one would discover the "trembling baby within."[29] In *Women*, the autobiographical novel by the "toughest of the tough," Charles Bukowski, sex scenes and scenes of vomiting alternate. The author spews out his hatred of women, his alcoholic excesses, his fear of not being a man. Then he criticizes himself before sobbing like a little child.[30] The same behaviors and the same anguish appear in a number of Norman Mailer's characters. In *Tough Guys Don't Dance*, he explores the most secret places of the American male (himself?), torn between the temptations of machismo and homosexuality. Alcoholic, evasive, the hero searches desperately for a virility that escapes him. As he tries to extirpate his latent homosexuality by an utterly mad climb, he ends by collapsing in tears, dead drunk. He confesses that like his father—who seemed so virile—he has lost his balls.[31]

It is true that within the context of a male hegemony, the genital organs are the object of an obsessional valorization. This is hardly surprising when the sex alone is supposed to sum up a person's gender or even the quality of the entire person. "To have or not to have" tends to be substituted for "to be or not to be."

THE OVERVALORIZATION OF THE PENIS

Of course men did not wait for psychoanalysis to magnify the penis and construct imposing obelisks to its glory. However, Freud, and after him Lacan, have each in their way contributed a decisive theoretical guaranty to the superiority and uniqueness of the male organ, even if only as a symbol.

The Freudian theory of female penis envy[32] has played a decisive role. Many psychoanalysts (Karen Horney, Ernest Jones, Melanie Klein)[33] have tried to diminish its importance, either by considering this envy to be a secondary formation, or by countering it with its symmetrical male opposite: envy of women's breasts and reproductive functions. Until recently, it has been women psychoanalysts[34] who have been preoccupied with attracting attention to this male desire, which has never had the same influence, as a theory, as penis envy.

The Lacanian theory of the primacy of the Phallus[35]—not to be confused with the real, biological sex called the penis— which achieved a great success in the 1960s and 1970s, managed to give the male sex an incomparable status. Behind this theory is the idea that the human subject is structured in and through language. The human subject and human sexual identity are produced simultaneously when the child enters the symbolic order of language. Now Lacan maintains that the reduction of sexual difference to the presence or absence of the phallus is a symbolic law produced by the patriarchy: the Law of the Father. Like Lévi-Strauss, Lacan considers the patriarchy a universal system of power. It has been pointed out that "the primacy of the Phallus as unique emblem of the human is necessary in order to maintain the preeminence of the father as Father: in effect, if there must be preference for the Father, if he is the origin and the representative of Culture and Law, if he alone gives access to language, it is because he possesses the phallus, which he can give or refuse."[36]

The Phallus is the major signifier, the signifier of signifiers that rules all the others and causes the human being to enter into the order of the culture.[37] The ultimate stroke of this hymn of praise in honor of the Phallus is its relation to the *Nous* and the *Logos*.[38]

How tenacious narcissism is, once it lays hold of us! Marecelle Marini thinks Lacan can go as far as he likes because he has first asserted the radical separation between the penis, a simple organ, and the phallus, a pure signifier. In fact, Lacan does not hesitate to recall that there is only *one* libido, a masculine one, and to emphasize the profound asymmetry that defines the two sexes. "For him, *one* sex has been chosen to accede to the level of signifier of sexuation: there is no `signifier of the female sex,' not even a `signifier of the difference between the sexes.' The phallus alone is the sex unit." "The man is not without having it" and "the woman is without having it."[39]

Numerous criticisms—and not only feminist ones—have been addressed to the Lacanian theory. Beyond the fact that the Phallus offers the penis a transcendental meaning it does not claim, its status as primary signifier makes differences other than genital ones "insignificant." What is more, the theory of the eternal and necessary patriarchy on which he depends to justify the primacy of the Phallus is decaying by now: the power of men over women defined as object of exchange appears to us to belong to another world.[40] Others point out that the power of the Phallus is only symbolic. Despite Lacan's denials, his theory makes use of "an anatomical elision between the Phallus and the penis. . . . Men, by virtue of their penis, can aspire to a position of power and control within the symbolic order."[41] Women, who have no penis, have no place in the symbolic order.

The theoretical criticisms addressed to Freud and Lacan change nothing about the intense valorization of this visible organ with its magical properties. Stoltenberg's psychological explanation is interesting: the boy learns that he has a penis and that his mother does not. If he cannot feel his penis, he will surely become like her. Later, his eroticism will be uniquely concentrated on his penis, that part of himself that distinguishes him from his mother.[42] It is thus through his sex and sexual activity that a man most effectively becomes aware of his identity and his virility—which also means that after ejaculation, when the erotic sensations of his penis disappear, he feels a sort of absence, the death of his phallic life. Whence the frenetic activity of a Don Juan, ceaselessly attempting to hold death at bay. In order to do this, he must objectify his body and consider it a machine that is unacquainted with anguish, fatigue, and different states of mind. Many men, obsessed by their virility, do not really consider their sex an organ of pleasure, but a tool, an instrument in a performance, a thing separate from themselves. Many also confess to having conversations with their penis, cajoling it, asking it to stay erect.[43] Alberto Moravia has described amusingly the dissociation between a man, a failed writer, and his sex, which leads its life quite independently. Unlike the Don Juan, Moravia's pitiable hero controls nothing at all. The intellectual who dreams of sublimating himself in a great work finds himself once again obeying the whims of his penis, "stupidly voluminous, idiotically available, hefty . . . giving him an inferiority complex."[44]

Symbol of omnipotence (a "love machine") or of the most extreme weakness (Moravia's hero), the penis, metonymy for the man, is also his obsessive master. The part lays down the law to the whole since it defines the whole. Psychic uneasiness naturally translates into sexual difficulties. Leonore Tiefer, a specialist in sexual disturbances, notes, like all her colleagues, a considerable increase in the number of men seeking treatment in medical centers since 1970. In more than half the cases, those who complain of a complete or partial loss of the ability to have an erection are looking for the perfect penis.[45] There is nothing surprising about this demand when it is seen in the context of the conviction that sexual activity confirms gender: a man is a man when he is in a state of erection. Thus, any difficulty with his penis is a source of profound humiliation and despair, a sign of the loss of his masculinity. To remedy this, some men are prepared to do anything, including receive penile implants, either inflatable or rigid.[46]

At the end of the 1970s, certain (young) men declared that they no longer recognized themselves in this kind of masculinity. Pascal Bruckner, Alain Finkielkraut, and Emmanuel Reynaud undertook to demystify the omnipotence of the penis and to rethink masculine sexuality. First, a man's sex is the most vulnerable part of his being[47]—"It is in woman that sexual power is based, in fact. For the real phallus is not the frail penis that only rises proudly up when it is made confident, that must be tenderly petted so that it will consent to expel its little white treasure; the real indefatigable and ever-valiant phallus is the woman's sex." In terms of power and performance, the man is beaten.[48] Second, the man does not know how to enjoy himself—"Caught between his fear of letting himself go and his use of the phallus as a means of appropriation,"[49] he has a sexuality that is blocked and sad, that is ignorant of many pleasures, because it is subject to the dictates of the genital. *Le Nouveau désordre amoureux* speaks at some length in praise of caresses, the anus, body games, and passivity on the part of the male: "Shared onanism, the man deliciously inert, abandoning himself to the zealous attentions of a woman who is both expert and perverse."[50] Praise is also given to the whore, with whom one can let oneself go: during the brief minutes of the assignation, the client "will be the most infantilized, the most passive body possible. No woman is more motherly than the prostitute. . . . The client is merely a little boy who gets an erection and whose erection, far from being an attribute of virility, is the very sign of his need of assistance." Third, the authors conclude by killing off the myth of the tough guy—"If a man pays, he does so in order to abdicate his masculinity, rid his eroticism of its supposedly active character: to climax without doing anything, in a sort of muscular catatonia, to bathe in Nirvana, in the degree zero of activity of motion."[51]

If in the eyes of some, the ideal of the hard man is a negative myth, it remains powerful in the male unconscious. At the origin of many frustrations, it engenders a great deal of violence against others and against oneself.

A DANGEROUS VIRILITY

Male violence is not universal. It varies from one society to another and from one individual to another. Certainly, where the male mystique continues to dominate, as in the United States, violence by men is a perpetual danger. In America, in the early 1970s, the National Commission on the Causes and Prevention of Violence noted that the country was experiencing a much higher rate of homicides, rapes, and thefts than any other modern, stable, democratic nation.[52] The commission added that most of this criminal violence was committed by men between fifteen and twenty-four years of age. To prove one's virility, explained the report, required frequent displays of toughness, the exploitation of women, and quick and aggressive responses.

In the last twenty years, the situation has distinctly worsened, and the gap has widened even more between America and Europe. I have already mentioned male violence against homosexuals. But nothing compares to that of which women are the victims, either beaten or raped. Rape is the crime that is increasing the most in the United States.[53] The FBI estimates that if this tendency continues, one woman out of four will be raped once in her life.[54] If one adds that the number of women beaten by their husbands every year is estimated at 1.8 million, one will have some idea of the violence that surrounds them and the fear of men they legitimately feel. The threat of rape—which has nothing to do with the fantasies of the hysteric—has caused one woman to say: "It alters the meaning and feel of the night . . . and it is night half the time."[55] More generally, the fear of being raped looms over the daily life of all women. In 1971 the feminist Susan Griffin evoked a response in the public when she declared: "I have never been able to rid myself of

my fear of being raped."[56] In her eyes, the guilty party is mainly the patriarchy, because it encourages the rape of women as
the symbolic expression of male power. Even more radical,
Susan Brownmiller[57] and Andrea Dworkin[58] assert that rape is
an integral part of male sexuality, necessary for establishing
male domination. Since the patriarchy is a universal given, one
comes to believe that all men are potential rapists. One man
goes so far as to assert: "The difference between a rapist, in the
literal and legal sense of the term, and other men is that most
of us stop at a lower degree of coercion and violence."[59]

The theory of the "rapist male" is fiercely challenged by
anthropologists and psychologists. The English feminist
anthropologist Peggy Reeves Sanday has shown that the
propensity to rape varies considerably from one society to
another.[60] In Sumatra, for instance, rape is extremely rare, for
in these societies women are respected and play an important
role in collective decisions. Here, the relationship between the
sexes tends toward equality. The same is true among the Arapesh Indians of America studied by Margaret Mead, among the
Tahitians described by Robert Levy, and in certain African
hunter-gatherer societies. Even without going to such remote
spots, we have to note that in our Western societies, the rate of
rape varies from one to seventeen between England and the
United States,[61] and from one to twenty between France and
the United States.[62]

The theory according to which rape is inherent to male sexuality has never been demonstrated. What is more, it is injuri-
ous to the male sex. Psychologists who have studied rapists
tend to think that rape is a pathology of virility and not the
expression of normal virility, a problem of gender and not of
sex. According to the work of David Lisak, rape is first of all the
consequence of a failure of male identification and an excessive
repression of one's femininity, which he calls "self- mutilation."[63] The psychological profile of the rapist cannot be
extended to all men—far from it. Rape implies a hatred of the
other, and many men confide that they could not have sexual

140

relations in such conditions. What remains true is that the model of the hypervirile man, dematricized, defeminized, is a source of real uneasiness with respect to identity and is responsible for two types of violence—violence toward others and violence toward oneself.

For almost twenty years now, we have suspected that our old masculine ideal is fatal to men themselves. A Canadian psychologist, Sidney Jourard, was the first to formulate this hypothesis.[64] The point of departure for this psychosocial hypothesis is the following: in 1900 life expectancy in the United States was 48.3 years for women and 46.3 years for men. In 1975 it was 76.5 years for women and 68.7 years for men.[65] Today, the gap is about eight years in all Western countries.[66] Two questions: why this gap in longevity between the two sexes, and why has the gap widened to this point since the beginning of the century?

The biogenetic hypothesis maintained by Ashley Montague (1953) attributes the higher mortality of males (prenatal, infantile, and adult) to the fragility of the y chromosome, which carries less genetic information than the x chromosome.[67] But this finding does not answer the second question. Moreover, biology does not supply the proof that female cells, tissues, or organisms are in themselves more viable than those of men. The psychosocial hypothesis that prevails today takes a close look at all the constraints that the masculine role imposes so heavily on men.

Jourard postulates that men have fundamentally the same psychological needs as women (to love and be loved, to communicate emotions and feelings, to be active and passive). However, the ideal of masculinity forbids men to satisfy these "human" needs. Others[68] have insisted on the physical dangers that lie in wait for the *tough guy*: boys are forced to take risks that end in accidents (e.g., various sports); they smoke, drink, and use motorcycles and cars as symbols of virility. Some of them find confirmation of their virility only in violence, either personal or collective. In addition, the competition and stress that follow in their professional life, and their obsession with performance, only add to men's fragility. The efforts demanded of men to conform to the masculine ideal cause anguish, emotional difficulties, fear of failure, and potentially dangerous and destructive compensatory behaviors.[69] When one sizes up the psychosomatic uniqueness of the human being, the influence of psychic distress on physical illness, and when one realizes that men find it harder to consult medical doctors and psychologists and do so less often than women,[70] then the shorter life expectancy of men is easier to understand. If one adds that in our society the life of a man is worth less than that of a woman (women and children first!),[71] that he serves as cannon fodder in time of war, and that the depiction of his death (in the movies and on television) has become mere routine, a cliché of virility, one has good reason to regard traditional masculinity as life-threatening.

Many have seen the lesson that should be learned from this. It is time, they say, that men understand that the ideal of virility comes at a high price[72] and that masculinity will only become less harmful to our health when we stop defining it by opposition to femininity.[73] It is urgent that we teach boys another model of virility that allows room for an acknowledgment of vulnerability. Boys must learn to express their emotions, ask for help, be motherly and cooperative, and resolve conflicts in a nonviolent way; to accept attitudes and behaviors traditionally labeled as feminine as necessary to the development of every human being (thus to reduce homophobia and misogyny)—which amounts to saying they must learn to love girls and other boys.[74]

The Soft Man

As noted above, the concept of the "soft man" comes from Scandinavia. But this type of man, as new as he is strange, has appeared here and there in countries where the *tough guy* has flourished the most, and thus where feminism has been the most militant: in the United States, in Germany, in English-speaking countries much more than in France. The *soft man* follows the *tough guy* as his absolute opposite.

In order to please women who were castigating the macho man in the 1970s, certain men felt they had to abandon all virility and adopt the most traditional female values and behaviors. The tough guy, with his repressed femininity, was replaced by the soft man, whose masculinity was ignored. The Danish *soft man* (*Den Blo/de Mand*) is a contradiction in terms, unlike the Norwegian appellation, the *gentle man* (*Den Myke Mann*). In the first case, there is no more virility, whereas the second evokes the image of another kind of virility. In French, the word *soft* means: "yielding easily to pressure; allowing itself to be cut effortlessly; flabby and limp,"[75] which is obviously incompatible with masculinity! Even if the dictionary likens it to *gentle*—the two words have a feminine connotation—there is a difference in nature between them as soon as they qualify a man. Gentle and tender is not synonymous with soft and flabby.[76]

The soft man, who had so few followers in France that one cannot consider him a social phenomenon there, turned out to be a failure everywhere he appeared. However, he still has advocates who confuse him with the gentle man.

HOW THE TOUGH GUY ENGENDERED THE SOFT MAN
As early as the seventeenth century, refined Englishwomen (along with the *précieuses*) dreamed of a more feminine man— "soft, urbanized, and weak."[77] We know how they were received! Three centuries later, in 1977, an American magazine surveyed twenty-eight thousand of its readers about masculinity. A majority of the men responded that they wanted to be warmer, gentler, and more loving, and that they despised aggressivity, competition, and sexual "conquests."[78] In France, in a study in which men were asked which qualities seemed most important to them in a man, they answered in order of

priority: honesty (66 percent), determination (40 percent), and tenderness (37 percent), followed by intelligence, good manners, seductiveness, and, last of all, virility, which garnered only 8 percent of the votes.[79]

It is true that for a long time women have shared these values[80] and that they have contributed a great deal to upsetting the ideal of masculinity. The dream of equality dismantled traditional masculinity and put an end to its prestige. This was expressed by a rejection of masculine values and an idealization of feminine values. Most men felt they were among the accused. Anguish, guilt, and aggressivity were the most common reactions. Philip Roth was one of their spokesmen when he attacked the feminists (who certainly paid him back in kind). One of his characters, suffering from a serious depression, says: "I can't stand the hypocrisy of the self-righteous [feminists]." And at a later point: "I really like the feminists, because they are so dumb. For them, exploitation is a guy fucking a woman."[81] As to this, the average Southerner in the United States reacts exactly the same way as a New York Jewish intellectual. The hero of *The Prince of Tides*, thirty years old, begins by attacking women "uniting to crush the penis once and for all." He ridicules feminists, whom he finds "terrifying." But at the same time, he internalizes their criticisms.[82]

In addition to those anguished men who can no longer manage to fulfill the obligations of the traditional role, as well as the skeptics who see only its disadvantages, certain men have become feminists for moral and political reasons. Human rights militants, pacifists, and ecologists were among the first to criticize the masculine values summed up in these three words: war, competition, and domination. Quite naturally, they called for the opposite values: life, compassion, forgiveness, tenderness, everything women are supposed to embody in the traditional ideology. These feminine values were declared morally superior to masculine values, which were systematically denigrated. The equation male = bad prevailed everywhere.[83]

But, in another of history's many ironies, while women were demanding gentler, kinder, less aggressive men, they themselves were encouraged to be fighters and conquerors. At the very moment when the new female warrior was being glorified, men were being discouraged from being warriors! Jérome Bernstein points out that we are witnessing the birth of the "female hero,"[84] active, competent, and a formidable rival for men.

Having roused her masculine elements, woman asserts herself more and more, using well-known weapons. By becoming a "female hero," she is now the one who, according to Bernstein, puts an end to her need for dependence on men as soon as these ties prevent her from achieving her goals. She is the one seeking success, fulfillment, ego satisfaction, even at the price of great difficulties and loneliness. She has no intention of conforming to the femininity dreamed of by men, but will listen only to what she is feeling. To this extreme vitality in women, men who have been challenged in their virility have reacted with evasion, despair, or silent impassivity.

Thus the 1970s witnessed the appearance of the "soft male,"[85] thoughtful, attentive, charming, wanting to respond to the expectations of women like his mother and her friends. According to Robert Bly, these "lovely men" turned out to be lacking in vitality and joie de vivre. Companions of stable women who radiated a positive energy, they were "life-preserving" and not "life-giving"[86] like their women. Starting in the 1980s, these men began to express their discomfort and their distress. The "soft man" felt himself to be passive and destructured. In 1980, during an early men's studies conference in New Mexico, certain men began weeping as they told of "their immense pain" at being forbidden to be virile.[87] They described their sorrow at being distanced from their father. The soft man could experience the feelings of the female other—his mother had become his model—but could not say what he wanted and hold to it. He had become totally passive, terrorized by his aggressivity and his desire for self-affirmation. In short, it was easier for him to express his inner femininity, his affectivity, than his virility, associated as it was with an unacceptable violence. The "mama's boy" could not even attain the degree of virility that his mother—whether feminist or not—displayed quite naturally.

Certain men, like Günter Grass,[88] denounced men's mother complex as well as the matriarchy, which they judged to be more oppressive than the patriarchy. *The Flounder* simply advises tremulous men to cut the umbilical cord: "Go on. . . . Kill her, my son!"[89] The idea of putting an end to the mother-son couple is not accompanied, here, by any challenge to the father, "that cornered hero,"[90] himself a slave of the gynecocracy. It is up to the son to accomplish the matricide and put himself in the care of his father. By the end of the 1980s, the mother was no longer the one under attack.[91] The focus of attention had shifted to the father, so unaccustomed to blame. He was universally criticized, declared guilty of emasculating his own son. These days, historians, psychologists, sociologists, and novelists are pointing an accusing finger at him. Studies are multiplying on the "busy" father, absent, aggressive, cold, full of resentment for his son, whom he abandons to the mother's clutches. References are made to mythology (Chronos devouring his son, Laios ordering the death of his son Oedipus) and to religion (Abraham preparing to sacrifice Isaac; the last words of Christ on the cross: "Father, why hast thou abandoned me?") to show that cruelty on the part of fathers has always existed. Bad fathers are found in profusion in literature, which offers few examples of good fathers, protective and warm. Kafka's famous *Letter to His Father* remains a model of a son's distress: "For me you took on the enigmatic quality that all tyrants have whose rights are based on their person and not on reason. . . . You were . . . scarcely able to be with me even once a day, and therefore made all the more profound an impression on me. . . . What was always incomprehensible to me was your total lack of feeling for the suffering and shame you could inflict on me with your words and judgments. . . . How terrible for me was, for instance, that 'I'll tear you apart like a fish.'"[92] And what of all those hateful, violent, sadistic fathers described by Saul Bellow,[93] Edmund White,[94] Pat Conroy,[95] Peter Härtling,[96] or François-Marie Bannier?[97]

The evidence to be found in the humanities is damning. We have seen in the Shere Hite study how very rare good relations between fathers and sons are.[98] Sons have trouble talking spontaneously about their fathers. But in private conversation, they complain about their fathers' humiliations, criticisms, derision, and condescension. The psychologist Phyllis Chesler, who has taken a profound interest in this failed relationship, remarks: "Listening to them, I had the very distinct impression that many of the men had had the same father, *all* the fathers were based on a single character, an archetype of a father: an alien fantasm, half tyrant, half deposed despot and because of that, worthy of pity. A man who was awkward, ill at ease, or out of his element in his own home; a tense man who had trouble controlling his emotions." She specifies that the sons questioned made an effort to retrieve for me the memory of this stranger, their father, all the while manifesting a sort of embarrassed indifference.[99]

The sons complained of the father's *absence* even more than his violence. Here, "absence" is to be taken figuratively rather than literally. It is true that with the considerable increase in the number of single-parent families headed by women alone,[100] more and more sons do not live under the same roof as their father. Still, one can be a divorced father and take good care of one's son. The *absence* of which the sons complained concerned fathers who were present in the house, but spectral. Guy Corneau designates them by the expression "missing fathers," which is more general than "absent fathers."[101]

As the lovely title of Corneau's book says, these "lacking" fathers engender sons that "lack," "for lack of a father." The absence of attention (love?) on the part of a father prevents a son from identifying with him and establishing his own masculine identity.[102] As a consequence, this son, lacking a father's love, remains in the orbit of his mother, attracted by feminine values alone. He regards his father and his virility with the eyes of the mother. If the mother sees the father as "maybe brutal . . . unfeeling, obsessed . . . the son often grows up with a wounded image of his father" and refuses to be like him.[103]

The sickness is deeper than one would believe, even in France, though it is less apparent here than in other societies. One may smile at the American "men's movement" and snicker over Robert Bly's weekends in the forest, which bring men together in search of their true masculine nature.[104] More than 100,000 have already participated in them in just a few years. Comfortably established men in their forties, for the most part, they come to shed tears in peace over their masculine distress and talk about the poverty of their relationships with their fathers. These unfulfilled and pained sons share with others the wounds their identities received and express their common "thirst for a father."[105]

In a very enlightening study, the American psychoanalyst Samuel Osherson confirms the depth of the "father sickness."[106] At midlife (between thirty and forty years), a time when their own sons are leaving childhood,[107] men who need to rediscover their fathers too often run up against a wall. They feel abandoned, orphaned. Generally, they have interiorized a sad image of their father, or one of a categorical and angry judge. They complain that they know nothing about him because his vulnerability is taboo. The unapproachable father—who seems to avoid intimate conversations with his son—rarely expresses his love verbally, because he has inherited a model of masculinity that rejects the expression of feelings of tenderness.[108] This "wounded father,"[109] incapable of showing his emotions, in turn wounds his son, who lacks a model of access to the emotions. As a result, the image of the father oscillates between an "alien omnipotence" and an infinite weakness;[110] the son's feelings are divided between fear (of the father's hatred and rejection) and contempt. The deep need of the son to be acknowledged and confirmed by his father runs up against the law of silence. His masculinity, which requires constant reinforcement, is left unfinished because the father has run away. Edmund White has illustrated very well the irreparable harm this causes. Over and over again, the little boy calls upon his father for help in cutting the umbilical cord.[111] Each time, the father turns a deaf ear and rejects him.

In the end, the "soft man" is one of those "lacking" sons who have perhaps suffered less from maternal omnipotence than from the emotional absence of the father.[112] True, this absence is not a recent one, since it is tied both to the industrial society and to the traditional ideal of masculinity. But Osherson is right in saying that in the past men could be content with a silent homage to the father, comforted by a life that resembled his: paterfamilias, professional success, and so on. For the past thirty years, the women's revolution has intensified boys' sadness and their terror of losing their father. Participants in the conquest of the world, women present an image of strength and vitality that contrasts with the impassivity and uneasiness of the father.[113] This increases their attraction even more and makes the son's break with his mother all the harder.

A PORTRAIT OF THE SOFT MAN

The soft man is a destructured one. As the psychoanalysts note: to lack a father is to lack backbone.[114] "The absence of the father produces a negative father complex that consists in a lack of internal structures. The son's ideas are confused, and he experiences difficulties when he has to decide upon a goal, make choices, or recognize what is good for him and identify his own needs. Everything in him is mixed up: love with reason, sexual appetites with a simple need for affection."[115]

The destructured man experiences internal disorder, which can vary from a superficial confusion to a mental disorganization. Corneau, an analyst, has observed that face to face with this reality, men try to compensate by structuring themselves on something outside of themselves. Some become industrious ants so as never to have a free moment. The admiring looks of others sustain them, and they have a tendency to obey collective values. Others, the Don Juans, structure themselves by their numerous sexual experiences. Still others, by becoming involved in "body building." They compensate, by an external corporeal construction, for an internal deficiency. "The more fragile a man feels inside, the more he will try to create an outer carapace for himself to mislead people. . . . The more categorical his assertions are, and lacking in nuances, the more they will serve to mask a basic uncertainty. . . . By means of this external compensation, the failed sons avoid feeling their great thirst for love and understanding."[116]

Emotionally, the young man abandoned by his father and initiated by his mother risks remaining a "mama's boy" all his life: a nice boy, irresponsible, avoiding the commitments of an adult. Unconsciously, he wants to remain "his mother's little husband,"[117] or to find the same type of relationship (an infantile one) with other women. In the heyday of feminism, he adopted the values of the women's movement to please his mother. A child of divorced parents, with an absent father, Keith Thompson is one example of a "mama's boy": in his early twenties, his best friends were women, including some older than he—energetic persons who initiated him into politics, literature, and feminism. His friendships with them were platonic and resembled very closely the bonds between a teacher and a student. "So for almost ten years, through about age 24, my life was full of self-confident, experienced women friends and men friends who, like me, placed a premium on vulnerability, gentleness, and sensitivity. . . . Yet a couple of years ago, I began to feel that something was missing."[118]

This sequence of experiences was shared by many men in the 1970s and 1980s in Germany, Scandinavia, and the United States.[119] But everywhere, it engendered a sort of uneasiness because there was too great a passivity and a feeling of lack of self-fulfillment—an arrest in the development of the personality. A "nice boy" is what the name indicates: a child, not a responsible adult. Jungians refer to him as the *puer aeternus*.[120] But he is also known as the Little Prince, Peter Pan, or the Flying Boy (the boy who flies away, who avoids difficulties).

The American John Lee has told the story of his own experience as a Flying Boy, a wounded man.[121] His personal itiner-
ary is exemplary and could be that of any of the others. He
needed many years in therapy for the wound to heal and the
child to give birth to the man. Like his mentor, Robert Bly, he
had an alcoholic father and a mother who treated him like a
"magical person," destined to fill the lacks in the marriage.
Both boys escaped the world of men and projected their souls
into the women they loved and then abandoned. "Flying boys"
have no male friends, reject their masculinity (identified with
the rejected father), and make use only of their feminine sensibility. John Lee describes himself, at twenty-five, as a nice boy,
completely dependent on his work, obsessed by sex but incapable of living with the woman he is in love with. He is so
afraid of commitment that he constantly avoids reality and
contrives each time to break away. A manic-depressive, he
embarks on an analysis that shows him that he is "his mother's mirror."[122] Most painful of all is his sadness and his fury
toward the absent father with whom he has never communicated. He discovers that he himself was his mother's real husband and that his father, jealous, withdrew his masculine affection from him. After a great deal of rage, tears, and physical suffering, the analysis allowed him to settle accounts with his
mother and to cut the umbilical cord ("she was the center of
the universe and I was a satellite").[123] Very soon, his appearance changed. The bohemian boy, with long hair and a unisex
style, was replaced by an adult man. The hardest part of the
analysis was attacking his father (a taboo subject for the son).
But by unleashing his rage, he was able to renew his ties with
him, accept him as he was, identify with him, and become a
man at last. By the end of his analysis, John Lee had reconciled
in himself, "like brother and sister,"[124] his femininity and his
virility. He has since devoted himself to male psychology.

Not all the "flying boys" have turned to psychoanalysis, and
many of them are unhappily married, suffering from impotence

and depression.[125] Others, such as divorced fathers who are disgusted at being deprived of their children, have turned their rage against women, like the fictional character who, having ditched his wife in order to go adventuring, confides to a friend: "I was fed up with my role as softy, trailing along behind the feminist movement."[126]

According to Gerlach-Nielsen, Scandinavian women have had enough of the soft man. Even the women most responsive to gentleness on the part of men want nothing more to do with these men, who are ersatz traditional women. The men, for their part, are "tired of having to do the dishes and the housework in order to have the right to sleep with their wives. In 1984, the death of the soft man was proclaimed."[127] In fact, it is not certain that he is really dead. Reading the radical American feminists, or the champions of pure and uncompromising ecology, one would gather that some thinkers continue to associate masculinity with its pathological aspects—violence, rape, and so on—and to compare the penis to a weapon. Although they may be rearguard fighters, certain men are not the last to call for the execution of the male "gender,"[128] the elimination of manly values,[129] even the renunciation of all aggressivity and the (temporary) choice of passivity in order to put an end to "male hegemony,"[130] or, finally, to raise boys in the same way as girls,[131] who are considered to be naturally more tender and cooperative.

The solution proposed by Bly and a number of other Jungians—the reuniting of each man with his "inner warrior," a reversion to the condition of primitive and savage man (the "Wildman," which he has some trouble distinguishing from the cruel "Savage man," who exteriorizes his violence) by means of periods spent in the forest, the use of masks and drums—is hardly convincing. What is more, nostalgia for the patriarchal olden days (Greece, the Middle Ages) is so strong in Bly and his followers—despite their constant denials—that they bring us back willy-nilly to a dualism of the sexes incompatible with changing customs and our increasing knowledge.

More generally, those in favor of the tough guy or the soft man are making the mistake of thinking that there exist certain qualities exclusively characteristic of one sex and alien to the other, such as aggressivity, supposed to be specifically masculine, and compassion, essentially feminine. In fact, whether one considers aggressivity as an innate virtue or an acquired disease, one would have to be blind to say that women are not aggressive. Even if the patriarchal education and culture have taught them—more than men—to turn it against themselves, women are thoroughly familiar with this human impulse. They are, like men, influenced by the degree of violence in the social environment.[132] Aggressivity is characteristic of both sexes, even if it is expressed differently.[133] What is more, it should not be identified merely with a destructive, gratuitous violence. It is not only that, as Freud saw.[134] It can also be equivalent to survival, action, and creation. Its absolute contrary is passivity and death, and its absence can mean loss of freedom and human dignity. The slogan of the German "Green Party," so fashionable in the 1970s ("Better Red Than Dead"), can only be explained by the past history of those who proclaimed it. Sons or grandsons of torturers, they feared more than anything else repeating the sins of their fathers. In their case, more than elsewhere, tough guys produced soft men. Passivity and submission to the enemy were favored over revolt and resistance. The viewpoint of the sons of victims is exactly the opposite. They tend to believe that the preservation of dignity is as important as life itself, and that a human being (man or woman) may take pride in risking his or her life in order to safeguard freedom and refuse to submit to what is unacceptable.

Is the Homosexual a Mutilated Man?

Assuming we have dealt with the crudest prejudices concerning homosexuals,[135] the uncertain and contradictory positions

153

of the experts, particularly psychiatrists and psychoanalysts, cast a shadow over the status of the homosexual. It is he, more than any other, who is suspected of being mutilated.

THE PSYCHIATRISTS' AMBIGUOUS POSITION

Freud's courageous opposition to his disciples in defense of homosexuals has been noted. But the fact that the homosexual was neither a criminal nor sick did not necessarily mean, for Freud, that homosexuality was as "normal" and desirable as heterosexuality. In his letter to the American mother of a homosexual son, he says, in so many words: "We consider it [homosexuality] as a variation of the sexual function, *provoked by a certain arrest in the sexual development.*"[136] The last words amount to a stigma. To speak of "arrest in the development" evokes something unfinished, morbid, abnormal. One may be implying that a homosexual is not a complete man, or an adult completely emerged from childhood, since he has not reached the stage of sexual maturity. Freud's message turns out to be ambiguous: the homosexual is an "abnormal" man who is not sick.

The current doctrine of psychiatrists and psychologists is hardly clearer. The manner in which the American Psychiatric Association (the APA) decided to strike homosexuality from the official list of mental disorders, by *referendum*, attests to both an ideological uneasiness and a scientific ignorance.[137] Pierre Thuillier, who told the story of homosexuality's "adventure" with American psychiatry, refers quite rightly to an "epistemological scandal."[138] Indeed, since when does science separate truth from falsehood by referendum? The point of departure of this curious affair was the revelation of the publication of a handbook of mental illnesses that still included homosexuality in its list in 1968. This was how far American "shrinks" were from Freud's liberalism! On December 15, 1973, the governing body of the APA organized an initial vote: thirteen members out of fifteen voted in favor of eliminating homosexuality from the notorious list. "Henceforth it would no longer be considered anything more than a disturbance of sexual orientation . . . which would concern, not all homosexuals, but only those who were not satisfied with their situation (and therefore judged themselves to be `sick')."[139] Homosexuals were jubilant at no longer being considered sick men, but a number of psychoanalysts and psychiatrists did not accept the decision of the governing body and demanded that it be annulled. They proposed that a referendum be organized. Homosexuals campaigned—and in April 1974 more than ten thousand psychiatrists and psychoanalysts voted: 58 percent of the votes confirmed the governing body's decision to exclude homosexuality from the list of mental disorders.

This democratic vote, even though it was hardly scientific, did not prevent the proponents of homosexuality-as-illness from continuing to preach their ideas and to counsel treatment.[140] To the great detriment of homosexuals, they perpetrated a negative view of homosexuality and intensified the anxieties and prejudices of homophobes of all kinds. In the eyes of psychiatrists and psychoanalysts close to Freud's position, if homosexuality was no longer an illness, it constituted a "deviance" or a "dysfunction," which did not come within their province. "The snag," as Thuillier points out, "is that one does not know where 'deviance' ends and 'illness' begins. . . . Once again we are face to face with the philosophical problem: how to define the limits of 'normal' sexuality?"[141]

THE GAYS' RESPONSE

Homosexuals, and particularly gay studies, reacted first defensively and then went on the attack.

The classic response to the idea of "an arrest in the sexual development" consists in countering Freud . . . with Freud himself, as he was the first to develop the argument of essential human bisexuality. For Freud, homosexuality is certainly a universal impulse, but it is nevertheless a stage to be passed. When one maintains that homosexuality has the same place as heterosexuality and that a double sexuality is everyone's natural state, one betrays Freud's thought in favor of the dissident theories of a thinker like Groddeck. As we know, the latter has described[142]—not without courage—his alternating homosexual and heterosexual experiences and that from them he has deduced his theory of a universal double sexuality that endures throughout one's life.[143]

In Groddeck's eyes, homosexuality has the same status as heterosexuality, and it is the latter that becomes a problem in itself when it claims to be exclusive: the sign of an excessive repression. There is nothing to prove that the theories of Groddeck, well known for his originality, are correct. But he has perhaps contributed, if not to making homosexuality commonplace, at least to removing some of its drama. This is an attitude adopted by many people today, homosexual or not, one example being the fact that Robert Brannon compares homosexuality to the phenomenon of left-handedness: the origins and causes of both behaviors remain unknown. Like the homosexual, the left-handed person is part of a minority that exists in every human society, and there is no more reason, Brannon says, to consider homosexuality contrary to nature than to take that view of left-handedness.[144]

The practical consequences of this have been noticed by a number of homosexuals. Having observed that a great many psychoanalysts continue to treat them as sick people whose sexual orientation must be changed,[145] and that numerous therapists are homophobic, which is disastrous for the patient, they advise homosexuals who want to enter therapy to deal only with analysts who are themselves homosexual. The latter, more than others, make an effort to offer a positive therapy, their objective being to induce the patient to accept his homosexuality and to help him integrate it with the other aspects of his personality.[146]

The second response, which appeared in gay studies at the end of the 1980s, takes a more offensive position. The aim is no longer to convince anyone of the universality of homosexuality but to question heterosexual imperialism. Two studies that appeared in 1990—one concerning more particularly male homosexuality,[147] the other exclusively lesbianism[148]—view heterosexuality not as a natural and eternal given, but as an "institution" that was imposed as a constraining norm at the end of the nineteenth century. The sexologists are accused of having created this institution, first by inventing the word *heterosexuality*[149] as a positive counterpoint to *homosexuality*, and then by declaring it to be the only normal sexuality.

According to Katz, the twentieth century has seen the amplification of a "heterosexual mystique"[150] that culminated, after World War II, in a veritable "heterosexual hegemony."[151] It was not until the end of the 1960s that people began to question heterosexual normality. In 1968 *Time*, and then the *New York Times*, printed long "histories" of heterosexuality. This was the point at which gays began making demands. The expression "the dictatorship of heterosexuality," first used by the writer Christopher Isherwood, was brought back into fashion. Lesbian feminists spoke, beginning in 1976, of "compulsory heterosexuality,"[152] and in 1979 of "heterocentrism."[153] All over, people increasingly questioned "heterosexism,"[154] which, like racism or sexism, established a hierarchical relationship between one group and another. By the 1980s the fight against the imperial domination of heterosexuality[155] was so virulent that, for the first time, a California psychoanalyst felt obliged to publish a *Defense of Heterosexuality*![156]

Even allowing for the homosexual militantism in these repeated attacks—sometimes tendentious—on heterosexuality, the debate will not have been in vain. In an authoritative history of sexuality in America, John d'Emilio and Estelle B. Freedman take cognizance of the vast diversity in the history of sexual emotions and behaviors.[157]

THE MUTILATED AND THE OTHERS

Without denying the diversity of the homosexual world, we can note the existence of dominant "styles" that differ from one period to another. At the end of the nineteenth century, the definition of the male homosexual described an extremely feminine subject. People talked about a female soul in a man's body. The mannerisms of the obvious homosexual (gait, elocution, appearance, and so on) evoked a parody of the traditionally feminine. The words *pansy, queer,* and *fag* designated the passive homosexual who appeared—wrongly—to represent all homosexuals. For a century homosexuals were divided into two unequal categories: a minority that exhibited a flashy femininity and a majority that was invisible, "in the closet," and sought to hide a furtive sexuality, experienced in shame. The gay movement certainly contributed to freeing a good number of homosexuals from their guilt. But it did not succeed in exploding the stereotypes and caricatures.

At the beginning of the 1980s, Dennis Altman noted that the once-dominant feminine model had been replaced by another: "A new type of man has become visible in most of the big American cities—and to a lesser degree in all Western urban centers. Having abandoned the effeminate style, the new homosexual expresses his sexuality in a theatrically masculine way. Denims, studded leather, etc. The androgynous style, the long hair of the 1970s, had become the style of the heterosexuals, whereas the homosexuals favored the supermacho image."[158] In France research among more than one thousand homosexuals shows that 83 percent seek partners with a virile appearance, compared to only 13 percent who prefer effeminate-looking men.[159]

Whereas heterosexuals are trying to eliminate sexual stereotypes, most hypermacho homosexuals emphasize them in an insistent homage to traditional virility with its associations of violence and contempt for things feminine. In the United States there has been a proliferation of "sadomasochist" bars, haunted by homosexuals fascinated by typically male objects, such as chains, boots, peaked caps. In these "leather bars," people play at being men, "real" men.[160] Seymour Kleinberg explains this 180-degree change of style as a desire to appear strong, free, and active; no longer to be systematically compared to the anally passive and orally active man, the object of every kind of contempt.[161] In fact, the "macho" culture turns out to be just as alienating as the earlier one—not only because it prohibits other expressions of homosexuality (it displays the same disdain for the effeminate as did the heterosexual of an earlier period), but most of all because it shows a total submission to heterosexual stereotypes. Between the mannered homosexual of earlier times who played the "pansy" in order to enter the caricatured world that society had created out of homosexuality, and the hypermacho man miming the old masculine ideal, there is scarcely any difference. Kleinberg points out that the latter is neither freer nor stronger than the preceding one; in addition, "it is dangerous to dress up like one's enemy, and worse, it can tie one to him as helplessly as ever. It still says that he, the powerful brute, is the definer, to which we then react. . . . Effeminacy acknowledged the rage of being oppressed in defiance; macho denies that there *is* rage and oppression. . . . Passing for the enemy does not exempt one from the wrath. Men in leather are already the easiest marks for violent teenagers on a drunken rampage."[162]

Both the hypermacho and the "pansy" are victims of an alienating imitation of the heterosexual male or female stereotype. Both are mutilated men, like the tough and soft heterosexuals already described. All are involuntary victims of self-hatred, prisoners of the ideology of the oppositional dualism of the genders. According to Gary Kinsman, only if the stereotypes (male and female) are challenged by heterosexuals of both sexes will homosexuals be freed from the prison of gender.[163]

The most badly mutilated of all are the homosexuals who have interiorized heterosexual rejection, namely, the homophobic homosexuals.[164]

Yet however difficult homosexuals' experience may be, not all of them are mutilated men. Quite probably, the proportion of stable, "well-adjusted"[165] homosexuals is nearly equal to that of nonmutilated heterosexuals. Neither "pansy" nor "hypermacho," the homosexual who accepts himself is well removed from the stereotypes of earlier times. He neither makes a display of himself nor hides himself, and wants to live the way everyone else does. Feeling that homosexuality is a source of happiness equal to heterosexuality,[166] he believes in love, lives as part of a couple, and has a profound and sustained emotional life. He feels he is a born father and would definitely like to be able to raise a child.[167] This homosexual now knows that the sick man requiring treatment is not he, but the homophobe,[168] who, as his name indicates, suffers from a phobia. Unfortunately, homosexual well-being depends largely on the evolution of the heterosexual majority. It is only when *mutilated men* are replaced by *reconciled men* that homosexuals will be able, in their turn, to live in peace.

CHAPTER SIX

THE RECONCILED MAN

The reconciled man is not some sort of synthesis of the two preceding types of mutilated man. Neither a spineless "soft man" nor a tough one incapable of expressing his feelings, he is the "gentle man,"[1] able to combine reliability and sensitivity, one who has found his father and rediscovered his mother— that is, one who has become a man without wounding the maternal-feminine. To express the dialectical character of this process, the concept of "reconciled man" seems preferable to that of "gentle man." Reconciliation illustrates better the idea of a duality of elements that must have separated, even opposed each other, before returning to each other. It takes into account the notion of time, stages to be reached, conflicts to resolve. Today, like yesterday, a boy cannot live with a male differentiation that translates into a distancing of his mother and the adoption of another mode of identification. But reconciliation cannot be achieved by the elimination of one of the two parts. The reunion of the adult man with his early femininity is at the opposite pole from the self-hatred that proceeds by exclusion. It is true that the reconciled man has not been raised with the same contempt for and fear of the feminine that characterized the education of his grandfather, and that therefore the reunion is less difficult and dramatic than it would have been in earlier times.

In the end, the reconciled man can only come into being

through a far-reaching revolution involving the father. This revolution, scarcely begun twenty or so years ago, will require several generations to be fully effective. It calls for a radical change of mentality and a profound transformation of the conditions of private and professional life, one that cannot be accomplished in a mere decade.

Integrated and Alternating Duality

Males and females become fully human only in androgyny, which has two elements or does not exist at all. Unfortunately, androgyny has always had a bad reputation. Its origins in mythology associate it with the hermaphroditic monster; Greek philosophy, mysticism, or the decadent literature of the nineteenth century have proposed other interpretations that add even more to its extraordinariness and confusion. And the current use of the concept of androgyny often refers to one of its earlier conceptions.

THE ANDROGYNE HAS TWO ELEMENTS

As we can see from its Greek etymology (*andr-*, *aner*, "man" and *gyne*, "woman"), the androgyne is a mixture of man and woman, though this does not mean it is a creature endowed with two sexes.[2]

The coexistence of the two heterogeneous elements (male and female) is so difficult to imagine that Jean Libis speaks rightly of the "ontological enigma of the dyad" or of the "paradoxical union."[3] Should the androgyne be seen as incorporating an image of juxtaposition, "of accumulation or prosthesis" of male and female, their powers being added together? Or is it "a fusion, a synthesis" that dissolves the two elements in one new entity?[4] Or perhaps the androgyne, as it manifests itself these days, is not, properly speaking, either juxtaposition or fusion.

In order to try to understand what the human androgyne is, we must first eliminate the most prevalent confusions, all of which tend to obscure the fundamental duality. Some people confuse anydrogyny with feminization, others liken it to masculinism, and still others identify it with the absence of all sexual characteristics. Thus, the decadent literature of the end of the nineteenth century, fascinated by the figure of the androgyne, represented it in the form of an effeminate young man. The bisexual being was presented as a young ephebe who resembled a boy taking communion for the first time. The Peladan[5] androgyne is a nonsexed being, a virgin adolescent who will cease to exist once he succumbs to a woman: "Virginity is what best defines the androgyne. . . . At the first assertion of sex, it resolves into male and into female."[6] The aesthetes of the time admired the beauty of the male androgyne more than female beauty, even though it was essentially feminine: the beardless, long-haired young man shows no sign of virility. On the other hand, a woman who displays an obvious masculinity is no longer experienced as a female being. Frédéric Monneyron points out that in the case of a woman, the masculine form no longer adds to the feminine essence but denies it.

The confusion of the androgyne with the feminine still persists today. Many people believed that the feminized man of the 1970s marked the advent of the anydrogyne.[7] They quickly changed their minds when they observed that this soft man no longer had anything virile about him.

Others, however, denounce the current tendency toward a "unilateral masculinization: the world is governed by male reason, and in their fight for equal rights, women for the most part deny their femininity in order to promote their masculine qualities. The two sexes have become more alike, and both have slipped into the male world."[8] This criticism raises several questions: must women necessarily adhere to what has been the traditionally female? Do men have a feminine aspect and can they express it? Under the pretext of questioning masculinized androgynes, isn't it the very notion of the androgyne that is being questioned?

A third possible error consists in confusing the androgyne

and the neuter, which totally obliterates sexual dualism. Roland Barthes clearly described this "neuter gender which is *neither* masculine *nor* feminine," a sexed nothingness.[9] Defined thus, the only androgynes would, at the very most, be infants who do not yet have access to sexual differentiation, perhaps old men who have become indifferent, and certainly the little angels who were so dear to the symbolists (and who, as we know, have never had a sex). Even young Westerners who adopt a unisex style (half-masculine, half-feminine) are not so much opting for the indeterminate and the neuter as they are in actuality manifesting the incompleteness of their process of sexual determination. Now, the human androgyne can come into being only after the long detour in which one acquires one's sexual identity. One is not born a man—one becomes a man, and it is only then that one can rediscover the other and aspire to the androgyny that characterizes the reconciled and completed man.

THE ANDROGYNE IS THE COMPLETION OF A PROCESS

Often, adulthood is confused with the age at which one becomes a full citizen. At eighteen one is considered a man, fit for citizenship, marriage, fatherhood, and war. However, a young man of that age seems quite far from being an adult. Not only has he not yet completed the acquisition of his male identity, he is still far from the last stage: that of reconciliation with his femininity, which defines the true androgyne.

Carl Jung was not only the first to conceptualize the duality of the human soul (*animus/anima*); he was also the one who drew attention to the ages of life and the fact that a man's fortieth year is an essential turning point. Only halfway through the journey does a man become fully adult, later than a woman.[10] At this time of his life, male norms are changing. Less exclusively centered on himself, his power, and his success, a man can turn toward others, be attentive, and manifest his tenderness and his other so-called feminine qualities. Perhaps this is in fact the ideal age for being a father, if one agrees with Erik

Erikson's characterization of it as "the age of generativity."[11]

Daniel Levinson, whose studies of the male life cycle are authoritative, believes that maturity is acquired between the ages of eighteen and forty, in accordance with a process that involves different stages followed by the questioning of certain aspects of virility.[12] Between the ages of twenty and thirty, a young man still has to control and repress his inner femininity. He seeks to assert himself outside the world of the family, struggles to make his mark in his professional life, measures his masculinity by the criteria of competition, success, and his recognition by men as one of them and by women as an attractive person. By the age of thirty, he has settled in, is successfully disciplining himself, and is working hard to confirm his virility. During this long period, which ends in the construction of his masculine identity, he tends to confuse the whole of his personality with the latter. At about forty, he is assumed to have proved himself.[13]

The time of androgyny has come. As Levinson says it so elegantly, he can at last begin the process of "detribalization"[14] in order to become a human being in the full sense of the word.

This conception of the androgyne, as the outcome of a process, is unlike earlier representations. The modern androgyne results from neither a conjunction of the two sexes nor a fusion that eliminates them. The potentially bisexual human being is not androgynous to begin with. Unlike the hermaphrodite, which exhibits both sexes at birth, the small version of the man is born into sexual indeterminacy and cannot avoid his apprenticeship first in femininity and then masculinity— two stages for girls, three for boys (who achieve a return to femininity). To deny the need for these stages and the need to be taught to differentiate can only lead to confusion of identity. The suggestion made by the American feminist psychologist Sandra Bem—a great advocate of androgyny—that children be raised "outside the schema of gender"[15] appears to me inspired by a misunderstanding of the androgyne that is more alienating than it is liberating. One must first learn that one is a boy or a girl, and the difference in the genital organs alone—contrary to what Sandra Bem says[16]—is not enough to construct a sense of sexual identity.[17]

By the end of the journey, the androgynous human being is not the "vague gender" desired by the Québecois Marc Chabot.[18] Nor is it *simultaneously* female and male. It *alternates* the expression of its two components according to the exigencies of the moment. Women make very good use of this alternation with respect to the stages of life or circumstances. Men can do the same. A father can be successively feminine with his baby and openly virile with an older child!

Nurturer, football player.... The androgynous identity allows a coming and going of feminine and masculine qualities that is comparable neither to "the economy of separation and distance" of earlier times nor to "the ecology of fusion."[19] It resembles a game between complementary elements whose intensity varies from one individual to another. His sexual identity interiorized, each makes use of his duality in his own way.

The human androgyne is a sexed being, distinct from the other, who can only integrate otherness when he has found himself. Of course, men and women have never resembled each other more than they do now; the genders have never shown less difference.[20] But resemblance is not identity, and *subtle differences* remain.[21] Children of androgynous parents always detect them in the end.

The Revolution in Fatherhood[22]

The end of the patriarchy marks the beginning of an entirely new kind of fatherhood. The reconciled man scarcely resembles the father of earlier times at all. The patriarch was the embodiment of law, authority, distance—but one hardly paid any attention to the fact that the patriarchy was also defined by the abandonment of babies by their fathers. As an inevitable consequence, the small child was the exclusive property of the mother. The beginning of its life thus unfolded in quasi ignorance of its father. The gradual disappearance of the patriarchy and research done over the past twenty years or so are causing an entirely different image of the father and his function to emerge, notably with respect to his son. In the United States and Scandinavia, numerous studies of troubled boys have produced identical conclusions that upset many beliefs: "It is in the course of *the first two years* of their existence that boys absolutely need their fathers."[23] Henry Biller is even more specific: "Boys who have suffered the absence of their fathers at the very beginning of their lives are more severely handicapped with respect to many dimensions of their personality than those who were deprived of their fathers at a more advanced age."[24]

This calls to mind the old Aristotelian adage: it is men who produce men—but with radically different suppositions today than in earlier times.

AN OVERVIEW OF FATHERHOOD IN THE WEST

On both sides of the Atlantic, the subject of the father is as controversial as it can be. Without concern for subtle distinctions, people announce the decline or the rebirth of fathers. Points of view differ radically, depending on the attitudes and ideologies of experts in the field of families.[25] In truth, one can no longer paint a portrait of the typical father, so motley is the reality of fatherhood now. If the majority of fathers still live under the same roof as the mother and children,[26] increasing numbers of them are divorced or separated and live outside that home, though still having responsibility for their children.

The statistics of the French National Institute of Statistics and Economic Studies on the ways in which men and women use their time each day inspire the reader with the blackest pessimism. In 1985 a wage-earning mother devoted forty-six minutes a day to the material care of her children, whereas her male counterpart accorded them only six minutes![27] Even in households that aspire to be egalitarian, American studies evaluate the respective average involvement of the father and the mother at 35 percent and 65 percent.[28] Fathers spend four times less time than mothers in contact alone with a child and do not experience the same feeling of engagement with him or her.[29]

Diane Ehrensaft and Arlie Hochschild, who conducted in-depth studies of these "egalitarian" families, painted a similar portrait of this new father. He is a man of middle- or upper-class background with a higher-than-average education and income. He has a liberal profession that allows him, like his wife, to make freer use of his time, and he rejects the traditional male culture. Most such men say they have broken with the model they knew in childhood and do not wish at any price to reproduce the behavior of their own fathers, who are judged to have been "cold and distant." They hope to "repair" their own childhood.[30] Last, they live with women who do not want to be full-time mothers.

Generally speaking, fathers who participate actively in the care and upbringing of their children say they are happier with their fatherhood than those who are not very involved.[31] But it must also be said, more specifically, that satisfaction in fatherhood depends very much upon freedom of choice. In those cases, more and more numerous, where men and women reverse roles (she has a job and he is unemployed), "imposed" fatherhood has less positive consequences. G. Russell's studies on this type of family in Australia show that fathers who take care of their children full time complain—like many mothers in the same situation—of having a boring and repetitive life, of lacking social relations, and, in addition, of having to suffer the critical attitude of family and friends.[32] As soon as they can return to a professional activity, they revert to a more traditional family model. The same has been found to be true in Sweden, where paternal leave has existed since 1974. Fathers often take the shortest leave for the birth of a baby and rarely the longest ones for raising the child, despite advantageous financial conditions.[33] They certainly want to "share" with the mother, but not reverse roles. Despite the Swedish government's campaign urging fathers to take more care of their children, the men have shown that they do not want to devote themselves to it full time. On the other hand, in certain Norwegian families where father and mother work halftime and share parenting activities, the greatest percentage of both members of the couple registered satisfaction.[34]

The number of fathers raising their children alone is increasing in most Western societies. In France, in 1990, the number of children living with their fathers was estimated at 223,500.[35] In the United States this number increased by 100 percent between 1971 and 1981, and experts believe that this increase will continue at the same rate, even though the proportion of children committed to the care of their mothers and their fathers, respectively, is still the same.[36] Studies on these fathers show that they are responsible for boys more often than for girls, for preadolescents more often than for infants, and that they face the same problems as single mothers concerning time, money, childcare, and so on. They experience as much difficulty with their adolescent daughters as mothers do with their sons of the same age. On the whole, single fathers manage quite well,[37] especially when they are able to bring their femininity into play, in order to be father and mother at the same time.[38]

Most divorced fathers do not have custody of their children.[39] At the time of the divorce, only a minority of fathers ask for it. Several factors may explain this phenomenon. Over the past twenty years or so, breakups have been occurring earlier and earlier: in 1982 they reached their maximum at around the fourth year of the marriage,[40] that is, when the children were still small. Movements concerned with the conditions of fathers specifically and men in general join in accusing judges of sexism, because the latter systematically entrust small children to mothers.[41] But it is more likely that the particular import of the traditional model that sanctifies the mother-child dyad is accepted not only by the judge but also by the father and mother. The father does not dream of asking for custody, and the mother cannot imagine letting him have it.[42]

Why not admit that a number of fathers simply do not want to upset their way of life, slow down their professional careers, and curb their ambitions in order to take care of a small child? Single mothers who work full time know that children are a heavy responsibility. For some, the emotional compensations are well worth the price. But for others, the reasons for the choice have more to do with guilt and a sense of duty—pressures that as yet do not weigh very heavily on fathers!

A study carried out in 1985 by Henri Leridon and Catherine Villeneuve-Gokalp on relations of children with their separated parents shows the startling disparity between paternal and maternal behaviors (see table). "More than half the children lose contact with the noncustodial parent, mother as well as father, or have only episodic relations with him or her (less than once per month). Since eight out of ten of the children live with their mother, it is most often with the father that contacts are strained."[43] Out of sight, out of mind! There is nothing to prove that the statistics would not be reversed if large numbers of fathers had custody of their children. However, one figure gives one pause: 27 percent of the separated fathers *never* see the child again and more or less the same percentage never spend a penny on alimony. Whether this is a result of indifference, guilt, or anger against the mother, these statistics bluntly show that love for the child depends very much upon the continuity and intensity of relations. And one must really want such a relationship.

Finally, a category of fathers never discussed in France is beginning to be the object of studies in the United States and Canada: homosexual fathers.[44] Their number is difficult to evaluate for obvious reasons. In North America (the United States and Canada), the number of homosexuals who are married or fathers is estimated at six million,[45] and the number of openly gay fathers at one million.

Many will ask themselves: how can one be homosexual and a father? Generally, these men married in all good faith, ignor-

TABLE ONE: Frequency of Meetings of Children with Their Separated Parents

	Together	Children Whose Parents Are*				Age of the Child			
		Separated since the birth	Cohabiting never married	Divorced		0–4 years	5–8 years	9–12 years	13–16 years
				Total	Having joint custody				
*With the mother									
Living together[a]	81	94	78	82	70	89	82	83	75
Half the time	2	1	1	2	11	2	2	1	1
1 or 2 days per week	0	0	0	0	2	0	0	1	2
Every 2 weeks	4	2	3	5	7	4	3	4	4
One a month or all school vacations	1	0	0	1	2	0	2	1	1
Less than once a month	4	0	8	4	6	0	4	3	7
Never	6	1	10	4	0	5	5	7	7
No answer (unknown)	2	2	0	2	2	0	2	0	4
TOTAL	100	100	100	100	100	100	100	100	100
*With the father									
Living together[a]	12	5	20	13	14	5	10	11	18
Half the time	3	2	3	3	14	3	5	1	3
1 or 2 days per week	6	3	5	7	17	5	7	4	7
Every 2 weeks	13	2	5	18	9	14	15	14	10
Once a month or all school vacations	7	2	3	9	4	3	8	8	7
Less than once a month	21	12	20	23	26	22	23	22	18
Never	27	56	39	19	6	40	24	26	25
No answer (unknown)	11	18	5	8	10	8	8	14	12
TOTAL	100	100	100	100	100	100	100	100	100

SOURCE: Henri Leroidon and Catherine Villeneuve-Golkolp, "Enquête sur la situation des familles." In Institut national d'études démographiques (January 1988); reprinted in *Population et sociétés*, no. 220 (January 1988).

[a]Or: a meeting "almost every day."

ing their homosexual impulses.[46] In their eyes, to marry and have children constituted a certificate of normality. Most did not acknowledge their homosexuality until they were married and fathers. Such a realization is usually gradual, painful, and terribly guilt-inducing. David Leavitt has superbly described the difficult road of a family whose husband/father, terrified by the idea of hurting his wife and son and breaking up his home, will not be able to admit his homosexuality until after twenty-seven years of marriage.[47] A double life, lies, and fear of discovery make up the daily life of these men, who are afraid of stigmatization and their children's reactions. Those who choose to live with their masks off end by divorcing and find themselves in a situation that is legally and socially difficult. Often rejected by homosexuals and heterosexuals alike, who accuse them of having married in order to conceal themselves, gay fathers are frequently isolated and deprived of the custody of their children.[48] The worst part of it is having to reveal their sexual orientation to their children, at the risk of traumatizing them and losing their affection and respect.[49]

The silence surrounding homosexual fathers does not prevent the formation of a number of myths about them, each more negative than the next. Barret and Robinson have recorded a dozen.[50] Among the most widespread is the idea that gay fathers are sick men who risk transmitting their homosexuality to their children. Yet there exists no proof that the children of homosexuals have a greater tendency to homosexuality than others.[51] As one father interviewed remarked humorously: "My heterosexual parents did not succeed in making me a heterosexual. There is therefore no reason to believe that I will succeed in doing the opposite, even if I wanted to!"[52]

Another myth that is hard to kill: that the gay man is sexually obsessed and the homosexual father will tend to attack his own children, or allow his friends to do so. Now, nothing could be farther from the truth. All the studies prove that the homosexual is less often guilty of misdemeanors than the heterosexual.[53] According to the national statistics of the American police, 90 percent of children sexually molested are molested by heterosexuals.[54] Incestuous behaviors or indecent assault are extremely rare, even nonexistent among homosexual fathers. Yet this is one of the reasons most often invoked in American courtrooms for refusing them custody of their children.

One last argument against homosexual fathers: they would expose their children to persecution on the part of society. It is true that fathers who live their homosexuality openly cause their children to run the risk of being scorned and rejected by their peers and by adults. But studies show that these fathers are sensitive to this handicap and do what they can to protect their children from it. Contrary to the widespread fantasy, the homosexual father is not an irresponsible pervert. He loves his children like any father. The different studies available describe him as eager to have affectionate and stable relations with his children; often more maternal, he is also stricter in enforcing rules than the traditional father.[55]

These necessary clarifications should not obscure the difficulties encountered by children of homosexuals. There is, first of all, the need to keep the secret from one's friends, even the closest. Fear of betraying the father or of being mocked creates a feeling of painful isolation. If there is no secret to keep, the life of the child is hardly easier since he or she will be directly in the line of fire of society's undisguised homophobia—the worst part of this being that the child often interiorizes this homophobia. Finally, the available studies tend to show that girls accept their father's homosexuality better than boys, but that certain children may display disturbances of behavior or identity—though not notably more than the children of divorced heterosexual parents.[56]

From this aside on the homosexual father, one can gather that sexual orientation proves nothing as to the quality of the "parenting." Nevertheless, public opinion is much harsher concerning this type of father than for the father who drops out of his child's life.

THE GOOD FATHER: FROM MOTHERING TO FATHERING

For decades now, studies beyond number have been done to measure the consequences of the absent father. Their conclusions are controversial.[57] If it is true that boys raised without a father seem statistically to encounter more difficulties than others (relating to control of aggressivity, success in school, gender identity, and so on), this finding is flawed by significant exceptions. Not all children raised without a father necessarily have problems, and those who live under the same roof with him are not guaranteed a normal development. At the present time, no one is sure of the reasons for a child's success or failure. The presence or absence of the father alone is not enough to account for it.[58]

Now that mothers have entered the workplace in large numbers and "transitional" fathers have been called upon to take care of their children,[59] more recent research is reversing the problematics and attempting to measure the effects of the father's presence, notably on very young children. A man begins his career as a father with the birth of his child. During the infant's first months, he is, properly speaking, a father-mother,[60] or, if you like, a masculine mother, more mother than masculine in order to satisfy the needs of the baby. Contrary to the cultural and linguistic tradition, "mothering" has no sex.[61] To avoid the trap of language, English speakers often prefer to opt, instead, for the more neutral *nurturing*, which means "nourishing physically and emotionally," or *parenting*. Both terms have the advantage of bypassing sexual distinctions.

Mothering is learned on the job. Men and women learn all the more quickly if they themselves have had mothering parents.[62] The quality of the mothering is also tied to opportunity: one study of fathers who are raising their babies alone shows that they adopt even more than married fathers a behavior close to that of a mothering woman. More than being a difference associated with gender, the mothering of a man or a woman depends on his or her own childhood, or on external circumstances that have nothing to do with one's physiology.[63]

In order to take good care of his baby, the father—like the mother—must mobilize all his early femininity. Furthermore, the reactivation of the latter often begins during his wife's pregnancy. The "expectant father" is subject to psychological upheavals that are increasingly well known. He must confront his return to his primary maternal femininity and to the unconscious memory of his fusion.[64]

This is an experience that certain men have great difficulty enduring, as is clear from the thousand little ailments they experience during the pregnancy or the fact that they stay away from home.[65] There is no question that, for certain men, the adoption of a coherent identity as a father is the most difficult task of integration of the adult years.[66]

After the baby is born, the father's effectiveness at mothering will depend on the extent to which he can reactivate his very earliest relations with his mother. Contrary to Chodorow's theories maintaining that men do not have the same capacities for relating as women, experience proves that, because they have in common an early femininity, they are on an equal footing where mothering is concerned. The more the father allows himself to be pervaded by his femininity, the more intimate he will be with his baby and the better father he will be. The numerous studies on the father-infant relationship as observed over the course of the first six months are categorical: fathers are capable of mothering just as well as mothers,[67] and in almost the same way as mothers.[68] This assertion is confirmed by observation of single fathers or married fathers who have the principal mothering role.[69] The father can, like the mother, establish a truly symbiotic relationship with his baby,[70] provided he is able to suspend his traditional masculinity, for the pure macho man, the toughest of the tough, may very well be essentially incapable of fatherhood.[71] The only good parents are those who are able to make use of their bisexuality.

However, if the father can mother as well as the mother, experts in the father-infant relationship observe subtle differences between male and female mothering. Michael Yogman has noted that the father tends to play with the small baby more than the mother, and his games are generally more stimulating, more vigorous, more exciting, and more perturbing for the baby.[72] The father also indulges very early in tactile and motion games during which he seeks to excite the child, whereas the mother prefers visual games that induce the child to focus its attention. The same observations hold true when the child is eight months of age and older. Starting at birth, the father, who in other areas behaves like the mother, tends to hold the child and rock it more. During interviews with Yogman, fathers stressed the importance of physical contact, of the "sensation of the baby moving against them."[73] These differences in manners of playing and in the quality of the stimulation are found in all studies of the nontraditional father, whether American or Swedish, English or Australian.[74]

There is another difference between the mothering of the father and of the mother: the father behaves differently with a male baby than he does with a female baby, especially after the child is a year old. Unlike the mother, who treats a boy and a girl in the same way, the father is more preoccupied with the virility of his male baby. Not only does he tend to spend more time playing with him,[75] he also encourages virile qualities such as physical activity, independence, and exploration, whereas he is more tender with his daughter and stimulates her feminine characteristics: gentleness, passivity, tranquility. Another sexual difference: it was observed that parents touched the genitals of a child of the same sex more than those of a child of the opposite sex.[76] The account of a father reflecting on his fatherly feelings is eloquent: to give a bath to his seventeen-month-old son is an acknowledged sensual pleasure: "After all, he is the only man whose penis, amusing little appendage, I can touch without directly violating the taboo of homosexuality. Kisses, which we call cuddles, are given in the greatest camaraderie." There was nothing of the sort with his daughter, ten or so years before: "I was a bewildered young father, fascinated by the beauty of this little woman. . . . But totally respectful, almost inhibited where her sex was concerned. When I wiped the insides of her labia majora with cotton balls . . . I immediately transformed myself into a nursery nurse, cold and professional."[77]

In truth, no good fatherhood is possible without an acceptance of one's latent homosexuality and a suspicion of pedophilia! It is time that we acknowledge in the father what we have always granted the mother.

The advantages of the father-mother are considerable for the small child. Beyond the fact that he represents a new source of stimulation and another object of love besides the mother, he turns out to be a very good model for identification for his son. But not in the expected way. The work of Henry Biller[78] and Michael Lamb[79] have demonstrated that the father's masculinity matters less than the intimacy and warmth of the father-son relationship. In other words, it is the father's "feminine" characteristics that give his son the desire to take him as a model. Of course, he will be more androgynous than the son of a traditional father, less avid for a distinction in sexual roles, but as he grows up the boy will be able to identify with a love object of the same sex as himself. Starting at eighteen months (the phallic phase), the son actively seeks the presence of his father, imitates him, and prefers him.[80] This has nothing to do with a feminine, passive attitude, nor with the love he feels for his mother. According to Loewald, the early attachment to the father is based on identification with an ideal. In this way, a positive pre-Oedipal triangular relationship is established that helps the son to find his way out of the maternal dilemma and lessens his fear of women.[81] It does not prevent the occurrence of the Oedipus complex nor the castration anxiety but does diminish their more dramatic effects.

The new father-mother strikingly belies the theory of an infant's exclusive attachment to its mother (John Bowlby), and the consequence thereof: that a baby cannot be attached to more than a single person at a time.[82] The precursory work of

Lamb or Yogman shows that this is not at all true. It is the parent who invests the most in the baby who becomes the main object of attachment—without distinction of sex—and this preferential relationship does not exclude others. What is more, preferences change with age. If a majority of children seem closer to their mother in the first year, all of them will change favorite parents several times in the course of the next two years. These changes will depend on psychological stages, the sex of the child, and external circumstances.[83] But whatever the evolution of its feelings, the child interiorizes its two available parents and is no longer locked in a one-on-one relationship that risks stifling it.

It is very easy to measure the advantages of this new type of family, particularly for the little boy. There is no need of barbarous rituals to separate him from his mother and bring him into the world of men. Close contacts with his father starting at his birth will spare him in an advantageous way the sorrows and pains of masculinization. But the latter will be less differentiated, less evident than the earlier masculinization. It will be organized around *subtle differences*, as essential tomorrow as the oppositional dualism used to be. Once the earliest years are past, the father must mobilize all his virility to transmit it to his son. He must make use of his bisexuality and be able to evolve from the father-mother to the father-mentor. These are the two stages of fatherly love, one as necessary as the other. But until now, few fathers have been able to pass from one to the other.

THE CONDITIONS OF THE REVOLUTION IN FATHERHOOD

The revolution in fatherhood, barely perceptible today, ought to cause great upheavals for generations to come and most notably lead to a new masculinity, more diversified and subtler. But it presupposes more democratic relations between members of a couple than those that we know today and is dependent on more than just the good will of individuals. At the present time, the powers-that-be in Western societies have not yet integrated the idea that a woman is worth as much as a man and still less that a father is worth as much as a mother.[84]

Almost two-thirds of mothers work outside their homes.[85] Even if Danish mothers work three times more often than Spanish mothers, there is no question that a new model of motherhood is very rapidly imposing itself on Western society as a whole—though the injustices of which these mothers are the victims have not yet been recorded in full.[86] French mothers, who are not the worst off,[87] often express their weariness with an inequality whose end they do not see. Quite naturally, they appeal to their companions, who generally turn a deaf ear.

This familiar scenario, experienced by a majority of women, should not conceal another, less often mentioned situation: the resistance on the part of mothers to sharing their motherhood. All the studies show that paternal involvement also depends on the willingness of the mother.[88] Yet many women do not want to see their companion become more occupied with the children. In the 1980s two studies showed that fathers who wanted to involve themselves a little more were not encouraged to do so: 60 percent to 80 percent of their spouses were not in favor.[89]

To explain their rejecting attitude, many women mention their husband's incompetence, which makes more work for them than it saves. But on a deeper level, they experience their maternal preeminence as a form of power that they do not want to share, even at the price of physical and mental exhaustion.[90] In fact, their attitude toward involvement on the father's part has changed very little in fifteen years.[91] And one may suppose that it will not change fundamentally as long as society as a whole has not ratified a new distribution of male and female powers. Even among women who say they want greater participation on the part of the father, there may exist more ambivalence than is indicated by the results of Pleck's 1982 study. Russell's research on Australian fathers who look after the house and the children has revealed a real dissatisfaction on the part of their wives, a source of conjugal friction.[92]

Diane Ehrensaft's valuable study on these new families shows that the mothers are often jealous of the bonds between father and child.[93] They feel excluded and complain of not having the same intimacy with their husband as that which he shares with the child. The implication of this for Ehrensaft is that when the mother loses her preeminent role, she must confront the idea that the child is not an extension of herself—the child also belongs to and identifies with someone else. This feeling is even more painful if the child is a boy. Curiously enough, the study showed no symmetrical jealousy on the part of the father with regard to the mother-child dyad.

But the couples scrutinized so closely by Ehrensaft constitute a tiny exception to the general rule. These parents, who share everything 100 percent, without any distinction of roles, are absolutely not representative of the current family reality. It would be false and dishonest to imply that men are merely victims of the women who prevent them from fathering. Alongside a certain number of fathers who would happily do a little more, there is still an army of men who feel neither a desire nor any obligation to do more. These are not fathers "prevented" by their wives but rather men who are recipients of the legacy of the tough guy—the man who forbids *himself* to be a father.

THE ADVANTAGES AND DISADVANTAGES OF PARENTAL SHARING

Two models are possible: one in which fathers and mothers perform exactly the same tasks; the other in which parents share out the tasks between them. The first model, even rarer than the second, is the one adopted by the forty couples observed by Ehrensaft. Starting from the birth of the child, the parents chose to perform all tasks (except for nursing, when it occurred) without discrimination and to show the child that mom and dad were interchangeable. The results as recorded are not without ambiguity, for the child and the couple itself.

There is no sign of confusion or anxiety in the children of

such couples, even if, when little, they use the words *daddy* and *mommy* interchangeably and not always correctly. Ehrensaft, at first uneasy, understood as she observed them that, for them, these appellations referred more to social categories than to proper names. When a child called its mother, it was sometimes the father who appeared. In other words, it was the closest parent who responded to the appellation "mommy" and the child learned that two persons could fill the same role. The most common criticism addressed to this mode of parenting is that the children risk having a confused sense of their sexual identity. Yet none of these children manifested any problem with identity ("core gender"). On the other hand, they did not have a clear notion of the usual sexual roles ("gender role identity") since mom and dad did the same things. They acquired it later, in contact with the outside world, and through a perception of *subtle difference* between father and mother. Even the children of particularly androgynous parents feel the need, when the time comes (that is, at three or four years of age), to define their gender identity—like, for example, little Sonia (whose mother and long-haired father basically lived in jeans), who got herself up as a model little girl (with curled hair, a well-groomed appearance, and frilly dresses) in order to assert her femininity. Once she became an adolescent, both feminine and athletic, she liked boys but had a well-established awareness of the equality of the sexes.

On the other hand, certain young boys expressed their femininity first,[94] to the great distress of the parents, who feared their sons were homosexual. The demand for masculinity came later and was less marked than the girls' insistence on femininity.

The greatest disadvantages of this model are probably for the parents. The unclear division of work between them results in their never knowing who is supposed to do what. The constant double parental responsibility ends in an overinvestment in the child which benefits neither him nor them. The "overparenting" yields more egocentric children, who expect to be loved and cared for at every moment. By putting the child before everything else, the parents lose their intimacy as a couple and risk exhausting their feelings of personal and sexual interest. In addition, all egalitarian parents recognize the need for negotiations concerning the child, which require a great expenditure of energy and time. If this mode of parenting favors the parents' solidarity, it has its limits. The couple can be in danger when the children leave home.

The second and more common model is a fifty-fifty sharing: equal participation, but different tasks. More precisely, there are certain sorts of care given to the child indiscriminately by mother or father, and others more specific to one or the other of the parents. Advocates of the radical disappearance of sexual roles disapprove of this model, which they accuse of prolonging stereotypes. However, there is very little danger of this since those who choose this model have already taken the essential step beyond the conventions. There is an economical use of time, access to the child by both its parents, and greater parental solidarity than in the traditional model, thus strengthening the couple without threatening it. What is more, the children seem more secure and less anxious.

Whatever the model adopted, the revolution in fatherhood will not put an end to misunderstandings between couples nor to divorce. Children will continue to be shared between father and mother. But if the fathers achieve their revolution, these children will have a greater chance of preserving continuous and warm relations with them. When one has greatly loved, cared for, and invested in a small child, one does not easily abandon it. Women still have to admit the sharing of responsibilities, and magistrates, employers, and other institutions to take cognizance of this evolution.

Utopian talk, some will say: real life is chaotic and full of conflict, and the selfishness of some, the passion of others, the eternal settling of accounts, will cause such schemas to fail. Not necessarily, because everyone's interest is at stake: the interest of the child, definitely (even if we know this is not always enough to determine his parents' behavior), but also the interest of the parents themselves because, in the long run, nothing is more painful and guilt-inducing than to see one's child in trouble—provided, of course, that one has learned to love him.

Man in Mutation

Twofold fatherhood (moving from the father-mother to the father-mentor) will take some time to compel recognition, and along with it the conditions for masculine reconciliation. This does not mean that men of the present generations are condemned to the alternative of mutilation. The tough guy and the soft man are only two prototypes that do not claim to describe male reality in all its diversity. There have always been men who have refused the imposed forms, warm and attentive fathers who have allowed their femininity to speak, tender men who have loved their wives as their equals. But it takes courage to defy the dominant models, no matter what era one is living in.

Today, young men do not identify either with the caricatured virility of the past or with a total rejection of masculinity. They are already the heirs to a first generation of mutants. Sons of more virile women and more feminine men, they sometimes have trouble identifying with their fathers. Among the latter, there are many who have taken a step outside the traditional model—either out of conviction or to please their companion—without really giving it up. Caught between modernist discourse and actual practice, they feel out of phase with respect to women and offer their sons a contradictory image of masculinity. Others, rarer, have rejected traditional virility but then found themselves without any model of masculinity. They have tried their hand at being father-mothers without being able to turn the attempt into anything else, since they no longer knew what masculinity to transmit. Con-

fronted with women who cheerfully put to use their new virility, these men thought they could join them on the terrain of
androgyny by being more feminine than they. This inversion
of identities has not necessarily been very attractive to sons.
Some, we know, have turned unwillingly to their mothers to
learn the secret of virility and unconsciously resent their
emasculated father.

At present, fathers who offer their sons an image of a reconciled man are still the exception. This is hardly surprising. One
would have to be ignorant of identity problems to believe that
one and the same generation of men, brought up with the old
model, could succeed all at once in performing the dangerous
triple somersault: first, questioning an ancestral virility, then
accepting a feared femininity, and last, inventing a different
masculinity compatible with that femininity. The fact that
one challenges the identity of one's fathers does not mean one
is psychologically ready to reconcile oneself with one's femininity. Nor does the fact that one has accepted the latter mean
that one has also discovered a suitable form of virility—especially when this word has become the object of so many questions and polemics.

It is time to tell our sons that Terminator, far from being a
superman, is a miserable parody. Even more important, it is
also high time to sing the praises of masculine virtues that are
not acquired either passively or easily but that find expression
in effort and struggle. These virtues are: self-control, the desire
to surpass oneself, a love of risk and challenge, and resistance
to oppression, among others. They are the conditions for creation, but also for dignity. They belong to every human being in
the same way as the feminine virtues. The latter preserve the
world, the former widen its boundaries. Far from being incompatible, they are inseparable if one is to claim to be a human
being. Even though a centuries-old tradition has opposed them
by attributing them to one or the other sex, we are gradually
becoming aware that having one set of qualities without the
other risks turning into a nightmare: self-control can become

neurosis, a love of risk may be suicidal, resistance can change into aggression. Inversely, the feminine virtues, so celebrated these days, can, if they are not tempered by masculine virtues, lead to passivity and subordination.

Women have understood this a little earlier than men and rejoice in incarnating their reconciled humanity. But they are wrong to be surprised that men are slow to join them. Contrary to the old story of the damnation of Eve, God has made her his accomplice. Not only did he deny the procreative power to Adam and give it to Adam's companion but, at the same time, he granted women the privilege of being born from a belly of the same sex. He thus spared them all the work of differentiation and opposition that so indelibly marks a man's fate. The father-mother may lessen the pains of separation and facilitate the acquisition of a male identity, but he will never be able to cancel the effects of the original fusion. As long as women give birth to men, as long as the xy develops within an xx, it will always take a little longer and be a little more difficult to make a man than to make a woman. To convince oneself of this, one has only to imagine the reverse hypothesis: if women were born from a male belly, what would be their fate?

When men became aware of this natural disadvantage, they created a far-reaching cultural palliative: the patriarchal system. Today, forced to bid the patriarchy good-bye, they must reinvent the father and, along with him, his own new form of virility. Women, observing these mutants with tenderness, are holding their breath . . .

NOTES

Preface

1. The formula for woman is XX.
2. Cf. the works of J. H. Tjio and A. Levant in Swedish, esp. *Hereditas* 42, no. 1 (1956).

Prologue: The Enigma of Masculinity—the Big X

1. Jean Jacques Rousseau, *Emile* (1762), book 5.
2. David D. Gilmore, *Manhood in the Making: Cultural Concepts of Masculinity*, p. 2.
3. Pierre Bourdieu, "La domination masculine," *Actes de la recherche en sciences sociales*, no. 84 (September 1990): p. 21.
4. Günter Grass, *The Flounder*.
5. Except for Marc Feigen-Fasteau's book *Le Robot mâle*, published in 1974 in the United States and in 1980 by Denoël-Gontier, they have not been translated. They are Warren Farrell, *The Liberated Man* (1975), Joseph H. Pleck and Janet Sayers, eds., *Men and Masculinity* (1974), and Deborah S. David and Robert Brannon, *The Forty-Nine Percent Majority: The Male Sex Role* (1976).
6. Lynne Segal, *Slow Motion: Changing Masculinities, Changing Men*, p. ix.
7. Catharine Stimpson, Harry Brod, ed., *The Making of Masculinities: The New Men's Studies*, p. xi.
8. I should, however, mention the earlier work of Emmanuel Reynaud, *La Sainte virilité*.

9. Philippe Djian, *Lent dehors*, pp. 44, 63.

10. Gilles Lipovetsky, *L'Ere du vide* (Paris: Gallimard, 1983), p. 80.

11. Elisabeth Badinter, *L'Un est l'autre: Des relations entre hommes et femmes*, part 3, "The Resemblance Between the Sexes."

12. Bourdieu, "La domination masculine," p. 21.

13. There are more than two hundred men's studies departments in the United States.

14. This passage is inspired by the American Thomas Laqueur's brilliant book *Making Sex: Body and Gender from the Greeks to Freud*.

15. It was Galen who most fully developed the structural identity of the male and female organs of reproduction. He maintained that women were essentially men who lacked vital heat, the sign of perfection. This lack of heat was the reason they contained inside them what men bore on the outside. In keeping with this point of view, the vagina was conceived as an internal penis, the uterus as a scrotum, and the ovaries as testicles. Galen based his theories on the dissections of the Alexandrian anatomist Herophilus in the third century B.C.

16. Diderot, *Le Rêve de d'Alembert* (1769), in Vernière, ed., *Oeuvres philosophiques*, p. 328.

17. Herophilus called the ovaries *dydumos*, "the twins," a name also attributed to the testicles. Likewise, there exists no technical name for the vagina in Latin, Greek, or the European languages before 1668.

18. In his *Histoire naturelle de la femme*, Jacques-Louis Moreau (1771–1826) describes the relationship between man and woman as "a series of oppositions and contrasts" (quoted by Laqueur, *Making Sex*, p. 5).

19. In 1889 the biologist Patrick Geddes believed he had found the ultimate proof through his observations of female and male cells under the microscope. The former were "more passive, conservative, apathetic, and stable," whereas the latter were "more active, energetic, impatient, passionate, and variable" (cited in Laqueur, *Making Sex*, p. 6).

20. Annelise Maugue, *L'Identité masculine en crise au tournant du siècle*, p. 7.

21. Brod, ed., *The Making of Masculinities*, p. 2.

22. Michael S. Kimmel and Michael A. Messner, eds., *Men's Lives*, p. 2.

23. Ibid.
24. Although the French word *virilité* signifies, first, the collection of physical and sexual attributes and characteristics of a man, it is also used in the more general sense of "nature of a man" and as a synonym for masculinity. On the other hand, the same word in English, *virility*, is confined to the first meaning, and American feminists detect a "macho" sense to the word and refrain from using it.
25. Michael S. Kimmel, ed., *Changing Men: New Directions in Research on Men and Masculinity*, p. 12.
26. During this period, France's rural population represented 80 percent of the country's total.
27. Once she could claim a certain social status, the Frenchwoman would hire a nurse to care for her child and then used her time as she liked. Elisabeth Badinter, *L'Amour en plus: Histoire de l'amour maternel du XVIIe au XXe siècle;* cf. part 1, "L'Amour absent."
28. See Georges Mongrédien, *Les Précieux et les précieuses,* pp. 149–50, on the diatribe against marriage: husband, children, and in-laws were all mercilessly relegated to the rank of women's misfortunes.
29. See *Sylvia's Complaint* (1688), quoted by Michael S. Kimmel, "The Contemporary Crisis of Masculinity in Historical Perspective," in Brod, ed., *The Making of Masculinities,* p. 132.
30. Kimmel, "The Contemporary Crisis of Masculinity," p. 133.
31. "Ladies this was ill luck, but you
    Have much the worser of the two;
    The world is chang'd I know not how,
    For men Kiss Men, not Women now." (quoted in Kimmel, "The Contemporary Crisis of Masculinity," p. 135)
32. "So strangely does Parisian air
    Change English Youth, that half a year
    Makes 'em forget all Native Custome
    To bring French modes, and Gallic Lust home;
    Nothing will these Apostates please
    But Gallic health and French disease." (quoted in Kimmel, "The Contemporary Crisis of Masculinity," pp. 136–37)
33. *Condorcet, Prudhomme, Guyomar . . . paroles d'hommes (1790–1793),* with an introduction by Elisabeth Badinter.
34. Maugue, *L'Identité masculine en crise,* and "L'Eve nouvelle et le vieil Adam," in Duby and Perrot, eds., *Histoire des femmes* 4:527–43.

35. Maugue, "L'Eve nouvelle et le vieil Adam," p. 528.
36. Maugue, *L'Identité masculine en crise*, p. 37.
37. *Les Bas bleus* (1878), quoted in ibid., p. 52.
38. Maugue, *L'Identité masculine en crise*, p. 52. Several antifeminist women writers, such as Ida Sée, *Le Devoir maternel* (1911) and Colette Yver, *Les Cervelines* (1908), added their contribution to this masculine resistance.
39. Maugue, "L'Eve nouvelle et le vieil Adam," p. 534.
40. Barrès, quoted in Maugue, *L'Identité masculine en crise*, p. 73.
41. This entire passage owes a great deal to the work of Jacques Le Rider, one of the best French experts on Viennese modernity. See especially *Modernité viennoise et crises de l'identité*; "Ludwig Wittgenstein et Otto Weininger"; "Otto Weininger: Féminisme et virilité à Vienne," *L'Infini*, no. 4 (Fall 1983): 4–20; "Misères de la virilité à la belle époque," *Le Genre humain*, no. 10 (June 1984): 117–37.
42. Bruno Bettelheim, *Le Poids d'une vie*, pp. 15–40.
43. Le Rider, *Modernité viennoise*, p. 55.
44. Robert Musil (1880–1942), *The Man Without Qualities* (Der Mann ohne Eigenshaften), 3 vols., published in Austria in 1930, 1932, and 1942.
45. Musil, "Oedipe menacé," in *Oeuvres pré-posthumes* (Paris: Seuil, 1931), translated by Phillipe Jaccottet in 1965.
46. Le Rider, *Le Cas Otto Weininger*, p. 67.
47. Otto Weininger, *Sexe et caractère* (1903), trans. Daniel Renaud, p. 73.
48. Le Rider, "Otto Weininger," p. 14. "Intermediate forms" signified homosexuality—in other words, vice, decadence, or shameful disease.
49. Cf. Le Rider, *Le Cas Otto Weininger*, pp. 71–76.
50. See Arthur Schopenhauer, "Essai sur les femmes," in *Parerga and Paralipomena* (1851), trans. Jean Bourdeau, enlarged with a preface by Didier Raymond (Arles: Actes Sud, 1981); and Friedrich Nietzsche, notably *Beyond Good and Evil*, trans. Walter Kaufmann (New York: Random House, 1966), sec. 238–39.
51. The treatise *Sur l'imbécillité physiologique de la femme* [On the physiological imbecility of woman] by the physician Paul Julius Moebius was a veritable bestseller. Published in 1900, it was reprinted nine times between 1900 and 1908 and had the same success as Weininger's *Sexe*

et caractère. Its subject, as the title indicates, is woman's "imbecility" and hence her relative irresponsibility legally. "One can define her by situating her midway between idiocy and normal comportment. It is not inappropriate to abandon the abstract idea of 'human kind' in order to speak henceforth of human kinds. Compared to that of man, the comportment of woman appears pathological, like that of Negroes compared to that of Europeans," writes Moebius (quoted by Le Rider, *Le Cas Otto Weininger*, p. 75).

52. In France, Dumas fils compared women to "Redskins with pink skin" and to "plump and dimpled negresses with white hands." If W. Vogt and Baudelaire compared her to a Jew, whose adaptability, indiscretion, and cunning she shared, this analogy is less often seen in the writings of a Frenchman than those of an Austrian or a German.

53. See in particular Georg Groddeck and Otto Gross.

54. Le Rider, "Misères de la virilité," p. 119.

55. On Rosa Mayreder, cf. Le Rider, *Modernité viennoise*, pp. 186–89; *Le Cas Otto Weininger*, pp. 165–66; "Misères de la virilité," pp. 128–29.

56. Klaus Theweleit, *Male Fantasies*, vol. 1, *Women, Flood, Bodies, History*, trans. Stephen Carway.

57. Maugue, *L'Identité masculine en crise*, p. 159.

58. Kimmel, "The Contemporary Crisis of Masculinity," pp. 143–53.

59. Peter G. Filene, *Him/Her/Self: Sex Roles in Modern America*; Joe L. Dubbert, "Progressivism and the Masculinity Crisis," in Pleck and Pleck, eds., *The American Man*, pp. 303–19.

60. Dubbert, "Progressivism and the Masculinity Crisis," p. 308.

61. Kimmel, "The Contemporary Crisis of Masculinity," p. 138.

62. Ibid.

63. Filene, *Him/Her/Self*, pp. 78–79.

64. Unlike Europe, the United States was already experiencing a crisis on the domestic scene. Beginning in the 1890s, books and women's magazines complained bitterly about the lack of servants or any other household help, which condemned the mistress of the house to perform so many repetitive tasks. At the same time, in Europe, even very modest homes enjoyed the help of a "maid," as

is shown in Emile Zola's twenty-volume *Rougon-Mac-quart* cycle (1871–1893).

65. In the United States, going to college meant leaving the family home and being exposed to coeducation in studies, sports, and social life. In 1890 there were 3,000 girls with college degrees as compared to 13,000 boys. At the beginning of the twentieth century, girls represented 40 percent of all graduates and did not intend to return home to perform the same tasks as their mothers. Peter Filene reports that between 1880 and 1890 the number of women who worked more than doubled. Between 1900 and 1910 it increased by another 50 percent. Filene, *Him/Her/Self*, p. 26, and Kimmel, "The Contemporary Crisis of Masculinity," p. 144.

66. Kimmel, "The Contemporary Crisis of Masculinity," p. 144.

67. Filene, *Him/Her/Self*, pp. 40–41. From 1,300 children under five per one thousand mothers in 1800, the figure had fallen to 700 children in 1900.

68. Henry James's *The Bostonians* (1886) illustrates this fear of feminization.

69. Kimmel, "The Contemporary Crisis of Masculinity," p. 146.

70. *The Independent*, quoted by Dubbert, "Progressivism and the Masculinity Crisis," p. 179.

71. Filene, *Him/Her/Self*, p. 95. The institution of the Boy Scouts was created in England by Gen. Robert Baden-Powell in 1907.

72. Ibid., p. 94. The first novel of this type, *The Virginian* (1902) by Owen Wister, was very successful. Within less than a year, fifteen novels in the same genre appeared.

73. One has only to read the correspondence of the writer John Dos Passos to be convinced of this. His letters home from France, where he was sent to fight, resound with a passionate violence. He confesses to his friend Arthur McComb that he has never been as happy as he is when under fire: "I constantly feel the need of the drunken excitement of a good bombardment. . . . And through it all I feel more alive than ever before" (Filene, *Him/Her/Self*, p. 101).

74. Edward O. Wilson, *Sociobiology: The New Synthesis*, and *On Human Nature*. Wilson defines sociobiology as "the systematic study of the biological bases of all social behaviors."

75. Unlike Desmond Morris, whose *Naked Ape* was highly successful, Lionel Tiger (*Men in Groups*, 1964) and Edward O. Wilson, translated into French, succeeded in convincing only the theoreticians of the New Right.
76. Jeffrey Weeks, *Sexuality and Its Discontents*, p. 114.
77. Ruth Bleier, *Science and Gender: A Critique of Biology and Its Theory on Women* (Tarrytown, N.Y.: Pergamon, 1984), p. 19.
78. Bleier, *Science and Gender*, p. 20.
79. David Barash, *The Whisperings Within*, pp. 30–31. Barash's books are very popular in the United States—and are also very severely criticized.
80. The first in the United States to maintain these positions were the lesbian separatists. They were followed by others who call themselves radicals. In France, it is Luce Irigaray who represents this trend of thought.
81. A term coined by Catharine Stimpson in 1980 to designate the feminists who stress sexual differences in opposition to the minimalists.
82. Cf. Ti-Grace Atkinson, "Le Nationalisme féminin," *Nouvelles questions féministes*, no. 13 (1984): 5–35.
83. Maryse Guerlais, "Vers une nouvelle idéologie du droit statutaire: Le temps de la différence de Luce Irigaray," *Nouvelles questions féministes*, nos. 16–17–18 (1991): 71.
84. Luce Irigaray, *Le Temps de la différence*, p. 71.
85. Adrienne Rich, *Of Woman Born* (New York: Norton, 1976).
86. Likewise, Irigaray calls upon girls to remain in their mother's lap and to rediscover "the great mother-daughter couples in mythology: Demeter-Kore, Clytemnestra-Iphigenia, Jocasta-Antigone." Going further, she demands the creation of an exclusively female language and civil code. The strategy of the separation of the sexes taken to its extreme results in the creation of a world of women. This is, in her eyes, the only way to thwart "a patriarchal culture based on sacrifice, crime, and war." Cf. *Le temps de la différence*, pp. 23 and 27.
87. Adrienne Rich, "Compulsory Heterosexuality and Lesbian Existence," *Signs* 5 (1980): 631–60. This article caused quite a stir in the United States.
88. Supporting their case with the work of Nancy Chodorow (*The Reproduction of Mothering*) and Carol Gilligan (*In a Different Voice*), who attempt to demonstrate women's "social" and moral superiority, "maternalist" feminists

declare that women's experience as mothers gives them a moral capacity that alone can oppose the individualist world of the liberal male. In *The Reproduction of Mothering*, the author's purpose is to show that women's ability to communicate and to establish bonds with others is a more positive human quality than the male's need to keep his distance.

89. Mary G. Diez, "Feminism and Theories of Citizenship," in Conway, Bourque, and Scott, eds., *Gender, Politics, and Power*, p. 11.

90. Linda Birke, *Women, Feminism, and Biology*, pp. 116–25.

91. Cf. the journal *Sorcières*, esp. no. 20 (1980), "La nature assassinée," in which a case is made for the woman/nature identification. In it the notion that bisexuality may possibly drain femininity is criticized (p. 15). See also the magazine *Le Sauvage*, associated with the same movement, as well as numerous works celebrating the body, menstruation, and the uterus. Caught up in the momentum of this way of thinking, some went so far as to revalorize housework as being more pacific and closer to nature than the work done by men. Cf. Annie Leclerc, *Paroles de femmes* (Paris: Grasset, 1976), p. 114.

92. Cf. A. Brown, *Who Cares for Animals?* (London: Heinemann, 1974), pp. 1–35.

93. Carol Adams, "The Oedipus Complex: Feminism and Vegetarianism," in Gina Covina and Laurel Galana, eds., *The Lesbian Reader* (Oakland, Calif.: Amazon Press, 1975), pp. 149–50.

94. Norma Benney, "All of One Flesh: The Rights of Animals," in Caldecott and Leland, quoted by Birke, *Women, Feminism, and Biology*, p. 121.

95. Margaret Mead, *Male and Female* (1949), translated into French (*L'Un et l'autre sexe*) and published by Denoël-Gontier in 1966. Recent criticisms of one of her most famous books (*Coming of Age in Samoa*, 1928) do not challenge the validity of her last work on the diversity of types; cf. Derek Freeman, *Margaret Mead and Samoa: The Making and Unmaking of an Anthropological Myth* (Cambridge: Harvard University Press, 1983).

96. Mead, *Male and Female*, pp. 67 and 70.

97. Gilmore, *Manhood in the Making*.

98. The tribes of New Guinea, for instance. See Maurice Godelier, *La Production des grands hommes*, which

reports observations made by the author in 1967 and 1975 on the Baruyas; see also Gilbert H. Herdt, ed., *Rituals of Manhood: Male Initiation in Papua New Guinea*.

99. On the Tahitians, see Robert I. Levy, *The Tahitians: Mind and Experience in the Society Islands*.

100. The Semai believe that aggressiveness is the worst of calamities and that frustration of another person is an absolute evil. As a result, they are neither jealous, authoritarian, nor scornful. They cultivate noncompetitive qualities, are rather passive and shy, and readily efface themselves before others, men or women. Little concerned by the difference between the sexes, they do not pressure their male children to distinguish themselves from the girls and become tough little boys. Cf. Gilmore, *Manhood in the Making*, pp. 209–19. See also Robert K. Dentan, *The Semai: A Non-Violent People of Malaysia*.

101. Anthony Astrachan, *How Men Feel*.

102. Robert Staples, "Stereotypes of Black Male Sexuality," in Kimmel and Messner, eds., *Men's Lives*, p. 4.

103. See part 2, chap. 6 of the present volume.

104. Lucien Malson, *Wolf Children and the Problem of Human Nature*. Translated by Edwin Fawcett, Peter Ayrton, and Joan White (New York: Monthly Review Press, 1972). In French, *Les Enfants sauvages*, collection 10/18, 1964, pp. 81–82.

105. Ibid.

106. Suzanne J. Kessler and Wendy McKenna, *Gender: An Ethno-Methodological Approach* (New York: Wiley, 1978). They challenge the dualism of genders as being arbitrary categories, as does Holly Devor, *Gender Blending: Confronting the Limits of Duality*, p. 33.

107. Judith Butler, *Gender Trouble: Feminism and Subversion of Identity*. Her objective is to destabilize the distinction. She insists on the fact that the body itself is a construction (p. 8).

108. Marcia Yudkin, "Transsexualism and Women: A Critical Perspective," *Feminist Studies* 4, no. 3 (October 1978): 97–106.

109. Marc Chabot, "Genre masculin ou genre flou" (lecture given at Laval University in Quebec, 1990, a copy of which the author was kind enough to send me), has been published in *Des hommes et du masculin*, pp. 177–91.

Part One: Constructing a Male (Y)

1. There are two sorts of intersexuality which pose problems of identity. In one case, the external genital organs are immediately ambiguous in appearance. In the other, they are normal in appearance, but the development of the secondary sexual characteristics at puberty is in contradiction to this appearance. Cf. Léon Kreisler, "Les intersexuels avec ambiguïté génitale," *La Psychiatrie de l'enfant* 13, no. 1 (1970): 5–127.

2. Michel Foucault, ed., *Herculine Barbin, dite Alexina B.* This text contains the journal and the medical-legal file of a male hermaphrodite who was declared a girl at his birth in 1838 and was forced to change his official identity after adolescence, when he turned out to be more masculine than feminine. The mental shock was so great that he committed suicide in 1868, unable to accept his masculine identity.

3. See Erik Erikson, *Childhood and Society* (1950) and esp. *Identity and the Life Cycle* (1959).

4. Alex Mucchielli, *L'Identité*, "Que Sais-Je?" series (Paris: PUF, 1986).

5. To describe this, Americans have a more precise vocabulary at their disposal than the French. Robert Stoller, expert in transsexuality, insisted as far back as 1963 that one distinguish among sex, gender, and core gender identity. The word *sex* (the condition of being male or female) refers to the domain of biology. To determine sex, one must analyze chromosomes, external and internal genital organs, gonads, the hormonal state, and secondary sexual characteristics. *Gender* has psychological or cultural connotations. *Gender identity* begins with the perception that one belongs to one sex and not the other. The *core gender identity* is the conviction that the assignation of one's sex was correct. "I am a male" asserts itself before the age of two and generally persists in an unalterable manner.

6. The fact of identification perhaps authorizes a literal use of the expression: plurality of psychic personae: Freud, in *Naissance de la psychanalyse*, annotations to letter dated May 2, 1897 (Paris: PUF, 1986), p. 176.

7. John Money and Anke A. Ehrhardt, *Man and Woman, Boy and Girl*, p. 13.

8. Ibid., p. 19.

9. Le Rider, "Misères de la virilité," pp. 121–22.

10. Spinoza, in a letter to Jarig Jelles, La Haye, June 2, 1674, in Baruch Spinoza, *Letters to Friend and Foe* (New York: Philosophical Library, 1966), p. 80.

11. Ruth Hartley, "Sex Role Pressures," *Psychological Reports* 5 (1959): 458.

12. Cf. Edmund White, *A Boy's Own Story*, and its sequel, *The Beautiful Room Is Empty*.

13. White, *The Beautiful Room Is Empty*.

14. Helen Mayer Hacker, "The New Burdens of Masculinity," *Marriage and Family Living* 19, no. 3 (August 1957): 231.

15. Cf. Segal, *Slow Motion*, p. 75; Gerald Fogel, ed., *The Psychology of Men*, p. 6; John Munder-Ross, "Beyond the Phallic Illusion," in Fogel, ed.

16. Jacques Ruffié, *Le Sexe et la mort*, p. 81: more boys than girls die in utero. In addition, the Sécurité Sociale reported that in 1991 a male child from 0 to 12 months cost the nation Fr 1,714 more than a female during the same period. At the adult stage, we find an average of 160 women to every 115 men (whereas more boys than girls are born: 104.5 to 108.3 boys to every 100 girls, depending on the years and the country) and the gap will only grow with time.

17. Philippe Chevalier, "Population infantile consultant pour des troubles psychologiques," *Population*, no. 3 (May–June 1988): 611–38. Pooling eighteen statistical studies on children being treated for psychological problems, he found two shared characteristics: a preponderance of boys and a triggering role on the part of school.

18. Ibid., pp. 615–16. See also the detailed article by the American psychiatrist Leon Eisenberg, "La répartition differentielle des troubles psychiques selon le sexe," in Beverly I. Fagot, *Le Fait féminin: Qu'est-ce qu'une femme?* pp. 313–27: "In the United States, total admissions in outpatient treatment of children under 14 years show a proportion of 2.5 boys to 1 girl. Between 14 and 17, admissions are roughly equal."

19. *Allele*: gene symmetrical to another gene and situated in the corresponding locus on the second chromosome of the pair. Cf. glossary in Fagot, *Le Fait féminin*, p. 517.

20. Money and Ehrhardt, *Man and Woman*, p. 148.

21. Out of more than one hundred recent novels written by

men, close to two-thirds show the hero in tears at least once, or even several times.

1: Y; or, Sexual Dualism

1. The spermatozoon carrying an x chromosome yields a female embryo and the spermatozoon carrying a y chromosome, a male embryo.

2. Notably, the set of factors involved in a program of gonadic differentiation.

3. 44xo, or Turner's Syndrome, yields a feminine type of human being. It affects one woman in 2,700 and is not an obstacle to fertility.

4. 44xxx: cytogenetic variant of the preceding case, affecting one woman in 500, with no fertility problems. This information and the following are taken from an article by Nacer Abbas, Colin Bishop, and Marc Fellous, "Le déterminisme génétique du sexe," *La Recherche* 20, no. 213 (September 1989): 1036–46.

5. xyy appears to involve one man in 500. The subject is normal and fertile. xxy (Klinefelter's Syndrome) is also masculine in type, with a small penis, atrophied testicles, and sterility problems. One man in 700 is affected.

6. As the American edition of the present book was about to go to press, the journal *Nature Genetics* 7 (August 1994): 497–501, published a discovery of fundamental importance by the Italian-American team of Giovanna Camerino, namely, the existence of a so-called dss gene, situated on the short arm of the x chromosome, that apparently plays a role in the development of a female parallel to that played by the sry gene in the development of a male. This discovery has led me to remove from my original text a number of reflections that are no longer justified, particularly regarding what was considered, in the light of current scientific knowledge, the masculine exception.

7. Money and Ehrhardt, *Man and Woman*, pp. 3–4.

8. The y chromosome carries a very great number of genes disproportionate to its size, which is small. As recently as July 1990, the English researcher Peter Goodfellow identified the gene that causes the embryo to develop as a male: known as sry, it emits chemical signals about eight weeks after fertilization which influence the sexu-

al glands so that they become testicles rather than ovaries (*Nature*, July 19, 1990). Confirming their discovery, the English succeeded in changing the sex of a female mouse embryo by injecting it with the SRY gene, which they had isolated. The embryo continued its gestation and developed normally as a male; it was able to mate several times but remained sterile (*Nature*, May 11, 1991).

9. One hormone, called the "Anti-Müllerian Hormone," or AMH, secreted by the immature, fetal testicle, acts to inhibit, in the male fetus, the development of the rudimentary oviduct and uterus, called the canals of Müller. For its part, testosterone assures the maintenance of the canals of Wolff, as well as the masculinization of the urogenital sinus and the external genital organs. "In the genetically male fetus, the internal program of development is thwarted. . . . In the female fetus, the development of the genital organs simply follows the preestablished program without the intervention of any specific feminizing factors" (cf. Vigier and Picard, "L'AMH: Hormone clé de différenciation sexuelle," p. 24).

10. Androgens (male hormones), as well as estrogens and progesterone (female hormones), are present in the blood of both. But a man produces close to six times more testosterone than a woman. As Betty Yorberg points out, to describe androgens and estrogens as male or female is deceptive, since both types of hormones are produced by men and women, but in different quantities. Cf. *Sexual Identity*, p. 20.

11. Fausto-Sterling, *Myths of Gender*, p. 85.

12. Zella Luria, "Genre et étiquetage: L'effet Pirandello," in Fagot, *Le Fait féminin*, p. 237. See also Beverly I. Fagot, "Sex Differences in Toddlers' Behavior and Parental Reaction," *Developmental Psychology* 10 (1974): 554–58, and "Sex-related Stereotyping of Toddlers' Behaviors," *Developmental Psychology* 9 (1973): 429.

13. Another experiment, dubbed "Baby X," uses a similar paradigm and comes to the same conclusions. The object of the experiment is a flesh-and-blood baby dressed in yellow. Forty-two adults are divided into three groups. The first group is told that the baby is a girl, the second that it is a boy, and the third that it is a three-month-old baby, without specifying its sex. Then the adults are asked to play with the baby. As before, the most striking

result was that the adults related differently to the same child, depending on whether it was stated to be male or female. When this information was not given, the men were more anxious than the women, and most of the subjects attributed a sex to the child, justifying this choice by signs that conform to stereotypes, for example the baby's strength or fragility. C. A. Seavey, P. A. Katz, and S. R. Zalk, "Baby X: The Effect of Gender Labels on Adult Responses to Infants," *Sex Roles* 1 (1975): 103–10.

14. Specialists in intersexuality try to assign a sex to the child as quickly as possible and begin surgical and hormonal treatment as early as possible. But the diagnosis cannot be completed in one day. It requires: a chromosomal analysis; cytological tracking; hormonal, gonadotropine, and steroid evaluations; and manual and X-ray examinations. Cf. Suzanne J. Kessler, "The Medical Construction of Gender," *Signs* 16 (Fall 1990): 3–26.

15. If it is decided that the child is of the male sex, the first stage of repairing the penis occurs during the first year. It is completed by other operations before school age. If it is decided that the child is female, the operation on the vulva and the reduction of the clitoris may be done as early as the third month. It is easier to form female genital organs that are close to normal than male genital organs. It is not yet known how to create a penis that is normal in appearance and functional. Cf. Kessler, "The Medical Construction of Gender," pp. 6 and 8.

16. Robert Stoller, *Recherches sur l'identité sexuelle*, pp. 60–70.

17. This context being: a very bisexual mother, superficially feminine, sexually neutral, depressive, without interest in sexuality or particular attachment to the child's father, and a profound sense of incompleteness. And an absent father, both physically and emotionally, who is not affected by seeing his son dress like a girl and display unusual behavior. Stoller, *Recherches sur l'identité sexuelle*, pp. 119–22.

18. "Psychic" refers to the formally registered sex as understood vis-à-vis one's own personal sense of one's identity—that is, the core gender identity, in Stoller's terminology.

19. Cases of "feminizing testicles" involve xy subjects who have all the appearances of a woman. These are women—sometimes very pretty ones—who present a female's

external genital aspect and a perfect female type of mor-
phological development, but who upon examination
prove to have a male set of chromosomes and a male's
internal genital apparatus.

20. Quoted in *Libération*, January 28, 1992, p. 3 (emphasis
added).

2: *Masculine Differentiation*

1. John Bowlby, *Attachement et perte*, vol. 1, *L'Attachement*; and P. H. Gray, "Theory and Evidence of Imprinting in Human Infants," *Journal of Psychology* 46 (1958):
155–66.

2. "The libidinal investment attached to the symbiosis . . .
protects the rudimentary ego from all premature and
non-adapted tension": Margaret Mahler, *Psychose infantile*, pp. 21–22. Some thinkers have recently criticized
the notion of symbiosis, like Daniel Stern, *Interpersonal World of the Infant* (New York: Basic Books, 1985), p.
10. He believes there is never any confusion between the
self and the other in the baby's mind.

3. Sigmund Freud, *Abrégé de psychanalyse* (1940).

4. In his autobiography Philip Roth wrote, "The link to my
father was never so voluptuously tangible as the colossal
bond to my mother's flesh, whose metamorphosed
incarnation was a sleek black sealskin coat into which I,
the younger, the privileged, the pampered papoose, bliss-
fully wormed myself . . . the unnameable animal-me
bearing her dead father's name, the protoplasm-me, boy-
baby, and body-burrower-in-training, joined by every
nerve ending to her smile and her sealskin coat." Roth,
The Facts: A Novelist's Autobiography, p. 18.

5. The expression is taken from Austrian writer Peter
Rosei's *Homme et femme S.A.R.L.*, p. 179.

6. Georg Groddeck, *Le Livre du ça* (1923).

7. Freud, *A General Introduction to Psychoanalysis*. When
the infant falls asleep sated next to his mother's breast,
he wears an expression of happy satisfaction that one
sees again later after sexual satisfaction.

8. Ibid., p. 294: "I wouldn't be able to give you a precise
enough idea of the importance of this first object—the
mother's breast—in all later searching for sexual objects,
of the profound influence it exerts on all its transforma-

tions and substitutions, even in the remotest areas of our psychic life."

9. Pat Conroy, among many others, refers to the "mother's solitary and innocently seductive advances," in *The Prince of Tides*, p. 111.

10. Janine Chasseguet-Smirgel, "Masculin et féminin"; Robert Stoller, "Féminité primaire," pp. 59–82.

11. Stoller, *Masculin ou féminin?* pp. 307–8.

12. Cf. the work of Margaret Mahler.

13. Stoller, "Faits et hypothèses," *Nouvelle revue de psychanalyse*, no. 7 (Spring 1973), p. 150.

14. Ibid., p. 151 (emphasis added).

15. Ibid.: "An experience imprinted with happiness, which, though it has been buried, is active deep within the identity and will be, throughout life, a sort of magnetized focal point capable of attracting the individual toward a regression to this primitive union."

16. Stoller, *Masculin ou féminin?* pp. 310–11.

17. Ibid., p. 311 (emphasis added).

18. Miriam M. Johnson, *Strong Mothers, Weak Wives*, p. 109.

19. "The fact of internalizing positive maternal behaviors allows the child to acquire his first psychic structures, which are the early beginnings of his self-esteem. If he is obliged to reject identification with his mother too early, the child is also disturbed in his capacity to develop a memory that allows him to recall, as often as he feels the need, the mother's consoling and soothing functions." Margarete Mitscherlich and Helga Dierichs, *Des Hommes*, pp. 49–50.

20. Phyllis Chesler, *La Mâle donne*, p. 53.

21. Freud, *New Introductory Lectures on Psychoanalysis*, *SE*, vol. 22.

22. Jean Laplanche and J. B. Pontalis. *Vocabulaire de psychanalyse*. Paris: PUF, 1967.

23. This paper, delivered in July 1967 in Copenhagen, was subsequently published under the title "Dis-Identifying from Mother," *International Psycho-Analytic Journal* 49 (1968): 370–73.

24. Fogel, ed., *The Psychology of Men*, p. 10.

25. Stoller, *Masculin ou féminin?* p. 309.

26. Godelier, *La Production des grands hommes*, and Herdt, ed., *Rituals of Manhood*. See also the article by Stoller and Herdt, "The Development of Masculinity," *Journal*

of the American Psychoanalytic Association 30 (1982): 29–59; also, translated into French in Stoller, *Masculin ou féminin?* pp. 307–38.

27. They forbid the parents all sexual activity until the child is in its second year.

28. Joe Dubbert, "Shaping the Ideal During the Masculine Century," p. 20.

29. Kenneth S. Lynn, *Hemingway*, p. 43.

30. Hemingway's father committed suicide on December 6, 1928, with a bullet through the head.

31. Aside from certain of Hemingway's novellas, like *The Garden of Eden*, written at the end of his life and expressing veritable transsexual fantasies, there is no question that the psychological portrait of his (homosexual) mother corresponds completely to the typical mother of the transsexual boy described by Stoller.

32. Hermann Burger, *La Mère artificielle*, p. 197. Born in 1942, the author committed suicide in 1989.

33. Bourdieu, "La domination masculine," p. 23.

34. Bettelheim, *Symbolic Wounds*.

35. Herman Numberg, *Problems of Bisexuality as Reflected in Circumcision* (London: Imago, 1949), p. 8.

36. Groddeck, "Le double sexe de l'être humain," trans. R. Lewinter, *Nouvelle revue de psychanalyse*, no. 7 (Spring 1973): 194; text published in *La Maladie: L'art et le symbole* (Paris: Gallimard, 1969). Lewinter explains that Judaism appears as the extremely exacerbated assertion of unisexuality, artificially established, the division of male and female roles "intended to be absolutely unequivocal. . . . Circumcision is truly the emblem of the human project, the individual fully guaranteeing his finitude in relation to the infinite." Cf. Lewinter, "Groddeck: (anti)judaïsme et bisexualité," in the same issue of *Nouvelle revue de psychanalyse*, pp. 199–200.

37. Gilligan, *In a Different Voice*.

38. Chodorow, *The Reproduction of Mothering*, p. 176. Her analysis is based in part on Stoller's research.

39. Lillian Rubin, *Intimate Strangers*.

40. Jean Jacques Rousseau, *Lettre à d'Alembert* (1758), pp. 195–96 (emphasis added).

41. Christopher Franck, *Le Rêve du singe fou*, pp. 33, 107, 116, 140.

42. Grass, *The Flounder*.

43. Burger, *La Mère artificielle*, pp. 75–76.

44. Why a breast? he asks himself. "A longing in me, deep down in my molten center, a churning longing to be utterly and blessedly helpless, to be a big brainless bag of tissue, desirable, dumb, passive, immobile, acted upon instead of acting, hanging, *there*, as a breast hangs and is *there*. Or think of it as a form of hibernation, a long winter's sleep buried in the mountains of the female anatomy. . . . Think of the breast as my cocoon, first cousin to that sac in which I had tread my mother's waters." Philip Roth, *The Breast*, p. 61.

45. Philip Roth, *My Life as a Man*, p. 78.

46. Michka Assayas, *Les Années vides*, pp. 38–39.

47. We find the theme of murdering the mother in Günter Grass, Michaël Krüger, Peter Rosei, Hermann Burger, and Thomas Bernhard, among others.

48. Chasseguet-Smirgel, "Masculin et féminin," p. 62.

49. The psychoanalyst also stresses that one of the slips heard most often in French is the word *mort* (death) for the word *mère* (mother). And it is not by chance that "the great writings on femininity [by Freud] are contemporaneous with the introduction of the death instinct and indisputably bear the mark of death" (ibid., pp. 85 and 86).

50. Philip Roth, *The Counterlife*, pp. 246 and 248 (1985). In French: *La Contre-vie*.

51. Roth, *My Life as a Man*, pp. 55–56.

52. Roth, *The Facts*, p. 19.

53. Philip Roth, *Portnoy's Complaint*, p. 56 (1969). In French: *Portnoy et son complexe*.

54. Roth, *Portnoy's Complaint*, p. 65.

55. Ibid., pp. 58–59.

56. Ibid., p 43. His mother threatens him with a knife when he won't eat!

57. Ibid., pp. 184–85.

58. Roth, *My Life as a Man* and *The Professor of Desire*.

59. Roth, *My Life as a Man*, p. 213.

60. Ibid., p. 183. Roth constantly returns to the theme of the infant, notably in *The Anatomy Lesson*, which tells the story of his terrible depression.

61. Grass, *The Flounder*.

62. Michaël Krüger, *Pourquoi moi? Et autres récits*, pp. 21–39.

63. Rosei, *Homme et femme S.A.R.L.*

64. Burger, *La Mère artificielle*, p. 262; Saul Bellow, *Seize*

the Day; Pat Conroy, *The Prince of Tides;* Knut Fald-bakken, *La Séduction,* pp. 84–86, and *Le Monarque,* pp. 131 and 215.

65. Faldbakken's expression in *Le Monarque,* p. 17. See also Dominique Fernandez, *L'Ecole du Sud;* Vitaliano Brancati, *Les Années perdues;* Philippe Sollers, *Femmes;* Roland Jaccard, *Les Chemins de la désillusion* and *Lou;* Hervé Guibert, *Mes Parents.*

66. Christian Giudicelli, *Station balnéaire;* Ludovic Janvier, *Monstre, va!;* François Weyergans, *Le Pitre,* and his work in general; Edgar Smadja, *Lubie;* Alfredo Bryce-Echenique, *L'Ultime déménagement de Felipe Carrillo.*

67. Roland Clément, *Fausse note.*

68. René Belletto, *La Machine.*

69. Janvier, *Monstre, va!*

70. Robert W. Connell, "A Whole New World," *Gender and Society* 14, no. 4 (December 1990): p. 459.

71. Stanley H. Cath, Alan R. Gurwitt, John Munder-Ross, eds., *Father and Child,* p. 163.

72. Devor, *Gender Blending,* p. 46.

73. Cf. Joseph H. Pleck, *The Myth of Masculinity,* as well as a number of articles.

74. Levy, *The Tahitians,* pp. 189–90.

75. Eleanor E. Maccoby, "Le sexe, catégorie sociale," *Actes de la recherche en sciences sociales,* no. 83 (June 1990): 16. Maccoby makes use of the work of Luria and Herzog; Barry Thorne, "Girls and Boys Together . . . but Mostly Apart" (1986), reprinted in Kimmel and Messner, eds., *Men's Lives,* pp. 138–53; as well as of his own research with Carol N. Jacklin, *The Psychology of Sex Difference* and "Gender Segregation in Childhood," in E. H. Reese, ed., *Advances in Child Development and Behavior* 20:239–87.

76. Beverly Fagot reports, in a study on children in nursery school, that boys and girls react favorably to "reinforcements" mainly when they come from children of the same sex, but hardly react at all when they come from children of the opposite sex. However, it is observed that girls are more sensitive to the influence of boys than vice versa. Boys and girls form groups with different cultures, the boys' group being characterized by domination, hierarchy, order-giving, bragging, and threats, while the girls express agreement more often, more readily allow others to talk, and are less sensitive to hierarchy. Fagot,

"Beyond the Reinforcement Principle," *Developmental Psychology* 21 (1985): 1097–1104.

77. Money and Ehrhardt cite a group of girls who had undergone prenatal androgenization and who differed from other little girls in their preference for boys as playmates (*Man and Woman*).

78. The categories *male* and *female* are fundamental binary categories acquired well in advance of those of *masculine* and *feminine*, which are vague and relative aggregates.

79. Badinter, *L'Amour en plus*.

80. Bowlby, *Attachement et perte*.

81. D. W. Winnicott, "La préoccupation maternelle primaire" (1956), in *De la Pédiatrie à la psychanalyse* (Paris: Payot, 1978), pp. 168–74. See also Alice Balint, "Love for the Mother and Mother Love," in Michael Balint, ed., *Primary Love and Psycho-Analytic Technique* (New York: Liveright, 1965), pp. 91–108.

82. Winnicott, "La préoccupation maternelle primaire," p. 170.

83. H. Deutsch defines the normal, "feminine" woman as the following: one formed by the harmonious interaction of narcissistic tendencies and the masochistic ability to tolerate suffering. The narcissistic desire to be loved metamorphoses in a maternal woman through a transfer of the ego onto the child, who is merely a substitute for the ego. Deutsch, *Psychologie des femmes* (Paris: PUF, 1949), 2:45.

84. D. W. Winnicott, *L'Enfant et sa famille* (Paris: Payot, 1973), pp. 117–18.

85. Winnicott, *L'Enfant et sa famille*, p. 120.

86. Ibid.: "The advantage of having two parents: one can continue to be experienced as loving, while the other is detested."

87. Balint, "Love for the Mother and Mother Love," pp. 98–100.

88. Françoise Dolto, *Lorsque l'enfant paraît* 2:71–72.

89. Badinter, *L'Amour en plus*, pp. 321–23.

90. William Ryan, *Blaming the Victim* (New York: Pantheon, 1970).

91. See part two, chapter 6, of the present volume.

92. Barbara J. Risman, "Men Who Mother: Intimate Relationships from a Microstructural Perspective," *Gender and Society* 1, no. 1 (March 1987): 6–32.

3: "It Is Man Who Engenders Man"

1. Aristotle, *Metaphysics* Z.7.1032a25.
2. Guy Corneau, *Père manquant, fils manqué*, p. 21 (emphasis added).
3. Nicole Loraux, "Blessures de virilité," *Le Genre humain*, no. 10 (June 1984): 39.
4. Georges Duby, *Mâle Moyen Age*, pp. 205–6.
5. Otto Rank, quoted by Herman Numberg, "Tentatives de rejet de la circoncision," *Nouvelle revue de la psychanalyse*, no. 7 (1973): 208.
6. Joseph H. Pleck, "Man to Man: Is Brotherhood Possible?" in N. Glazer-Malbin, ed., *Old Family/New Family*.
7. Gilmore, *Manhood in the Making*, p. 15.
8. Gilbert H. Herdt, *Guardians of the Flutes*, p. 305.
9. William Shakespeare, *Henry IV, Part 2*, act 3, scene 2, line 129.
10. Herdt, *Guardians of the Flutes*, pp. 58–59.
11. Godelier, *La Production des grands hommes*, p. 72.
12. Louis Carus Madih, Steven Foster, and Meredith Little, eds., *Betwixt and Between: Patterns of Masculine and Feminine Initiations*.
13. According to Victor Turner, who has drawn on the analyses of Van Gennep, initiation symbols are taken from biology, from death, from decomposition, or are modeled on the process of gestation. Victor Turner, *The Forest of Symbols: Aspects of Ndembu Ritual* (Ithaca and London: Cornell University Press, 1967), p. 95, as cited by Jan O. Stein and Murray Stein, in Madih, Foster, and Little, eds., *Betwixt and Between*, pp. 291–92.
14. In a subincision, a deep incision is made on the ventral surface of the penis, so deep it reaches the urethra. The incision is anywhere from a few centimeters long to the entire length of the penis, from the glans to the scrotum. Persons having the subincision urinate crouching down like women, have a diminution of their reproductive capacities, and display a radical deformation of the penis. Often the scar is reopened for ritual bleedings.
15. Gilmore, *Manhood in the Making*.
16. At the time of his circumcision, the young Masai does not even have the right to tremble or to blink or he will bring shame to his family.

17. The description that follows is borrowed from Fitz John Porter Pode, "The Ritual Forging of Identity: Aspects of Person and Self in Bimin-Kuskusmin Male Initiation," in Herdt, ed., *Rituals of Manhood*, pp. 100–151.

18. Mothers are called "diabolical soilers."

19. Herdt, *Guardians of the Flutes*, pp. 31–32.

20. Godelier, *La Production des grands hommes*, p. 84.

21. Dan De Kiley, *The Peter Pan Complex* (New York: Dodd, Mead, 1983).

22. Barbara Ehrenreich, *The Hearts of Men: American Dreams and the Flight from Commitment.*

23. Duby, *Guillaume le Maréchal ou le meilleur chevalier du monde* (Paris: Fayard, 1984), p. 82: "During this period [the twelfth century], a knight's sons left their father's house early; they went elsewhere to perform their apprenticeship in life and all except the oldest left this house forever, unless spared by some fortunate happenstance. After eight years, ten years, they were thus separated from their mother, from their sisters, from the women kinfolk among whom they had lived until then and who loved them dearly. . . . A twofold break—from the house of their birth, and from the female universe of the young children's room. And a very abrupt transfer to another world, that of the cavalcades, the stables, the armories, the hunts, the ambushes, and the manly revels."

24. Christine Heward, *Making a Man of Him* (London: Routledge, 1988), p. 55. See also Lynne Segal, *Slow Motion*, p. 108.

25. Segal, *Slow Motion*, pp. 108–9.

26. Gilmore, *Manhood in the Making*, p. 18.

27. Ray Raphaël, *The Men from the Boys*, p. 29.

28. Cooper Thompson, "A New Vision of Masculinity," in Kimmel and Messner, eds., *Men's Lives*, p. 587. See also William Arkin and Lynne R. Dobrofsky, "Military Socialization and Masculinity," *Journal of Social Issues* 34 (1978): 151–68.

29. Pat Conroy, *The Great Santini.*

30. Bernard Sergent, *L'Homosexualité initiatique dans l'Europe ancienne.*

31. In Plato's *Symposium*, Aristophanes says this very thing when he refers to androgynous males in his speech: "Those who are half male . . . love men and take pleasure in lying with them and being in their arms . . . are among the best because they are the most male in their nature.

Some say they are without modesty, this is a mistake: it is not through immodesty, but through boldness, courage, and manliness that they act thus . . . and here is a convincing proof of this, which is, that when they have attained their full development, boys of this nature are the only ones who devote themselves to governing the States" (Paris: Garnier-Flammarion, 1964), 192A, p. 51 (emphasis added).

32. Paul Veyne, "L'homosexualité à Rome," in Ariès and Bejin, eds., *Sexualités occidentales*, p. 43. Antinoüs drowned in 122.

33. Michel Foucault, *The History of Sexuality*, vol. 2, *The Use of Pleasure*, trans. Robert Hurley, p. 190.

34. Corneau, *Père manquant, fils manqué*, p. 74.

35. Michel Foucault, *La Volonté de savoir*, p. 82.

36. It is Plutarch, in his *Life of Pelopidas*, who gives the most details about the sacred batallion of Thebes, a military unit formed of three hundred elite men, *erastes* (initiators) and their novice *eromens*. This troop, formed of men who loved each other, possessed an unbreakable cohesion.

37. Plato in the *Symposium* recalls that in Elide, in Boetia, and in Sparta, the relationship between an adult and a young man has an obligatory sexual character, whereas in Athens the rule admitted of variations.

38. Plutarch, *Life of Lycurgus* 16–19, cited by Sergent, *L'Homosexualité initiatique*, pp. 75–76.

39. Sergent, *L'Homosexualité initiatique*, p. 120.

40. Aristophanes, *Clouds* 973–83, quoted by Sergent, *L'Homosexualité initiatique*, p. 121.

41. Godelier, *La Production des grands hommes*, pp. 91–92. This custom, which disappeared from among the Baruya with the arrival of Europeans in 1960, still survives in twenty other tribes that live in the less accessible mountains and forests. It still exists among the Sambia, and Gilbert Herdt has observed it in detail.

42. Robert Bly, "Initiations masculines contemporaines," in *Guides-ressources* 4, no. 2 (Montréal: November–December 1988); reprinted in English as "Men's Initiation Rites," in Kimmel and Messner, eds., *Men's Lives*, pp. 153–57.

43. "Psychodynamically, in a context of traumatic maternal separation, Sambia ritual attempts to use the flute as a . . . [means of] releasing feelings of helplessness and

fear, [and] supplants the mother as the preferred attachment figure by offering the culturally valued penis and homosexual relationships as sensual substitutes for the mother's breast and for the mother as a whole person." Herdt, *Guardians of the Flutes*, p. 79.

44. F. Buffière, *Eros adolescent: La pédérastie dans la Grèce antique* (Paris: Belles Lettres, 1980), pp. 605–7.

45. Sergent, *L'Homosexualité initiatique*, p. 113.

46. Foucault, *La Volonté de savoir*, p. 136.

47. "A boy having commerce with a man does not share like a woman the joys of love, he gazes with the coldness of a fasting man upon a man drunk with love." Cf. Xenophon, in Plato *Symposium* 7.21.

48. "He was expected to show his ardor, and to restrain it; he had gifts to make, services to render; he had functions to exercise with regard to the eromenos; and all this entitled him to expect a just reward. The other partner, the one who was loved and courted, had to be careful not to yield too easily. . . . He must also show gratitude for what the lover had done for him. . . . The sexual relation between man and boy did not 'go without saying': it had to be accompanied by conventions, rules of conduct, ways of going about it, by a whole game of delays and obstacles designed to put off the moment of closure." Foucault, *History of Sexuality* 2:196–97.

49. This echoes the beginning of Plato's *Laches*, 179C–D, cited by Sergent, *L'Homosexualité initiatique*, p. 120.

50. K. J. Dover, *Homosexualité grecque*, p. 86: "Allusions to the desires one feels for beautiful people are necessarily ambiguous, since the genitive plural is the same in the masculine and the feminine."

51. Diogenes Laërtius, *Lives of Eminent Philosophers* 4.7.49.

52. Foucault, *History of Sexuality* 2:188.

53. John Boswell, *Christianity, Social Tolerance, and Homosexuality*, p. 130.

54. Herdt, *Guardians of the Flutes*, p. 69.

55. Stoller, *Masculin ou féminin?* p. 321.

56. E. James Anthony, "Afterword," in Cath, Gurwitt, and Ross, eds., *Father and Child*, p. 575.

57. See Johnson, *Strong Mothers, Weak Wives*, pp. 108–9, on eroticism and a mother's sensuality with respect to her male and female children.

58. In their eyes, "Western homes are strictly skeletal. . . . How can you become a man in a place where you are

assigned only a single father? And what can you do if the latter does not suit you?" Suzanne Lallemand, "Le b.a. ba Africain," *Pères et Fils* in *Autrement*, no. 61 (June 1984): 180.

59. Mentor is the name of a character from the *Odyssey* (see 2.225), also popularized in France by François Fénelon's *Télémaque* (*Telemachus*, 1699).

60. Robert Bly, *Iron John: A Book About Men*. The book remained on the *New York Times Book Review* best-seller list for many weeks.

61. Samuel Osherson, *Finding Our Fathers*, pp. 44–45.

62. A form of literature in fashion in the nineteenth century as much in Europe as in the United States. Cf. Peter N. Stearns, *Be a Man! Males in Modern Society*, p. 57: he points out that fathers were still very frequently mentioned in 1830–1840, then less and less.

63. On the other hand, the image of the father is becoming obscure. His importance and his authority, so great, still, in the eighteenth century, are declining. At best he is defined by his function as provider and is granted authority as the ultimate arbiter of discipline ("I'll tell your father when he comes home"). At worst, if he does not work, like the French *rentier*, it is said quite complacently that he has better things to do and that in any case "he would be perfectly incapable of this delicate work [the moral and physical education of his child]." Cf. Badinter, *L'Amour en plus*, pp. 252–80.

64. In France he tends to be supplanted more and more by the State. School transmits to the son a knowledge often unfamiliar to the parents, and new institutions, protective of children, gradually assume his old functions and prerogatives. Social investigations, judges, "visiting nurses," all keep a close watch on the penniless and "unworthy" father. The laws of 1889 and 1898 concerning a father's forfeiture of rights as well as the generalization of social investigation in 1912 completed the curtailment of his centuries-old powers.

65. An image popularized by Gustave Droz in *Monsieur, Madame et Bébé* (1866), which—with over twenty printings—became an immense success in the bookstores.

66. Stearns, *Be a Man!* p. 156, asserts that nothing as dramatic had ever happened before as the separation of men's work and the home, along with the erosion of the patriarchy that followed from it.

67. Shere Hite, *The Hite Report on Male Sexuality*, pp. 19–20. Lacking similar studies in France, it is not possible to extrapolate Hite's results in the case of the French. If we are as yet poorly informed as to sons' relationship with their fathers, we do know that the man/woman relationship is not the same in France as in the United States. The image of the French mother does not evoke the all-powerful American mother that emerged in the nineteenth century. Last, the well-known anxiety of the young American boy over the idea of being a "mama's boy" has no real equivalent in France, where one is more likely to speak of being a "papa's son" than a "mama's son," and this expression designates a social situation more than a psychological bond.

68. Leon Edel, *Henry James: A Life*.

69. Edel, *Henry James*.

70. Ibid.

71. Ibid.

72. Ibid. He even believed, for a while, that men drew their strength from the women they married, and that for their part women could deprive men of both their strength and their lives. And he believed that it had not been otherwise for his father.

73. Henry James lived from 1843 to 1916 (ibid.) and Hemingway from 1899 to 1961 (Lynn, *Hemingway*).

74. With no money, no education, no culture, no wisdom, though affectionate and sensitive, this father "had no power to direct, command, or oppress. He was the one oppressed. . . . He had no cock, no balls. . . . If only my father had been my mother! And my mother my father!" Roth, *Portnoy's Complaint*, pp. 12–24, 42, 59–62.

75. David Cooper, *Mort de la famille* (Paris: Seuil, 1972), p. 110.

76. A theme that is increasingly common in North America, as witness the essays of the Québecois Guy Corneau and the Americans Robert Bly, Franklin Abbott, Samuel Osherson, and John Lee. See also Margarete Mitscherlich and Helga Dierichs's research on men (*Des Hommes*) conducted in Germany in 1980.

77. Gary Alan Fine, "The Dirty Play of Little Boys," in Kimmel and Messner, eds., *Men's Lives*, pp. 171–79.

78. See the description of sports locker rooms dominated by a frenzied machismo in Conroy's *The Great Santini*.

79. Régine Boyer, "Identité masculine, identité féminine," *Revue française de pédagogie*, no. 94 (January–March 1991): 16.

80. Michel Bozon, "Les Loisirs forment la jeunesse," *Données sociales* (1990): 217–22.

81. Jeffrey P. Hantover, "The Boy Scouts and the Validation of Masculinity," in Kimmel and Messner, eds., *Men's Lives*, p. 124.

82. The American historian E. Anthony Rotundo notes that, beginning in the 1860s, boys' colleges and most towns organized baseball and football games for young men of all backgrounds. Rotundo, "Boy Culture," in Carnes and Griffen, eds., *Meanings for Manhood*, p. 34.

83. Gary Alan Fine, "Little League Baseball and Growing Up Male," in Lewis, ed., *Men in Difficult Times*, p. 67.

84. Conroy, *The Great Santini* (see note 78, above).

85. Michael Messner, "Ah, Ya Throw Like a Girl," in Abbott, ed., *New Men, New Minds*, pp. 40–42.

86. Don Sabo, "Pigskin, Patriarchy and Pain," in Abbott, ed., *New Men, New Minds*, p. 47.

87. Ibid., p. 48.

88. Michael Messner, "The Life of a Man's Seasons," in Kimmel, ed., *Changing Men*, p. 59.

89. See Thomas Faber, *La Course du chien*, and Pat Conroy, *The Great Santini*.

90. See John Updike, *Rabbit Run* and *Rabbit Redux*.

91. See Philip Roth, *Portnoy's Complaint* and *The Great American Novel*; and Edmund White, *A Boy's Own Story*.

92. Christian Baudelot and Roger Establet, *Allez les filles!*, p. 227.

93. "Boys participate in large numbers in sports activities and outdoor activities and in the sociability which may be associated with them: football and ball games. . . . Attendance at sporting events among the young is also a male phenomenon and a group one. . . . There always exists a male tendency to assert oneself through physical activities outside the home within the framework of groups of peers which are not necessarily of mixed sex." Bozon, "Les Loisirs forment la jeunesse," p. 221.

94. Alain Finkielkraut, "La nostalgie de l'épreuve," *Le Genre humain*, no. 10 (June 1994): 57–63.

95. Douglas Gillette and Robert Moore, *King, Warrior, Magician, Lover*.

4: Identity and Sexual Orientation

1. The French magazine *Lui*, no. 50 (December 1991).

2. Weeks, *Sexuality and Its Discontents*, p. 90.

3. Montesquieu, *L'Esprit des lois* (1748), book 12, chap. 7, cited by Pierre Hahn, *Nos Ancêtres les pervers*, p. 19.

4. Hahn reports that in the early eighteenth century, sodomy seems to have been the privilege of the nobility. On the eve of the French Revolution, the situation changed. Mouffle d'Angerville acknowledged with disillusionment: "This vice that was once called the beautiful vice [what of the abominable vice?] because it was reserved for the great lords, the wits, or the Adonises, has become so fashionable that there is no order of the State, from the dukes to the lackeys and the people, that hasn't been infected by it." Hahn, *Nos Ancêtres les pervers*, pp. 90–91.

5. Cited by Hahn, *Nos Ancêtres les pervers*, pp. 21–22.

6. Ibid., p. 22.

7. Hahn makes note of another perplexing subject: sodomy between women, which already surprised the good ecclesiastic of the eighteenth century. In order to understand the idea of female sodomy, one must recall that up to and including the seventeenth century, the female sex was conceived by analogy with the male sex. From this point of view, the clitoris could be compared to the penis, whose characteristics it shares, if imperfectly. "Does it not also take the form of the penis when it is swollen?" It would not be until the nineteenth century that the model of the two opposite sexes would be imposed, and that women, at the same time, would be excluded from the category of sodomite. Hahn, *Nos Ancêtres les pervers*, p. 23.

8. Maurice Lever, *Les Bûchers de Sodome*, p. 239.

9. Voltaire, *Dictionnaire philosophique* (1764), cited by Lever, *Les Bûchers de Sodome*, p. 241.

10. Condorcet, *Notes sur Voltaire* (1789), in Arago, ed., *Oeuvres de Condorcet*, vol. 4 (Berlin: Friedrich Frammaun Verlag, 1968), p. 561.

11. Diderot, *Suite de l'Entretien*, in Vernière, ed., *Oeuvres philosophiques*, pp. 376 and 378.

12. Ibid., p. 377.

13. Ibid., p. 380: "I will therefore ask you, of two actions

equally limited to sensual pleasure (masturbation and homosexuality), which give only pleasure without usefulness, but of which one gives it only to the one who does it and the other shares it with a similar creature, male or female, for here the sex, and even the use of the sex, does not matter, in favor of which will common sense decide?"

14. *Pervert* is associated with *effeminate*, a person afflicted with sexual perversity. It was also in the nineteenth century that the terms *folle* and *tante* [*fairy* and *pansy*] appeared in the vocabulary.

15. In the same way, the more and more widespread use of the term *gay* in the 1970s would again change one's conception of them.

16. In Germany, which suppressed pederasty, it was the forensic pathologist Casper, of Berlin, who in 1852 published the first study on pederasts (cf. Hahn, *Nos Ancêtres les pervers*, p. 41).

17. The term entered the common speech of the English and French in the 1890s.

18. Ulrichs, *Recherche au sujet de l'énigme de l'amour de l'homme pour l'homme* (1864–1869), cited by Hahn, *Nos Ancêtres les pervers*, p. 80.

19. Hahn, *Nos Ancêtres les pervers*, p. 82; cf. also Robert A. Nye, "Sex Difference and Male Homosexuality in French Medical Discourse, 1830–1930," *Bulletin of the History of Medicine* 63 (1989): 32–51.

20. Jeffrey Weeks, "Questions of Identity," in Caplan, ed., *The Cultural Construction of Sexuality*, pp. 31–51.

21. *Les Psychopathies sexuelles* went through numerous editions between 1886 and 1903 and became the inspiration for thousands of publications on homosexuality.

22. Weeks, "Questions of Identity," p. 35.

23. Foucault, *La Volonté de savoir*, p. 59.

24. Jeffrey Weeks, *Sex, Politics and Society*, p. 10; and Nye, "Sex Difference and Male Homosexuality," p. 32.

25. Segal, *Slow Motion*, p. 134.

26. Nye, "Sex Difference and Male Homosexuality," p. 44.

27. Birke, *Women, Feminism, and Biology*, pp. 22–23.

28. Weeks, "Questions of Identity," p. 36.

29. Weeks, *Sexuality and Its Discontents*, p. 90.

30. Jonathan Ned Katz, "The Invention of Heterosexuality," *Socialist Review* 1 (1990): 7–34.

31. Weeks, *Sexuality and Its Discontents*.

32. Frederick L. Whitam, "Culturally Invariable Properties of Male Homosexuality," *Archives of Sexual Behavior* 12, no. 3 (1983): 207–26.

33. Freud, "L'analyse avec fin et l'analyse sans fin" (1937), in *Résultats, idées, problèmes*, vol. 2 (Paris: PUF, 1985), p. 259.

34. See the theories of Ulrichs and Hirschfeld.

35. Freud, *Three Essays on the Theory of Sexuality*, trans. Strachey.

36. Freud, *Leonardo da Vinci and a Memory of His Childhood*, trans. Tyson, p. 36.

37. Freud, *Three Essays on the Theory of Sexuality*.

38. Letter from Freud to Mrs. N. N., dated April 9, 1935, in *Letters of Sigmund Freud*, p. 423 (emphasis added, because this phrase will cause a great deal of ink to flow, as we shall later see).

39. Alfred Kinsey et al., *Sexual Behavior in the Human Male*. Some two decades later, William H. Masters and Virginia E. Johnson supported Kinsey's theory with their own research in *Homosexuality in Perspective*.

40. Kinsey's research on 16,000 white Americans was to show that if only 4 percent of the male population was exclusively homosexual from puberty on, 37 percent of men (and 19 percent of women) acknowledged having had at least one homosexual experience leading to orgasm between puberty and adulthood. Furthermore, 30 percent had had at least one casual homosexual experience between the ages of sixteen and fifty-five.

41. Alan P. Bell and Martin S. Weinberg, *Homosexualities*. In a previous article, Alan Bell makes this important clarification: "In regard to how they (adult homosexuals) rated themselves during adolescence, . . . about one-third of them were predominantly *heterosexual* in their behaviors . . . and more than a quarter in their feelings. . . . Forty percent of the males had changes in their feelings and behavior ratings during adolescence. . . . Almost two-thirds of both males and females experienced heterosexual arousal. . . . A lengthy and detailed explanation of a person's self ratings on the Kinsey scale over the course of his or her lifetime . . . enables [one] to get a sense of the ebb and flow of homosexual versus heterosexual experience, to challenge the commonly held assumption that one is *either* homosexual or heterosexual." Bell, in "The Appraisal of Homosexuality," an

unpublished paper for the Kinsey Summer Conference in 1976, quoted by Kenneth Plummer, *The Making of the Modern Homosexual*, pp. 58–59.

42. Hite, *The Hite Report on Male Sexuality*, p. 45.
43. Lonnie G. Nungesser, *Homosexual Acts: Actors and Identities*, p. viii.
44. Robert Stoller, *Sex and Gender*, vol. 2, *The Transsexual Experiment*, p. 199.
45. Henry Abelove, "Freud, Male Homosexuality and the Americans," *Dissent* 33 (Winter 1986): 68.
46. Richard C. Friedman, *Male Homosexuality*, p. xi.
47. Nungesser, *Homosexual Acts*, p. 27.
48. G. Dörner, *Hormones and Brain Differentiation* (Amsterdam: Elsinber, 1976). See also the works of Simon Levay cited by *Le Point*, September 21, 1991, p. 88.
49. Money, Schwartz, and Lewis have noticed the frequency of bisexuality or homosexuality in women who have been treated for an adrenogenital syndrome, as well as that of homosexuality among a group of boys suffering in adolescence from an excessive development of mammary tissues. But all these observations involve so many exceptions that one must refrain from generalizing. Money, Schwartz, and Lewis, "Adult Heterosexual Status and Fetal Hormonal Masculinization and Demasculinization," in *Psychoneuroendocrinology* 9, r 4 (1984): 405–15, cited by Friedman, *Male Homosexuality*, p. 15.
50. F. J. Kallman, *Heredity in Health and Mental Disorder* (New York: Norton, 1953).
51. Richard Green, *The "Sissy Boy Syndrome" and the Development of Homosexuality*; cf. also Green et al., "Masculine or Feminine Gender Identity in Boys," *Sex Roles* 12, nos. 11–12 (1985): 1155–62.
52. Bernard Zuger, "Early Effeminate Behaviors in Boys," *Journal of Nervous and Mental Disease* 172 (February 1984): 90–97.
53. Richard A. Isay, "Homosexuality in Homosexual and Heterosexual Men," in Fogel, ed., *The Psychology of Men*, pp. 277–99.
54. Green, *The "Sissy Boy Syndrome,"* p. 305.
55. Edmund White, *A Boy's Own Story*.
56. Ibid.
57. Edmund White, *The Beautiful Room Is Empty*.
58. Ibid.

59. Puig's novel has been made into a film, *Kiss of the Spider Woman* (United States–Brazil, 1985), as well as an award-winning Broadway musical.
60. Puig, *Kiss of the Spider Woman*, cf. p. 198.
61. Ibid., pp. 232–33.
62. On the origin and etymology of the word *gay*, cf. Cheris Kramare and Paula A. Treichler, *A Feminist Dictionary* (London: Pandora, 1985).
63. Gary Kinsman, "Men Loving Men: The Challenge of Gay Liberation," in Kimmel and Messner, eds., *Men's Lives*, p. 513.
64. Dennis Altman, *The Homosexualization of America, the Americanization of the Homosexual.*
65. A real gay community is not limited to bars, clubs, baths, restaurants . . . nor to a network of friendships. It is, rather, a collection of institutions, including social and political clubs, publications, bookstores, religious groups, community centers, radio stations, theater companies, etc., that represent at once a feeling of shared values and a desire to assert one's homosexuality as an important part of one's life and no longer as something private and hidden. Ibid.
66. Ibid., p. 39.
67. Weeks criticized the essentialism of Adrienne Rich, who maintains that all women are naturally lesbian (cf. Weeks, "Questions of Identity," pp. 47–48); cf. also Plummer, *The Making of the Modern Homosexual.*
68. Gregory M. Herek, "On Heterosexual Masculinity," *American Behavioral Scientist* 29 (May–June 1986): 569. Cf. also the writer Gore Vidal.
69. Katz, "The Invention of Heterosexuality," pp. 22–23.
70. Nungesser, *Homosexual Acts*, p. 26.
71. See, among others, Robert W. Connell, Tim Carrigan, and John Lee, "Toward a New Sociology of Masculinity," in Brod, ed., *The Making of Masculinities*, pp. 63–100. See also Herek, "On Heterosexual Masculinity."
72. Weeks, *Sexuality and Its Discontents*, p. 86.
73. Foucault, *History of Sexuality* 2:192.
74. Ibid., p. 190.
75. Thompson, "A New Vision of Masculinity," p. 76; Herek, "On Heterosexual Masculinity," p. 567.
77. Stephen F. Morin and Lonnie Nungesser, "Can Homophobia Be Cured?" in Lewis, ed., *Men in Difficult Times*, p. 266.

78. Bruce Feirstein, *Real Men Don't Eat Quiche!* (New York: Pocket Books, 1982).

79. The word was invented in 1972 by George Weinberg, who defined it as the "fear of being in contact with homosexuals."

80. Reynaud, *La Sainte virilité*, p. 76.

81. Stephen F. Morin and Ellen M. Garfinkle, "Male Homophobia," *Journal of Social Issues* 34 (1978): 37.

82. Gregory Lehne, "Homophobia Among Men," in Kimmel and Messner, eds., *Men's Lives*, pp. 416–29.

83. Cf. Wainwright Churchill, *Homosexual Behavior Among Males* (New York: Hawthorne, 1967; rpt., Englewood Cliffs, N.J.: Prentice-Hall, 1971); and Marion Brown and Donald M. Amoroso, "Attitudes Toward Homosexuality Among West Indian Male and Female College Students," *Journal of Social Psychology* 97 (February 1975): 163–68.

84. Seventy percent of heterosexual men and women questioned in 1977 answered that they thought "homosexual men are not fully masculine." Cf. Carol Tavris, "Men and Women Report Their Views on Masculinity," *Psychology Today* (January 1977): 35.

85. This explanation was given as early as 1914 by Sándor Ferenczi, "L'homoérotisme: Nosologie de l'homosexualité masculine," *Psychanalyse* 2 (Paris: Payot, 1978), pp. 117–29.

86. Dr. Richard A. Isay, in the *New York Times*, July 10, 1990.

87. In January 1981 the magazine *Elle* published a survey that revealed parents' inability to tolerate the idea of having a homosexual child; also, 61 percent of the persons questioned refused to have a homosexual president of the Republic, and 64 percent a homosexual educator. Only 24 percent thought homosexuality was one way of experiencing one's sexuality, compared to 42 percent who said it was an illness and 22 percent a sexual perversion to be fought. In July 1991, 37 percent of those surveyed confessed that they could not accept homosexuality as compared to 58 percent who did accept it (*L'Evénement du jeudi*, July 4–10, 1991).

88. In another study of 2,800 schoolchildren aged twelve to seventeen, 75 percent of the boys and 50 percent of the girls said they would not like to have a homosexual neighbor! Result: antigay violence is given the appear-

ance of legitimacy. Isay, *New York Times*, July 10, 1990.

89. The police department of the State of New York recorded three times more homosexual victims in the first six
months of 1990 than during the same period of the preceding year. In 1989 more than seven thousand incidents
of violence against homosexuals were counted in the
United States, including sixty-two murders. The figures
from the 1980s show a constant increase.

90. Isay, *New York Times*, July 10, 1990.

91. Morin and Garfinkle, "Male Homophobia," p. 32.

92. Cited by Herek, "On Heterosexual Masculinity," pp.
575.

93. *The Hite Report on Male Sexuality*, p. 25. Those who
experienced a friendship of this sort say it was only during their years as a student and that now they are no
longer close to that friend. A few others mention men in
their families to whom they are or have been close. But
many men do not have, and never have had, a best friend.
Shere Hite points out that many friendships between
men are based on admiration, but very few men describe
shared intimacy, even tenderness. Certain men even say
they could have had intimate friends but that they broke
off the friendship out of fear of homosexual feelings.

94. Freud, "Sur quelques mécanismes névrotiques dans la
jalousie, la paranoïa et l'homosexualité" (1922), in
Névrose, psychose et perversion (Paris: PUF, 1973), p. 281.

95. Robert R. Bell, *Worlds of Friendship*, p. 79. The same
observation is made by Lillian Rubin, *Intimate
Strangers*.

96. Morin and Garfinkle, "Male Homophobia," p. 41.

97. Guy Corneau, *Père manquant, fils manqué*, p. 29.

98. Ibid., p. 28.

Part Two: Being a Man (XY)

1. Paul Olsen, *Sons and Mothers*, p. 12.

2. Theweleit, *Male Fantasies*, vol. 1, *Women, Flood, Bodies, History*.

3. Le Rider, *Le Cas Otto Weininger*, p. 195: Weininger
gives the advantage to the Jew over the woman, even so.
She is mere nothingness, whereas the Jew embodies the
force of the negative.

4. Weininger, *Sexe et caractère*, p. 247 (emphasis added).

One finds similar analyses in Theodor Lessing, *La Haine de soi* (Berlin, 1930).

5. Cf. Le Rider, *Le Cas Otto Weininger* and *Modernité viennoise*.

6. Mary Dearborn, *The Happiest Man Alive: A Biography of Henry Miller*, pp. 84–86, 101, 147, 154–55, 161–76.

7. Emile Delavenay, *D. H. Lawrence*, pp. 93, 131, 175, 387–88.

8. Lynn, *Hemingway*, pp. 255, 324–25.

9. Freud, "Little Hans" (1909), in *Les Cinq psychanalyses* (*Five Lectures on Psychoanalysis* [1910]), p. 116n1. A similar analysis can be found in Freud's *Leonardo da Vinci and a Memory of His Childhood*.

10. John Stoltenberg's *Refusing to Be a Man* was hailed by many American feminists as being both "courageous" (Gloria Steinem) and liberating.

11. Stoltenberg, *Refusing to Be a Man*, p. 28.

12. Ibid.

13. Ibid., p. 88.

14. Published in Berlin in 1923, Hermann Ungar's *Les Mutilés* was not translated from the Czech and published in France until 1987.

15. A process advocated by Nietzsche to resolve the fundamental problem of man and woman. The mistake would be, in his eyes, to "deny the most abysmal antagonism between them and the necessity of an eternally hostile tension." Nietzsche, *Beyond Good and Evil*, trans. Walter Kaufmann (New York: Random House, 1966), sec. 238, p. 166.

16. Ferdinando Camon, *The Sickness Called Man*.

17. Mitscherlich and Dierichs, *Des Hommes*, p. 318.

18. See the many studies cited by Joseph Pleck, "The Contemporary Man," in Kimmel and Messner, eds., *Men's Lives*, pp. 593–94.

19. Michael S. Kimmel and Jeffrey Fracher, "Hard Issues and Soft Spots," in ibid., pp. 477, 481. See also the hero of Philip Roth's *The Counterlife*, who cannot get an erection and no longer feels like a man.

20. See, for example, Thomas McGuane's hero in *The Man Who Had Lost His Name*.

21. As witness, for instance, *A Weekend in Michigan* by Richard Ford (1986); *L'Insurrection* by Peter Rosei (1987); the heroes of *La Séduction* (1985) and *La Monarque* (1988) by Knut Faldbakken; *Money* (1984) by Martin

Amis; *Pourquoi moi?* (1984–1987) by Michaël Krüger; *Les Virginités* (1990) by Daniel Zimmerman; and *Drame privé* (1990) by Michael Delisle.

5: The Mutilated Man

1. I am borrowing much of what follows from the brilliant lecture by Merete Gerlach-Nielsen, "Essai sur l'évolution du rôle masculin au Danemark, 1975–1985," given in Athens in 1985 at the UNESCO international conference of experts on the new roles of men and women in private and public life. Part of this lecture was published by *La Gazette des femmes* 8 (Quebec, July–August 1986): 10–12.
2. "Le" is the first name of the novel's protagonist. In Danish it means both "death's scythe" and "laughter." The novel was published by Lindhardt and Ringhof in 1977.
3. Unlike "macho," which primarily signifies the superiority of men over women, "the tough guy" says more about the man himself: he is a machine-man who represses his feelings and treats his body like a tool.
4. Faldbakken, *Le Journal d'Adam*, p. 70.
5. Ibid., p. 113.
6. Ibid., p. 269.
7. Norman Mailer, *The Prisoner of Sex.*
8. Chesler, *La Mâle donne*, pp. 53ff.
9. Mitscherlich and Dierichs, *Des Hommes*, pp. 20–22, 368.
10. David and Brannon, *The Forty-Nine Percent Majority.*
11. If you can keep your head when all about you
   Are losing theirs and blaming it on you,
   If you can trust yourself when all men doubt you,
   But make allowance for their doubting too;
   If you can wait and not be tired by waiting,
   Or being lied about, don't deal in lies,
   Or being hated don't give way to hating,
   And yet don't look too good, nor talk too wise:
   If you can dream—and not make dreams your master;
   If you can think—and not make thoughts your aim;
   If you can meet with Triumph and Disaster
   And treat those two impostors just the same;
   If you can bear to hear the truth you've spoken
   Twisted by knaves to make a trap for fools,

Or watch the things you gave your life to, broken,
And stoop and build 'em up with worn-out tools:
If you can make one heap of all your winnings
And risk it on one turn of pitch-and-toss,
And lose, and start again at your beginnings
And never breathe a word about your loss;
If you can force your heart and nerve and sinew
To serve your turn long after they are gone,
And so hold on when there is nothing in you
Except the Will which says to them: "Hold on!"

If you can talk with crowds and keep your virtue,
Or walk with Kings—nor lose the common touch,
If neither foes nor loving friends can hurt you,
If all men count with you, but none too much;
If you can fill the unforgiving minute
With sixty seconds' worth of distance run,
Yours is the Earth and everything that's in it,
And—which is more—you'll be a Man, my son!

12. Expression used by Helga Dierichs in Mitscherlich and Dierichs, *Des hommes*, p. 12.

13. See Jack Balswick, "Types of Inexpressive Male Roles," in Lewis, ed., *Men in Difficult Times*, pp. 111–17; Robert W. Connell, *Gender and Power*; Filene, *Him/Her/Self*; Lydia Flem, "Le stade du cowboy," *Le Genre humain*, no. 10 (June 1984): 101–15.

14. Flem, "Le stade du cowboy," p. 103.

15. Balswick, "Types of Inexpressive Male Roles," pp. 114–15.

16. The cowboy is afraid of woman, who "distracts him from solitude, nomadism, the perfection and the aesthetic of heroic death. She harps upon forming roots, entering the flow of time . . . everything that is opposed to male fulguration. . . . Fundamentally virgin and solitary, despite his phallic asset, he is and remains affectively impotent." Flem, "Le stade du cowboy," pp. 104–5.

17. In *Rambo II* (1985), there is reason to think he feels something for a young woman warrior who is serving as his interpreter. But scarcely has she expressed her admiration for him than she is killed and disappears from the film.

18. File on *Terminator 2: Judgment Day* (1991) in *Mad Movies*, no. 73 (September 1991).

19. And for a good reason: a machine does not have a mother.

20. See the criticism of the male sexual role by Pleck, *The Myth of Masculinity*, p. 198.
21. Mitscherlich and Dierichs, *Des Hommes*, p. 35.
22. Connell, *Gender and Power*, pp. 185–88.
23. Peter Härtling, *Hubert; ou, Le retour à Casablanca* (1978), p. 252.
24. Cf. Lynn, *Hemingway*, p. 539.
25. "His chronic depression, his insomnia, his inferiority complexes, his fierce jealousy, his brutal competitiveness, the perverse humiliation of his friends, are constantly visible to the observer with a practiced eye. More and more, 'pure' masculinity took the form of an authentic paranoia, a self-destructiveness and a fear of death that culminated in a terrible nervous depression and suicide." Segal, *Slow Motion*, pp. 111–12.
26. The two members of the Garden of Eden (i.e., paradise) exchange sexual identities. Here Hemingway could enjoy the confusion of sexes that had plagued him from childhood on. In 1948 he wrote in his journal: "She [his wife Mary] has always wanted to be a boy and thinks as a boy. . . . She loves to be my girls [sic], which I love to be. . . . I loved feeling the embrace of Mary . . . quite outside of all tribal law. On the night of December 19th we worked out these things and I have never been happier." Cf. Lynn, *Hemingway*, p. 533.
27. Ibid., pp. 520–21.
28. Segal, *Slow Motion*, pp. 114–15.
29. Gilmore, *Manhood in the Making*, p. 77, has observed the ravages of this compulsive masculinity in all sorts of different patriarchal societies.
30. Bukowski, *Women*. These attitudes show up time and again in Bukowski's work.
31. Norman Mailer, *Tough Guys Don't Dance*.
32. Freud, "La féminité" (1932) in *New Introductory Lectures on Psychoanalysis* (1933), *SE*, vol. 22, and "Sur la sexualité féminine" (1931), in *La Vie sexuelle*, p. 146.
33. Janine Chasseguet-Smirgel is one of the latest to have reset the clock. Cf. *Le Deux arbres du jardin*, pp. 12–14.
34. See Danielle Flamant-Paparatti, *Le Journal de Lucas*. The author was also kind enough to show me an unpublished article: "L'envie des attributs sexuels féminins et des fonctions bio-psycho-socio-culturelles de l'autre sexe chez Louis XIII enfant," an analysis of the young king's desires based on the *Journal de Jean Héroard*, Fayard, 1989.

35. Jacques Lacan, "La signification du Phallus," lecture given in 1958 and published for the first time in his *Ecrits*, pp. 685–95.

36. Marcelle Marini, *Lacan*, p. 61. The proof lies in the psychosis known by the name of "exclusion from the Name of the Father," attributed to the failure of the paternal metaphor that has not allowed the subject "to evoke the signification of the phallus."

37. Lacan, *Ecrits*, p. 692: "One can say that this signifier is chosen as the most salient of what one can capture of the reality of sexual copulation: as also the most symbolic in the literal (topographical) sense of this word, since it is *equivalent* to the logical copula. One can also say that through its turgidity, it is the image of the vital flux as it passes in generation."

38. Ibid., p. 695.

39. In Marini, *Lacan*, p. 62.

40. Badinter, *L'Un est l'autre*. As is very often true of psychoanalysts, Lacan is totally indifferent to history, social reality, and the battle of the sexes.

41. Arthur Brittan, *Masculinity and Power*, p. 72.

42. Cited by Chesler, *La Mâle donne*, p. 225.

43. Michael S. Kimmel and Jeffrey Fracher, "Counseling Men About Sexuality," p. 475.

44. Alberto Moravia, *Moi et lui* (1971), p. 81.

45. Leonore Tiefer, "In Pursuit of the Perfect Penis," in Kimmel, ed., *Changing Men*, pp. 165–84; see also Geneviève Delaisi de Parseval, ed., *Les Sexes de l'homme*.

46. Tiefer, "In Pursuit of the Perfect Penis," p. 169, quotes the figure given by a French urologist according to whom, during the year 1970 alone, 5,000 men were implanted with a penile prosthesis.

47. Reynaud, *La Sainte virilité*, pp. 53–54.

48. Alain Finkielkraut and Pascal Bruckner, *Le Nouveau désordre amoureux*, p. 71.

49. Reynaud, *La Sainte virilité*, p. 73.

50. Finkielkraut and Bruckner, *Le Nouveau désordre amoureux*, p. 78.

51. Ibid., p. 96. Corneau, *Père manquant, fils manqué*, p. 100, also speaks of the fantasy of the motherly prostitute.

52. Excerpt quoted by Gloria Steinem, "The Myth of the Masculine Mystique," in Pleck and Sayers, eds., *Men and Masculinity*, p. 135.

53. Tim Beneke recalls that in September 1980, a survey by

Cosmopolitan magazine of 106,000 anonymous women showed that 24 percent of them had been raped (Beneke, *Men on Rape*). An excerpt from this book was reprinted in Kimmel and Messner, eds., *Men's Lives*, pp. 399–405.

54. In Los Angeles, one woman out of three will at some time in her life be the victim of an act of sexual aggression.

55. Quoted by Beneke in Kimmel and Messner, eds., *Men's Lives*, p. 400.

56. Susan Griffin, "Rape: The All-American Crime," *Ramparts*, September 1971.

57. Susan Brownmiller, *Against Our Will: Men, Women, and Rape.*

58. Andrea Dworkin, *Pornography: Men Possessing Women.*

59. Kendall Segel-Evans, "Rape Prevention and Masculinity," in Abbott, ed., *New Men, New Minds*, p. 118.

60. Peggy Reeves-Sanday, "Rape and the Silencing of the Feminine," in Tanaselli and Porter, eds., *Rape.*

61. Statistics cited by Segal, *Slow Motion*, pp. 239–40.

62. In 1980, 1,886 complaints of rape were lodged in France, compared to 4,582 in 1990 (*Statistiques de la police judiciaire: Documentation française*).

63. David Lisak, "Sexual Aggression, Masculinity, and Fathers," *Signs* 16 (Winter 1991): 238–62.

64. Sidney M. Jourard, *The Transparent Self.*

65. Statistics from the U.S. Department of Health (1976). Today, in France, life expectancy for women is 81.1 years and for men 73 years.

66. Iceland is an interesting exception: the gap between men's and women's mortality is 5.5 years. However, this country is known for its egalitarian policy with respect to the sexes.

67. Ashley Montague, *The Natural Superiority of Women* (New York: Macmillan, 1953).

68. Farrell, *The Liberated Man*; Feigen-Fasteau, *Le Robot mâle.*

69. In a very interesting article about men and AIDS, Michael S. Kimmel and Martin P. Levine show how the traditional model of manliness, which promotes adventure and risk, is contrary to prevention, which consists in avoiding them. All the AIDS prevention campaigns must be used to convince people that virility is not necessarily tied to a risk of death but is compatible with prudence. Cf. "Men and AIDS," in Kimmel and Messner, eds., *Men's Lives*, pp. 344–54.

70. James Harrison, "Warning: The Male Sex Role May Be Dangerous to Your Health," *Journal of Social Issues* 34 (1978): 71.

71. Kenneth Clatterbaugh, *Contemporary Perspectives on Masculinity*, p. 75.

72. In 1988 H. Wallot, a professor at the University of Quebec, expressed surprise that there was no Council on Men's Conditions, given the precariousness of men's health: he recalled that four men for every one woman suffered from drug addiction or alcoholism, and three for every one committed suicide; cf. Corneau, *Père manquant, fils manqué*, pp. 9–10.

73. Harrison, "Warning," p. 83.

74. Thompson, "A New Vision of Masculinity."

75. Definition in the *Dictionnaire Robert*.

76. Americans, such as Robert Bly, speak of the "soft male," or the "lovely boy." This lovely boy is closer to the soft man than the gentle man. Bly describes him as passive, evasive, and compares him to a "wet hen" (*Iron John* [New York: Vintage Books, 1990]).

77. Kimmel, "The Contemporary Crisis of Masculinity in Historical Perspective," p. 134.

78. Tavris, "Men and Women Report Their Views on Masculinity," pp. 35–42.

79. Sofres survey for *Le Nouvel Observateur*, June 13–19, 1991, p. 8.

80. Peter G. Filene, "Between a Rock and a Soft Place: A Century of American Manhood," *South Atlantic Quarterly* 84 (Fall 1985): 339–55.

81. Roth, *The Anatomy Lesson*.

82. "My manhood! How I loathed being a man, with its fierce responsibilities, its tale of ceaseless strength, its passionate and stupid bravado. . . . I knew the tyranny and the snare of maleness . . . a quivering mass of insecurities." Tom, the Southerner, will "go up" to New York to undergo psychoanalysis with a woman. He will confess to her that he is a permanently defeated man: "I'm a completely defeated male. . . . I've been neutered by life and circumstances." The most difficult thing about the male condition: "They don't teach us how to love. It's a secret they keep from us. . . . When a woman loves us we're overpowered by it, filled with dread, helpless and chastened before it. . . . We have nothing to return." Conroy, *The Prince of Tides*, pp. 55, 439–40.

83. A film ad promoting road safety in France, chastising the man at the wheel so intoxicated by speed that he causes an accident, concluded with this message: Macho = booboo.

84. Jerome Bernstein, "The Decline of Masculine Rites of Passage," in Madhi, Foster, and Littel, eds., *Betwixt and Between*, p. 145. He explains that he uses "female hero" rather than the more usual term "heroine," which depicts a weak, dependent, passive woman instead of emphasizing the "phallic" aspect of female power.

85. Bly, *Iron John: A Book About Men*, p. 2.

86. Ibid., p. 3.

87. Ibid., p. 4.

88. Günter Grass, *The Flounder*.

89. Ibid., p. 27.

90. Bernstein, "The Decline of Masculine Rites of Passage," p. 151.

91. Robert Bly, who takes great care to distinguish himself from vulgar macho men, warns his troops that "attacking the mother . . . probably does not accomplish much" (*Iron John*, p. 11).

92. Franz Kafka, *Letter to His Father*, pp. 21, 15, 25, 35. Another form of the terrifying father is given us by Henry Roth, in *L'or de la terre promise* (1933).

93. Bellow, *Seize the Day*.

94. White, *The Beautiful Room Is Empty*.

95. Conroy, *The Great Santini* and *The Prince of Tides*.

96. Härtling, *Hubert; ou, Le retour à Casablanca*.

97. François-Marie Bannier, *Balthazar, fils de famille*.

98. *The Hite Report on Male Sexuality*, pp. 17–24.

99. Chesler, *La mâle donne*, p. 215.

100. For the statistics concerning the United States, Canada, Quebec, France, and Switzerland, see Corneau, *Père manquant, fils manqué*, pp. 18–19.

101. The "missing father" refers "as much to the father's psychological absence as to his physical absence, absence of mind, emotional absence." The expression also contains the notion "of a father who, despite his physical presence, does not behave in an acceptable way; here I am thinking of authoritarian fathers, crushing and envious of the talents of their sons, in whom they trample any attempt at self-assertion; I am thinking of alcoholic fathers, whose emotional instability maintains the sons in a permanent state of insecurity." Ibid., p. 19.

102. "He was not able to feel sufficiently confirmed and rendered secure by the presence of his father to move on to the adult stage. Or, the example of a father who was violent, soft, or always drunk repelled him to the point that he flatly refused to identify with the male." Ibid., pp. 19–20.
103. Bly, *Iron John*, p. 24.
104. "Call of the Wild Men," *New York Times Magazine*, October 14, 1990, pp. 34–47.
105. Mitscherlich and Dierichs make the same observation for Germany (cf. *Des hommes*, pp. 322–23).
106. Osherson, *Finding Our Fathers*.
107. Ibid., p. 12.
108. Particularly toward other men.
109. This expression is often used by Bly and Osherson.
110. Robert Bly says that the absent father of the industrial society—who leaves the house early in the morning and does not return until late in the evening—is often fantasized by the little boy as "a demoniacal figure." Cf. "What Men Really Want," in Abbott, ed., *New Men, New Minds*, p. 178.
111. See especially White, *A Boy's Own Story*, pp. 143, 172.
112. Samuel Osherson, John Lee (in *The Flying Boy*), and numerous psychoanalysts have testified that, in therapy, sons are reconciled more quickly with their mothers than with their fathers.
113. Osherson, *Finding Our Fathers*, p. 40.
114. Corneau, *Père manquant, fils manqué*, p. 39.
115. Ibid., pp. 39–40.
116. Ibid., pp. 40–41.
117. This theme runs through the whole of Philip Roth's work and is also found in the autobiographical novels of Edmund White as well as in Jean-Marc Roberts's *Mon Père américain* (Paris: Seuil, 1988), pp. 130, 153.
118. Keith Thompson in Abbott, ed., *New Men, New Minds*, p. 174. See also the story of Julien in Corneau, *Père manquant, fils manqué*, pp. 75–76, as well as the case of the German Werner, in Mitscherlich and Dierichs, *Des Hommes*, pp. 29–31, 46, 59.
119. In Julia Kristeva's *Les Samouraïs* (Paris: Fayard, 1990), one of the female characters says that a man, a real man, is a rare phenomenon in the United States. One finds more women-men, child-men, and adolescent-men (pp. 307–8).

120. Marie-Louise von Franz, *Puer Aeternus* (Boston: Sigo, 1991).

121. Lee, *The Flying Boy*.

122. Ibid., pp. 8–9. Farther on he says: "My Stomach has always been connected to my mother's" (p. 22).

123. Ibid., p. 39.

124. Ibid., p. 109.

125. See the novels of the Norwegian Knut Faldbakken, or those of the Dane Hans-Jorgen Nielsen (e.g., *L'Ange du football*, 1979), as well as those of Soeren K. Barsoee (e.g., *Le Groupe masculin*, 1985).

126. Barsoee, *Le Group masculin*, quoted and translated by Gerlach-Nielsen.

127. Gerlach-Nielsen, text of the Athens Conference, 1985.

128. Cf. the Quebecois Marc Chabot or the American John Stoltenberg (*Refusing to Be a Man*).

129. Franklin Abbott, ed., *New Men, New Minds*, p. 2.

130. Connell, "A Whole New World," *Gender and Society* 14 (December 1990): 467.

131. Thompson, "A New Vision of Masculinity," p. 589.

132. Segal, *Slow Motion*, pp. 261–69, cites, in no particular order, the spectacular increase over the last fifteen years in the number of women implicated in violent crimes; the behavior of girls in gangs of hooligans; studies on women's prisons and the cruelty of their wardens in the nineteenth century, and so forth. More commonplace, though constantly denied, is maternal violence, visible or invisible. In France, 700 children die every year following parental abuse, 50,000 are tortured by their parents, not to mention all those who suffer mental and psychological violence that leaves no visible trace. It is known that in the great majority of cases, the mother is the one responsible for these acts.

133. In 1984 the two well-known American psychologists Eleanor E. Maccoby and Carol N. Jacklin published the results of a study on aggressiveness conducted over ten years on 275 children. Taking into account biological, psychological, and social factors, they concluded that the similarities between the sexes were much more significant than the differences. Cf. Maccoby and Jacklin, "Neonatal Sex-steroid Hormones and Muscular Strength of Boys and Girls in the First Three Years," *Developmental Psychobiology* 20, no. 3 (May 1984): 459–72.

134. Freud, *Civilization and Its Discontents* (1929), chap. 5.
135. See chapter 4 of the present volume, on homophobia. As noted, even today many French or American surveys show that a majority of the public finds the idea of a homosexual president or a homosexual educator shocking. In the eyes of many of our contemporaries, the homosexual is a person potentially dangerous to children.
136. Freud, *Letters of Sigmund Freud*, p. 423 (emphasis added): "*sexual* development" here refers to the broad (Freudian) meaning of psychic development.
137. In the APA the word *psychiatrist* is used in the broadest sense, which includes psychoanalysis (psychoanalysts).
138. Pierre Thuillier, "L'homosexualité devant la psychiatrie," *La Recherche* 20 (September 1989): 1128–39.
139. Ibid., p. 1128.
140. Brian Miller, "Gay Fathers and Their Children," *Family Coordinator* (October 1979): 545; see also Michel Bon and Antoine d'Arc, *Rapport sur l'homosexualité de l'homme*.
141. Thuillier, "L'homosexualité devant la psychiatrie," p. 1136.
142. Groddeck, *Le Livre du ça*, pp. 247–49.
143. "*The human being is bisexual throughout his life and remains such during his entire existence*. At the very most, one era or another will manage—in the guise of a concession to morality, to fashion—to curb homosexuality, meaning it is not annihilated, but only repressed. And just as there are no purely heterosexual people, there are no pure homosexuals." Ibid., p. 255 (emphasis added).
144. Cited by Lehne, "Homophobia Among Men," p. 419.
145. A number of therapists continue to advise homosexuals to start families as a cure for their illness. Cf. Robert L. Barret and Bryan E. Robinson, *Gay Fathers*, pp. 45–46.
146. Gordon Murray, "The Gay Side of Manhood," in Abbott, ed., *New Men, New Minds*, p. 135.
147. Katz, "The Invention of Heterosexuality," *Socialist Review* 1 (1990): 7–34.
148. Sheila Jeffreys, *Anticlimax: A Feminist Perspective and the Sexual Revolution*.
149. The word *heterosexuality* was not in use until the 1890s.
150. Katz, "The Invention of Heterosexuality," p. 16.
151. Ibid., p. 19.
152. An expression brought back into use with well-known

success by Adrienne Rich in 1980 in the journal *Signs*.

153. The word *heterocentrism* was coined by Lillian Faderman.

154. Kinsman, "Men Loving Men," p. 506.

155. Ibid., p. 515.

156. Stanley Keleman, *In Defense of Heterosexuality* (Berkeley, 1982), cited by Katz, "The Invention of Heterosexuality," p. 28.

157. John d'Emilio and Estelle B. Freedman, *Intimate Matters: A History of Sexuality in America*.

158. Altman, *The Homosexualization of America*, p. 1.

159. Bon and d'Arc, *Rapport sur l'homosexualité de l'homme*, p. 269.

160. Corneau, *Père manquant, fils manqué*, p. 68.

161. Seymour Kleinberg, "The New Masculinity of Gay Men, and Beyond," in Kimmel and Messner, eds., *Men's Lives*, pp. 101–14.

162. Kleinberg, "The New Masculinity of Gay Men," p. 89.

163. Kinsman, "Men Loving Men," p. 514.

164. In the large-scale study by Bell and Weinberg, nearly a quarter of homosexuals said they regretted their homosexuality (compared to the three-fourths who accepted it). The same proportion tended to think that "homosexuality was an emotional illness, that they would be upset if their own child was to become a homosexual and wished they had been given a magic pill for heterosexuality at birth." Bell and Weinberg, *Homosexualités*, pp. 152–54.

    A survey carried out among readers of the French homophile magazine *Arcadie* yielded noticeably different results. On a conscious level the great majority of Arcadians, who are by definition active militants in the homosexual movement, accept their homosexuality (93 percent answered yes, and 7 percent no). But whether French or American, those who reject it mention the suffering due to their environment, the rejection of society as a whole, conflicts with religion, regret at not having a child, and the problem of loneliness. Cf. Bon and d'Arc, *Rapport sur l'homosexualité de l'homme*, p. 459.

165. An expression used by the psychoanalyst Richard Isay, "Homosexuality in Homosexual and Heterosexual Men," p. 277.

166. Bon and d'Arc, *Rapport sur l'homosexualité de l'homme*, p. 458, and Bell and Weinberg, *Homosexualités*, pp. 245–46.

167. "Homos: La nouvelle vie," *Le Nouvel Observateur*, November 7–13, 1991, pp. 10–15.
168. Kenneth Plummer was the first to reverse the problematics of the illness (*The Making of the Modern Homosexual*, p. 61).

6: The Reconciled Man

1. John Misfud, "Men Cooperating for a Change," in Abbott, ed., *New Men, New Minds*, p. 140.
2. The *Dictionnaire Robert* is mistaken in identifying the androgyne with the hermaphrodite, known to geneticists and physiologists because he actually possesses elements of the genital organs of both sexes. Doctors concerned with this anomaly do not confuse the two terms. One designates a physical anomaly, the other a psychic reality.
3. Cf. Jean Libis, "L'Androgyne et le nocturne," *L'Androgyne* in *Cahiers de l'herméticisme*, pp. 11–26.
4. Ibid., pp. 11–12.
5. *De l'Androgyne* (Paris: Sansot, 1910). See Françoise Cachin, "L'Androgyne du temps de Gustave Moreau," in *Nouvelle revue de psychanalyse*, no. 7 (1973): 63–69.
6. Frédéric Monneyron, "Esthéticisme et androgyne," *L'Androgyne*, in *Cahiers de l'hermétisme*, p. 221.
7. Barbara Ehrenreich, in Kimmel and Messner, eds., *Men's Lives*, p. 34.
8. Sophie Latour, "L'archétype de l'androgyne chez Léopold Ziegler," *L'Androgyne*, in *Cahiers de l'hermétisme*, p. 205.
9. Roland Barthes, "Le Désir de neutre" (1978 lecture), published in *La Règle du jeu*, no. 5 (August 1991): 36–60.
10. John Moreland, "Age and Change in the Adult Male Sex Role," in Kimmel and Messner, eds., *Men's Lives*, pp. 115–24.
11. Erikson, *Childhood and Society*, pp. 266–68.
12. Daniel J. Levinson, *The Seasons of a Man's Life*, chaps. 9, 13, and 15. See also Levinson et al., "Periods of Adult Development in Men: Ages 18–44," *Counseling Psychologist* 6(1976): 21–25.
13. "He enters a transition phase which introduces new questions and different tasks. He looks back at his past, measures how far he has realized his youthful dreams

and all that he has left aside in order to devote himself to them. He can at last rejoin the feminine part of his being." Filene, "Between a Rock and a Soft Place," pp. 348–49.

14. Levinson, *The Seasons of a Man's Life*, p. 242.

15. Sandra Bem, "Gender Schema Theory and Its Implications for Child Development," *Signs*, no. 8 (1983): 598–616.

16. Ibid.

17. See chap. 2 of the present volume.

18. Marc Chabot ("Je viens plaider pour un genre flou"), in "Genre masculin ou genre flou," p. 182. See also Sandra Bem, "Au-delà de l'androgyne: Quelques précepts osés pour une identitésexuelle libérée," in Hurtig and Pichevin, eds., *La Différence des sexes*, p. 270.

19. Michel Maffesoli, *Au Creux des apparences*, p. 257.

20. Badinter, *L'Un est l'autre*.

21. By this I mean the differences duly observed in the way men and women hold a baby, play with it, talk to it, and so on—in other words, bodily differences, differences of voice, of projection.

22. Throughout this chapter, "father" means not only the child's biological father but also any father substitute who gives love and care to a child.

23. Corneau, *Père manquant, fils manqué*, p. 26, explains: "The boys observed were, for the most part, sons of soldiers, abandoned at an early age, or sons of marines whose fathers were absent nine months out the year. One finds in these boys the same atypical developments as in orphans placed in inadequate foster homes or in sons of single-parent families brought up in isolation and lacking father substitutes."

24. Henry B. Biller, "Fatherhood: Implications for Child and Adult Development," in Wolman, ed., *Handbook of Developmental Psychology*, p. 706. See also Henry B. Biller and D. L. Meredith, "Invisible American Father," *Sexual Behavior* 2 (1972): 16–22.

25. For instance, in the United States, researchers well known to the public express radically opposed points of view: the feminist Barbara Ehrenreich notes the evasion of family responsibilities on the part of American men, whereas Joseph Pleck, one of the founders of men's studies, maintains that men are becoming more and more involved in fathering.

26. *Population et Sociétés* (January 1988): in 1986, 86.2 percent were married or cohabiting, in this case.
27. Cf. Institut national des statistiques et des études économiques (hereafter, INSEE), *Les Femmes*, p. 141.
28. Joseph Pleck, "Men's Family Work: Three Perspectives and Some New Data," *Family Coordinator* (October 1979): 481–88.
29. Stanley H. Cath, Alan R. Gurwitt, and Linda Gunsberg, eds., *Fathers and Their Families*, p. 12. See also Diane Ehrensaft, *Parenting Together*; Arlie Hochschild, *The Second Shift*; Michael Kimmel, ed., *Changing Men*; and the English studies by Charles Lewis and Margaret O'Brien, eds., *Reassessing Fatherhood*.
30. Arlie Hochschild's research proves that the new egalitarian fathers who are reacting against their own fathers were nevertheless able to identify with satisfying men (stepfathers, older brothers, and so on), which allowed them to rediscover their mothers without fear of becoming too feminine. Hochschild, *The Second Shift*, pp. 216–18.
31. See the study by Frodi et al. on Swedish families in the *Scandinavian Journal of Psychology* 23 (1982): 53–62. On the Australians, see studies by G. Russell, "Share-Giving Families: An Australian Study," in Michael Lamb, ed., *Non-Traditional Families: Parenting and Child Development*, pp. 139–71; and Lawrence Erlbaum, *The Changing Role of Fathers* (St. Lucia: University of Queensland Press, 1983). See also, for the United States, N. Radin, "Primary Caregiving and Role-Sharing Fathers," in Lamb, ed., *The Father's Role*, pp. 29–57; or, for Israel, Sage in Lamb, ed., *Non-Traditional Families*.
32. See Russell, "Share-Giving Families" and "Problems in Role-Reversed Families," in Lewis and O'Brien, eds., *Reassessing Fatherhood*, pp. 161–79. Russell estimates that there are some 10,000 to 15,000 of this type of family in Australia—that is, about 1 to 2 percent of families in that country.
33. In Sweden, since 1988, parental insurance grants fifteen months' leave to parents for the birth of a child, of which twelve months have an indemnity representing 90 percent of the normal salary. The leave can be taken by both parents but not simultaneously. Up to now, men have been slow to take their parental leave: only one father in five do so, and this for shorter periods than

the maternity leaves taken by women. Cf. Stig Hadenius and Ann Lindgren, *Connaître la Suède* (Institut Suédois, 1990), p. 67. It is true that studies done in 1980 on fathers who had taken one month or more of parental leave showed that they had been the object of negative reactions on the part of their employer (studies cited by Joseph Pleck, "Employment and Fatherhood: Issues and Innovative Policies," in Lamb, ed., *The Father's Role*, pp. 401–2).

34. E. Gronseth, "Work Sharing: A Norwegian Example," in Rapoport and Rapoport, eds., *Working Couples*.

35. *Population et sociétés*, no. 269 (June 1992).

36. In 1984 one child out of five lived in a single-parent family: 90 percent (or 10.5 million) with their mother and 10 percent (or 1.5 million) with their father. Cf. Shirley M. Hanson, "Father-Child Relationships: Beyond Kramer vs. Kramer," *Marriage and Family Review* 9, nos. 3–4 (1986): 135–49.

37. Ibid., p. 145. See also Arnold J. Katz, "Lone Fathers: Perspectives and Implications for Family Policy," *Family Coordinator* (October 1979): 521–27, which enumerates all the studies done on this subject in the United States, Australia, and Canada.

38. Margaret O'Brien, who conducted an in-depth study of fifty-nine London fathers caring for children five to eleven years old, quotes this avowal by one of them: "I'm going to refer to myself as being a mother, because there is no male, no name for men doing the job that I'm doing." O'Brien, "Becoming a Lone Father: Differential Patterns and Experiences," in McKee and O'Brien, eds., *The Father Figure*, p. 184.

39. In 1984 fewer than 10 percent of French divorced fathers had custody of their children.

40. INSEE, *Données sociales*, p. 298.

41. See *Journal de la condition masculine*, nos. 50 (1987) and 62 (1990) and *L'Express*, June 13–19, 1991, p. 80.

42. Despite the absence of national statistics on fathers' demands for custody, a recent study conducted in the Paris law courts seems to confirm this hypothesis: "Of the 200 lawsuits studied, in 161 cases in which there was no conflict over the custody, the mother was awarded it in 145 cases, and the father in only 12 cases. The same study reveals that out of 14 cases of conflict, the mother obtained custody of the child in 9 cases, the

father in 5." Cf. Violette Gorny, *Priorité aux enfants: Un nouveau pouvoir*, p. 87.

43. Henri Leridon and Catherine Villeneuve-Gokalp, "Enquête sur la situation des familles," p. 19.

44. The study done in the early 1970s among the Arcadians indicated that if the great majority remained unmarried, 16 percent had been married at one time, 8 percent were still married at the time of the study, and 13 percent had children (10 percent conceived, 3 percent adopted). But one knows almost nothing about their fatherhood. Cf. Bon and d'Arc, *Rapport sur l'homosexualité de l'homme*, pp. 156 and 163. Alan P. Bell estimates at 20 percent the number of homosexual men who had been married (Bell and Weinberg, *Homosexualités*, p. 202).

45. F. W. Bozett, *Gay and Lesbian Parents*.

46. See Bon and d'Arc, *Rapport sur l'homosexualité*, pp. 166–70; Brian Miller, "Lifestyles of Gay Husbands and Fathers," in Kimmel and Messner, eds., *Men's Lives*, pp. 559–67, and "Gay Fathers and Their Children," *Family Coordinator* (October 1979): 544–52; and Barret and Robinson, *Gay Fathers*.

47. David Leavitt, *The Lost Language of Cranes*.

48. Miller, "Gay Fathers and Their Children," p. 549.

49. In 1977 a national study revealed that homosexuality was the most difficult subject to broach between parents and children (*The General Mills American Family Report* [Minneapolis: General Mills, Consumer Center, 1977]).

50. Barret and Robinson, *Gay Fathers*, pp. 32–33.

51. An in-depth study of forty homosexual fathers, whose forty-eight daughters and forty-two sons were old enough for their sexual preference to be known, belied this myth. Only one of the boys and three of the girls seemed oriented toward homosexuality. Miller, "Lifestyles of Gay Husbands and Fathers," p. 565, and "Gay Fathers and Their Children," pp. 546–47.

52. Miller, in "Gay Fathers and Their Children," p. 547.

53. Bell and Weinberg, *Homosexualités*; Acts of the International Congress, *Le Regard des autres*, p. 65; Barret and Robinson, *Gay Fathers*, pp. 42 and 80.

54. B. Voeller and J. Walters, "Gay Fathers," *Family Coordinator*, no. 27 (1978): 149–57; Miller, "Gay Fathers and Their Children," p. 546.

55. F. W. Bozett, "Gay Fathers: A Review of the Literature," *Journal of Homosexuality* 18 (1989): 137–62; J. Bigner and A. Jacobsen, "The Value of Children for Gay Versus Heterosexual Fathers," *Journal of Homosexuality* 18 (1989): 163–72.

56. Barret and Robinson, *Gay Fathers*, p. 89.

57. For a summary of these studies and controversies, cf. Michael Lamb, ed., *The Father's Role*, pp. 14–16, and Gregory G. Rochlin, *The Masculine Dilemma*.

58. Many factors come into play: for instance, the presence or absence of substitute fathers, or the closeness of the relationship between father and son, is certainly more important than the presence or absence of the father.

59. Theresa L. Jump and Linda Haas, "Fathers in Transition," in Kimmel, ed., *Changing Men*, pp. 98–114.

60. Badinter, *L'Amour en plus*, pp. 365–68.

61. Diane Ehrensaft uses the word *mothering* to designate the daily care given to the child, accompanied by the consciousness of being directly responsible for him or her, which has nothing to do with the few minutes per day that the traditional father devotes to his child. Ehrensaft, "When Women and Men Mother," *Socialist Review*, no. 49 (January–February 1980): 45–46.

62. See Robert A. Fein, "Research on Fathering," *Journal of Social Issues* 3–4, no. 1 (1978): 128. Cf. also Lamb, ed., *The Father's Role*, p. 11.

63. Risman, "Men Who Mother," *Gender and Society* 1 (March 1987): 8–11.

64. Osherson, *Finding Our Fathers*, pp. 133 and 140.

65. John Updike, *Rabbit Run*. The hero leaves after learning of his wife's pregnancy and later abandons his mistress, who is also pregnant. See also Genevieve Delaisi de Parseval, *La Part du père*, and Mary-Joan Gerson, "Tomorrow's Fathers," in Cath, Gurwitt, and Gunsberg, eds., *Fathers and Their Families*, pp. 127–44.

66. Mary-Joan Gerson, "Tomorrow's Fathers," p. 141.

67. In addition to the works already cited, cf. those of T. Berry Brazelton, Michaël Yogman, Kyle Pruett, and others.

68. "Children of three months interact perfectly well with their fathers as with their mothers, according to the same reciprocal and mutually regulated schema. . . . Fathers and mothers demonstrate the same capacity to make the infant play, to capture its attention." Cf. Michaël Yogman, "La Présence du père," *Autrement:*

Objectif bébé, no. 72 (1985): 143–44.

69. Kyle C. Pruett, "The Nurturing Male," in Cath, Gurwitt, and Gunsberg, eds., *Fathers and Their Families*, pp. 389–405; Fein, "Research on Fathering," pp. 127–31; McKee and O'Brien, eds., *The Father Figure*, pp. 56–60 and 162–67.

70. Peter B. Neubauer, "Fathers and Single Parents," in Cath, Gurwitt, and Gunsberg, eds., *Fathers and Their Families*, pp. 63–75.

71. Judith Kestenberg et al., "The Development of Paternal Attitudes," in Cath, Gurwitt, and Ross, eds., *Father and Child*, p. 206. Hochschild has noted that very involved fathers talked about fatherhood the way women talked about mothering (*The Second Shift*, pp. 228–29).

72. Yogman "La Présence du père," p. 144. See also Yogman, "Observations on the Father-Infant Relationship," in Cath, Gurwitt, and Ross, eds., *Father and Child*, pp. 101–22.

73. Yogman, "La Présence du père," p. 145.

74. Michael Lamb points out that we do not yet know if these differences are social or biological in origin.

75. Michael Lamb and Jamie Lamb, "The Nature and Importance of the Father-Infant Relationship," *Family Coordinator* (October 1976): 379–84. See also Michael Lamb, "The Development of Mother-Infant and Father-Infant Attachments in the Second Year of Life," *Developmental Psychology*, no. 13 (1977): 637–48. The same conclusions are reached by Charles Lewis, "The Observation of the Father-Infant Relationship," in McKee and O'Brien, eds., *The Father Figure*, p. 161.

76. Charles Lewis, "The Observation of the Father-Infant Relationship," p. 155.

77. Jules Chancel, "Le corps de B," *Pères et fils* in *Autrement*, no. 61 (June 1984): p. 210.

78. Henry B. Biller, *Father, Child, and Sex Role*.

79. Michael Lamb, *The Role of the Father in Child Development*.

80. Ibid. The little boy is very proud when his father teaches him to urinate standing up like a man.

81. See the work of John Munder-Ross (1977, 1979, 1982), and Peter Blos, *Son and Father: Before and Beyond the Oedipus Complex*. John Munder-Ross, who has interpreted the case of Little Hans, suggests another reason for his neurosis: the insufficient presence of his father

during his second year. Cf. Ross, "The Riddle of Little Hans," in Cath, Gurwitt, and Gunsberg, eds., *Fathers and Their Families*, pp. 267–83.

82. See Margaret S. Mahler, D. W. Winnicott, Françoise Dolto, among others.

83. Ehrensaft, *Parenting Together*, pp. 195–99.

84. In France, a man who stays home to take care of a sick child meets with even more disapproval than a woman who does the same. By contrast, in Sweden, parental insurance provides for a compensation for the parent who remains at home to take care of a sick child (at the most, ninety days per year and per child up to the age of twelve). Generally speaking, as many fathers as mothers stay home to take care of their sick children. Cf. Hadenius and Lindgren, *Connaître la Suède*, p. 67.

85. For the United States, cf. the Bureau of Labor Statistics, *Employment and Earning, Characteristics of Families: First Quarter* (Washington, D.C., U.S. Department of Labor, 1988). For Europe, cf. Julio Caycedo and Boyd C. Rollins, "Employment Status and Life Satisfaction of Women in Nine Western European Countries," *International Journal of Sociology of the Family* 19 (1989): 1–18.

86. An extremely detailed Danish study concluded in 1988: "It is true that men are sharing household tasks more and more, but it is still the women who do the bulk of the work" (Gunnar Viby Mogensen, *Time and Consumption in Denmark*, pp. 36 and 201). This voluminous Danish study proves the country's desire to uncover sexual inequalities.

87. Like American mothers, they work a total of nearly seven hours more per week than their companions— that is, fifteen days more per year!

88. See Radin, "Primary Caregiving and Role-Sharing Fathers," and Russell, "Share-Giving Families."

89. Robert Quinn and Graham Staines, *The 1977 Quality of Employment Survey* (Ann Arbor: Survey Research Center, Institute for Social Research, University of Michigan, 1979). See also Joseph Pleck, *Husbands' and Wives' Paid Work: Family, Work, and Adjustment* (Wellesley, Mass., 1982).

90. Michael Lamb and D. Oppenheim, "Fatherhood and Father-Child Relationships," in Cath, Gurwitt, and Gunsberg, eds., *Fathers and Their Families*, p. 18.

91.   Pleck, *Husbands' and Wives' Paid Work.*
92.   Russell, "Share-Giving Families."
93.   Ehrensaft, *Parenting Together*, pp. 151–63.
94.   Notably by putting on women's clothes. But unlike the "sissy boy," this behavior (which was merely the manifestation of a double sexual identification) was always transitory.

BIBLIOGRAPHY

Selected Novels Illuminating
the Contemporary Masculine Condition

Amis, Martin. *Money* (1984). New York: Penguin, 1986.

Assayas, Michka. *Les Années vides*. Paris: L'Arpenteur, 1990.

Bannier, François-Marie. *Balthazar, fils de famille*. Paris: Gallimard, 1985.

Bazot, Xavier. *Tableau de la passion*, Paris: POL, 1990.

Belletto, René. *La Machine*. Paris: POL, 1990.

Bellow, Saul. *More Die of Heartbreak*. New York: Morrow, 1987.

———. *Seize the Day*. New York: Viking, 1956; rpt., New York: Penguin, 1984.

Benoziglio, Jean-Louis. *Tableau d'une ex*. Paris: Seuil, 1985.

Bernhard, Thomas. All of his work, particularly the autobiographical sequence *L'Origine*, *La Cave*, *Le Souffle*, *Le Froid*, and *Un Enfant*. Paris: Gallimard, 1990.

———. *Extinction: Un effrondrement*. Paris: Gallimard, 1986.

Bonhomme, Frédéric. *L'Obsédé*. Paris: Robert Laffont, 1990.

Brancati, Vitaliano. *Les Années perdues* (1943). Translated from the Italian. Paris: Fayard, 1988.

———. *Don Juan en Sicile* (1942). Translated from the Italian. Paris: Gallimard, 1968; rpt., Paris: Fayard, 1990.

Braudeau, Michel. *L'Objet perdu de l'amour*. Paris: Seuil, 1988.

Brautigan, Richard. *The Abortion*. 1971.

Bruckner, Pascal. *Lunes de fiel*. Paris: Seuil, 1984.

Bryce-Echenique, Alfredo. *L'Ultime déménagement de Felipe Carrillo* (1988). Translated from the Spanish. Paris: Presses de la Renaissance, 1990.

Bukowski, Charles. *Women*. Santa Rosa, Calif.: Black Sparrow, 1978. In French: Paris: Collection de Poche, 1985.

Burger, Hermann. *La Mère artificielle* (1982). Translated from the German. Paris: Fayard, 1985.

Camon, Ferdinando. *The Sickness Called Man*. Translated by John Shepley. Marlboro, Conn.: Marlboro, 1992.

———. *La Femme aux liens* (1986). Translated from the Italian. Paris: Gallimard, 1987.

———. *Le Chant des baleines* (1989). Translated from the Italian. Paris: Gallimard, 1990.

Carrère, Emmanuel. *La Moustache*. Paris: POL, 1986.

Chardin, Philippe. *L'Obstination*. Paris: Jacqueline Chambon, 1990.

Charyn, Jerome. *The Catfish Man: A Conjured Life*. New York: Arbor House, 1980.

Clément, Roland. *Fausse note*. Paris: Editions Phébus, 1990.

Conroy, Pat. *The Great Santini*. Boston: Houghton Mifflin, 1976; New York: Bantam, 1976.

———. *The Prince of Tides*. Boston: Houghton Mifflin, 1986; New York: Bantam, 1987.

Cubertafond, Bernard. *On s'est manqué de peu: Chroniques d'un homme libéré*. Paris: Dumerchez-Naoum, 1987.

Dagerman, Stig. *Notre plage nocturne*. Translated from the Swedish. Paris: Maurice Nadeau, 1988.

———. *Notre besoin de consolation est impossible à rassasier*. Translated from the Swedish. Arles: Actes Sud, 1989.

Delisle, Michael. *Drame privé*. Paris: POL, 1990.

Djian, Philippe. *Lent dehors*. Paris: Bernard Barrault, 1991.

Domecq, Jean-Philippe. *Antichambre*. Paris: Quai Voltaire, 1990.

Donleavy, J. P. *De Alphonce Tennis: The Superlative Game of Eccentric Champions*. New York: Dutton, 1984.

———. *The Beastly Beatitudes of Balthazar B*. New York: Delacorte Press, 1968.

———. *A Singular Man*. Boston: Little, Brown, 1963.

Drieu, La Rochelle Pierre. *Journal, 1939–1945*. Paris: Gallimard, 1992.

Faber, Thomas. *La Course du chien*. Paris: Gallimard, 1984.

Faldbakken, Knut. *Le Journal d'Adam* (1978). Translated from the Norwegian. Paris: Presses de la Renaissance, 1991.

———. *Le Monarque* (1988). Translated from the Norwegian. Paris: Presses de la Renaissance, 1990.

———. *La Séduction* (1985). Translated from the Norwegian. Paris: Presses de la Renaissance, 1988.

Fernandez, Dominique. *L'Ecole du Sud*. Paris: Grasset, 1991.

———. *Porfirio et Constance*. Paris: Grasset, 1991.

Field, Michel. *Le Passeur de Lesbos*. Paris: Bernard Barrault, 1984.

Ford, Richard. *Rock Springs Stories*. New York: Atlantic Monthly Press, 1987.

——. *A Weekend in Michigan*. 1986.

Franck, Christopher. *Le Rêve du singe fou* (1976). Paris: Seuil-Poche, 1989.

Franck, Dan. *La Séparation*. Paris: Seuil, 1991.

Giudicelli, Christian. *Station balnéaire*. Paris: Gallimard, 1986.

Goytisolo, Juan. *Chasse gardée* (1985). Translated from the Spanish. Paris: Fayard, 1987.

——. *Les Royaumes déchirés* (1987). Translated from the Spanish. Paris: Fayard, 1988.

Grass, Günter. *The Flounder*. Translated by Ralph Manheim. New York: Harcourt Brace Jovanovich, 1978.

Grimm, Jacob and Wilhelm. "Iron Hans." *The Complete Grimm's Fairy Tales* (1944). New York: Pantheon, 1972.

Guibert, Hervé. *Mes Parents*. Paris: Gallimard, 1986.

Gustafson, Lars. *Musique funèbre* (1983). Translated from the Swedish. Paris: Presses de la Renaissance, 1985.

Haavardsholm, Espe. *Le Romantisme est mort, Anna* (1983). Translated from the Norwegian. Arles: Actes Sud, 1988.

Handke, Peter. *The Left-Handed Woman*. New York: Farrar, Straus, Giroux, 1978.

Härtling, Peter. *Felix Guttmann* (1985). Translated from the German. Paris: Seuil, 1985.

——. *Une femme* (1974). Translated from the German. Paris: Flammarion, 1977.

——. *Hubert; ou, Le retour à Casablanca* (1978). Translated from the German. Paris: Seuil, 1982.

Hemingway, Ernest. *The Nick Adams Stories*. New York: Scribner, 1972.

Irving, John. *Hotel New Hampshire*. New York: Dutton, 1981.

——. *The World According to Garp*. New York: Dutton, 1978.

Jaccard, Roland. *Les Chemins de la désillusion*. Paris: Grasset, 1979.

——. *Lou*. Paris: Grasset, 1982.

James, Henry. *The Bostonians* (1886). New York: Modern Library, 1956.

Janvier, Ludovic. *Monstre, va!* Paris: Gallimard, 1988.

Jarry, Alfred. *Le Surmâle*. Paris: Ramsay–J. J. Pauvert, 1990.

Kafka, Franz. *Letter to His Father*. Translated by Ernst Kaiser and Eithne Wilkins. New York: Schocken, 1966.

Kristeva, Julia. *The Samurai*. New York: Columbia University Press, 1992.

Krüger, Michaël. *Pourquoi moi? Et autres récits* (1984–1987). Translated from the German. Paris: Seuil, 1990.

Lawrence, D. H. *Sons and Lovers*. New York: Viking, 1913.

Leavitt, David. *Equal Affections*. New York: Weidenfeld and Nicolson, 1989.

——. *Family Dancing Stories*. New York: Knopf, 1986.

——. *The Lost Language of Cranes*. New York: Knopf, 1986.

Lees-Milne, James. *Another Myself*. 1970.

Lodge, David. *Society Game*. 1988.

Mailer, Norman. *The Prisoner of Sex*. Boston: Little, Brown, 1971.

——. *Tough Guys Don't Dance*. New York: Random House, 1984. In French: Paris: Collection de Poche, 1986.

Marek, Lionel. *Nouvelles d'un amour*. Paris: Denoël, 1990.

Matznef, Gabriel. *Isaïe, réjouis-toi*. Paris: La Table Ronde, 1974.

——. *Les Passions schismatiques*. Paris: Stock, 1977.

——. *Mes Amours décomposées*. Paris: Gallimard, 1990.

McCauley, Stephen. *The Object of My Affection*. New York: Simon and Schuster, 1987.

McGahern, John. *The Dark*. London: Faber and Faber, 1965.

McGuane, Thomas. *The Man Who Had Lost His Name*. 1989.

Michaels, Leonard. *The Men's Club*. New York: Farrar, Straus, Giroux, 1981.

Miller, Henry. *Crazy Cock*. New York: Grove Weidenfeld, 1991.

Mishima, Yukio. *Les Amours interdites* (1952). Translated from the Japanese. Paris: Gallimard, 1985.

——. *Confessions d'un masque* (1958). Translated from the Japanese. Paris: Folio, 1983.

Moravia, Alberto. *Moi et lui* (1971). Translated from the Italian. Paris: Folio, 1974.

——. *Brève autobiographie*. Translated from the Italian. Paris: Salvy, 1989.

Musil, Robert. *Journaux*. Translated from the German. 2 vols. Paris: Seuil, 1981.

——. *The Man Without Qualities* (Der Mann ohne Eigenshaften; 3 vols.: 1932–1942). New York: Coward-McCann, 1993.

——. *Trois femmes, suivi de noces*. Translated from the German. Paris: Seuil, 1963.

Nakagami, Kenji. *La Mer aux arbres morts* (1977). Translated from the Japanese. Paris: Fayard, 1985.

Paasilinna, Arto. *Le Lièvre de Vatanen* (1975). Translated from the Finnish. Paris: Denoël, 1989.

Patier, Xavier. *Le Migrateur*. Paris: La Table Ronde, 1990.

Puig, Manuel. *Kiss of the Spider Woman*. New York: Knopf, 1979.

Quignard, Pascal. *Les Escaliers de Chambord*. Paris: Gallimard, 1989.

Robert, Jean-Marc. *Mon père américain*. Paris: Seuil, 1988.

Rosei, Peter. *Homme et femme S.A.R.L.* (1984). Translated from the German. Paris: Fayard, 1987.

——. *L'Insurrection* (1987). Translated from the German. Paris: Fayard, 1990.

Roth, Henry. *L'Or de la terre promise* (1933). Translated from English. Paris: Grasset, 1968 (reissued, 1985).

Roth, Philip. *The Anatomy Lesson*. New York: Farrar, Straus, Giroux, 1983.

——. *The Breast*. New York: Holt, Rinehart and Winston, 1972.

——. *The Counterlife*. New York: Farrar, Straus, Giroux, 1986. In French: *La Contre-vie*. Paris: Gallimard, 1989.

——. *The Facts: A Novelist's Autobiography*. New York: Farrar, Straus, Giroux, 1988.

——. *The Great American Novel*. New York: Holt, Rinehart and Winston, 1973.

——. *My Life as a Man*. New York: Holt, Rinehart and Winston, 1974; Paris: Gallimard, 1976.

——. *Portnoy's Complaint*. New York: Random House, 1969. In French: *Portnoy et son complexe*. Published in 1970.

——. *The Professor of Desire*. Farrar, Straus, Giroux, 1977.

——. *Zuckerman Unbound*. Farrar, Straus, Giroux, 1981.

Rouart, Jean-Marie. *La Femme de proie*. Paris: Grasset, 1989.

Rozo Thierry. *Ce n'est pas la vie que je voulais*. Paris: Presses de la Renaissance, 1990.

Selby, Hubert. *Last Exit to Brooklyn*. New York: Grove, 1964.

Smadja, Edgar. *Lubie*. Paris: Bernard Barrault, 1990.

Sollers, Philippe. *Femmes*. Paris: Gallimard, 1983.

Stern, Richard. *Other Men's Daughters*. New York: Dutton, 1973.

Targowla, Olivier. *Narcisse sur un fil*. Paris: Maurice Nadeau, 1989.

——. *L'Homme ignoré*. Paris: Maurice Nadeau, 1990.

Toole, John Kennedy. *The Confederacy of Dunces*. Baton Rouge: Louisiana State University Press, 1980.

Toussain, Jean-Philippe. *La Salle de bains*. Paris: Éditions de Minuit, 1985.

Ungar, Hermann. *Les Mutilés* (1923). Translated from the Czech. Paris: Editions Ombres, 1987.

Updike, John. *Museums and Women and Other Stories*. New York: Knopf, 1972.

——. *Rabbit Is Rich*. New York: Knopf, 1981.

——. *Rabbit Redux*. New York: Knopf, 1971.

——. *Rabbit Run*. New York: Knopf, 1960.

Wägeus, Mats. *Scène de chasse en blanc* (1986). Translated from the Swedish. Paris: Presse de la Renaissance, 1990.

Weyergans, François. *Le Pitre*. Paris: Gallimard, 1983.

———. *Le Radeau de la Méduse*. Paris: Gallimard, 1983.

———. *Rire et pleurer*. Paris: Grasset, 1990.

White, Edmund. *The Beautiful Room Is Empty*. New York: Knopf, 1988.

———. *A Boy's Own Story*. New York: Dutton, 1982. In French: *Un Jeune américain* (Paris: Mazarine, 1984); and the sequel, *La Tendresse sur la peau* (Paris: Christian Bourgois, 1988).

Zimmermann, Daniel. *Les Virginités*. Levalloise-Perret: Manya, 1990.

GENERAL BIBLIOGRAPHY

Abbas, Nacer, Colin Bishop, and Marc Fellous. "Le déterminisme génétique du sexe." *La Sexualité* in *La Recherche* 20, no. 213 (September 1989): 1036–46.

Abbott, Franklin, ed. *New Men, New Minds: Breaking Male Tradition; How Today's Men Are Changing the Traditional Roles of Masculinity.* Freedom, Calif.: Crossing Press, 1987.

Abelove, Henry. "Freud, Male Homosexuality and the Americans." *Dissent* 33 (Winter 1986): 59–69.

Acts of the conference, colloque. *Enfances du père.* Paris: Editions GREC, 1989.

Acts of the conference. *Les Pères aujourd'hui.* Paris: INED, 1982.

Acts of the conference. *Le Père: Métaphore paternelle et fonctions du père.* L'espace analytique. Paris: Denoël, 1989.

Acts of the International Congress. *Le Regard des autres.* Paris: Arcadie, 1979.

Alcoff, Linda. "Cultural Feminism Versus Post-Structuralism: The Identity Crisis in Feminist Theory." *Signs* 13, no. 3 (Spring 1988): 405–36.

Altman, Dennis. *Homosexuality: Power and Politics.* London: Allison and Busby, 1980.

——. *The Homosexualization of America, the Americanization of the Homosexual.* New York: St. Martin's, 1982.

Anatrella, Tony. *Le Sexe oublié.* Paris: Flammarion, 1990.

Ariès, Philippe and André Bejin, eds. *Sexualités occidentales* in *Communications* 35. Paris: Points Seuil, 1982.

Arkin, William and Lynne R. Dobrofsky. "Military Socialization and Masculinity." *Journal of Social Issues* 34, no. 1 (1978): 151–68.

Astrachan, Anthony. *How Men Feel.* New York: Doubleday/ Anchor, 1986.

——. "Dividing Lines." In Kimmel and Messner, eds., *Men's Lives,* pp. 63–73.

August, Eugène R. *Men's Studies*. Englewood, Colo.: Libraries Unlimited, 1985.

Badinter, Elisabeth. *L'Amour en plus: Histoire de l'amour maternel du XVIIe au XXe siècle*. Paris: Flammarion, 1980.

———. *L'Un est l'autre: Des relations entre hommes et femmes*. Paris: Odile Jacob, 1986.

Balswick, Jack. "Types of Inexpressive Male Roles." In Lewis, ed., *Men in Difficult Times*, pp. 111–17.

———. *The Inexpressive Male*. Lexington, Mass.: Lexington Books, 1988.

Barash, David. *The Whisperings Within*. New York: Harper and Row, 1979.

Barber, Brian K. and Darwin L. Thomas. "Dimensions of Fathers' and Mothers' Supportive Behavior: The Case of Physical Affection." *Journal of Marriage and the Family* 48 (November 1986): 783–94.

Barnett, Rosalind C. and Grace K. Baruch. "Determinants of Fathers' Participation in Family Work." *Journal of Marriage and the Family* 49 (February 1987): 29–40.

Barret, Robert L. and Bryan E. Robinson. *Gay Fathers*. Lexington, Mass.: Lexington Books, 1990.

Barthes, Roland. "Masculin, Féminin, Neutre." *Le Masculin* in *Le Genre humain*, no. 10 (June 1984): 171–87.

———. "Le Désir de neutre" (lecture at the Collège de France in 1978). *La Règle du jeu*, no. 5 (August 1991): 36–60.

Baudelot, Christian and Roger Establet. *Allez les filles!* Paris: Seuil, 1992.

Bear, Sheryl, Michael Beyer, and Larry Wright. "Even Cowboys Sing the Blues." *Sex Roles* 5, no. 2 (1979).

Bell, Alan P. and Martin S. Weinberg. *Homosexualities*. New York: Simon and Schuster, 1978. In French: *Homosexualités*. Paris: Albin Michel, 1980.

Bell, Robert R. *Worlds of Friendship*. Newbury Park, Calif.: Sage, 1981.

Bem, Sandra. "Gender Schema Theory and Its Implications for Child Development: Raising Gender-Aschematic Children in a Gender-Schematic Society." *Signs*, no. 8 (1983): 598–616.

———. "The Measurement of Psychological Androgyny." *Journal of Clinical and Consulting Psychology* 42 (1974): 155–62.

———. "Sex Role Adaptability: One Consequence of Psychological Androgyny." *Journal of Personality and Social Psychology* 31 (1975): 634–43.

Beneke, Timothy. *Men on Rape*. New York: St. Martin's, 1982.

Bernard, Jessie. "The Good Provider Role." *American Psychologist* 36, no. 1 (January 1981): 1–12.

——. *Women, Wives, Mothers*. Chicago: Aldine, 1975.

Bernstein, Jerome. "The Decline of Masculine Rites of Passage." In Madih, Foster, and Little, eds., *Betwixt and Between*, pp. 135–58.

Bettelheim, Bruno. *Le Poids d'une vie*. Paris: Robert Laffont, 1991.

——. *Symbolic Wounds: Puberty Rites and Envious Males*. Glencoe, Ill.: Free Press, 1984.

Bigner J. and A. Jacobsen. "The Value of Children for Gay Versus Heterosexual Fathers." *Journal of Homosexuality* 18 (1989): 163–72.

Biller, Henry B. *Father, Child, and Sex Role*. Lexington, Mass.: Heath, 1971.

——. "Fatherhood: Implications for Child and Adult Development." In Benjamin B. Wolman, ed., *Handbook of Developmental Psychology*. Englewood Cliffs, N.J.: Prentice-Hall, 1982.

Biller, Henry B. and D. L. Meredith. *Father Power*. New York: Doubleday, 1975.

——. "Invisible American Father." *Sexual Behavior* 2 (1972): 16–22.

Birke, Linda. *Women, Feminism, and Biology: The Feminist Challenge*. New York: Metheun, 1986.

"Bisexualité et différence des sexes." *Nouvelle revue de psychanalyse*, no. 7 (Spring). Paris: Gallimard, 1973.

Blos, Peter. *Son and Father: Before and Beyond the Oedipus Complex*. New York: Free Press, 1985.

Bly, Robert. "The Erosion of Male Confidence." In Madih, Foster, and Little, eds., *Betwixt and Between*, pp. 187–89.

——. *Iron John: A Book About Men*. New York: Addison-Wesley, 1990.

——. "Men's Initiation Rites." In Kimmel and Messner, eds., *Men's Lives*, pp. 153–57.

——. "What Men Really Want." In Abbott, ed., *New Men, New Minds*.

Bon, Michel and Antoine d'Arc. *Rapport sur l'homosexualité de l'homme*. Paris: Editions universitaires, 1974.

Bonneau, Dominique and Marc Fellous. "Les accidents du programme: Ni, homme, ni femme." *L'un et autre sexe* in *Science et vie*, no. 171 (June 1990): 32–36.

Boswell, John. *Christianity, Social Tolerance and Homosexuality*. Chicago: University of Chicago Press, 1980.

Bourdieu, Pierre. "La domination masculine." *Actes de la recherche en sciences sociales*, no. 84 (September 1990): 2–31.

Bowlby, John. *Attachement et perte*. 2 vols. Vol. 1, *L'Attachement*. Paris: Presses Universitaires Francais (hereafter, PUF), 1978.

Boyer, Régine. "Identité masculine, identité féminine parmi les lycéens." *Revue française de pédagogie*, no. 94 (January–March 1991): 13–18.

Bozett, F. W. *Gay and Lesbian Parents*. New York: Praeger, 1987.
——. "Gay Fathers: A Review of the Literature." *Journal of Homosexuality* 18 (1989): 137–62.
Bozon, Michel. "Les Loisirs forment la jeunesse." *Données sociales* (1990): 217–22.
Breton, Stéphane. *La Mascarade des sexes: Fétichisme, inversion et travestissement rituels*. Paris: Calmann-Lévy, 1989.
Brittan, Arthur. *Masculinity and Power*. London: Blackwell, 1985.
Brod, Harry. "A Case for Men's Studies." In Kimmel, ed., *Changing Men*, pp. 263–77.
——. "Eros Thanatized: Pornography and Male Sexuality." *Humanities in Society* 7, nos. 1–2 (Winter/Spring 1984).
——. "Fraternity, Equality, Liberty." In Abbott, ed., *New Men, New Minds*, pp. 148–53.
——, ed. *The Making of Masculinities: The New Men's Studies*. Boston, Unwin Hyman, 1987.
Broughton, John M., ed. *Critical Theories of Psychological Development*. New York, Plenum, 1987.
Brown, Marion, John Dunbar, and Donald M. Amoroso. "Some Correlates of Attitudes Toward Homosexuality." *Journal of Social Psychology* 89 (February 1973): 271–79.
Brown, Marion and Donald M. Amoroso. "Attitudes Toward Homosexuality Among West Indian Male and Female College Students." *Journal of Social Psychology* 97 (February 1975): 163–68.
Brownmiller, Susan. *Against Our Will: Men, Women and Rape*. New York: Penguin, 1976.
Butler, Judith. *Gender Trouble: Feminism and Subversion of Identity*. London: Routledge, 1990.
Cachin, Françoise. "L'androgyne du temps de Gustave Moreau: Monsieur Vénus et l'ange de Sodome." *Nouvelle revue de psychanalyse*, no. 7 (1973): 63–69.
Cancian, Francesca M. "The Feminization of Love." *Signs* 11, no. 4 (Summer 1986): 692–709.
——. *Love in America: Gender and Self-Development*. Cambridge: Cambridge University Press, 1990.
Caplan, Pat, ed. *The Cultural Construction of Sexuality*. London: Routledge, 1987; New York: Tavistock, 1987.
Carnes, Mark C. and Clyde Griffen, eds. *Meanings for Manhood: Constructions of Masculinity in Victorian America*. Chicago: University of Chicago Press, 1990.
Castelain-Meunier, Christine. *Les Hommes aujourd'hui: Virilité et identité*. Paris: Acropole, 1988.
Cath, Stanley H., Alan R. Gurwitt, and John Munder-Ross, eds. *Father and Child*. Boston: Little, Brown, 1982.

Cath, Stanley H., Alan R. Gurwitt, and Linda Gunsberg, eds. *Fathers and Their Families*. New York: Analytic Press, 1989.

Caycedo, Julio C. and Boyd C. Rollins. "Employment Status and Life Satisfaction of Women in Nine Western European Countries." *International Journal of Sociology of the Family* 19 (Fall 1989): 1–18.

Chabot, Marc. *Chroniques masculines*. Quebec: Editions Pantoute, 1981.

——. "Genre masculin ou genre flou." In *Des Hommes et du masculin*, pp. 177–203.

——. *Des Hommes et de l'inimité*. Quebec: Editions Saint-Martin, 1987.

Chancel, Jules. "Le corps de B." *Pères et fils* in *Autrement*, no. 61 (June 1984).

Chasseguet-Smirgel, Janine. "Masculin et féminin." In *Les Deux arbres du jardin*. Paris: Des Femmes, 1988.

Chesler, Phyllis. *La Mâle donne*. Paris: Des Femmes, 1982.

Chevallier, Philippe. "Population infantile consultant pour des troubles psychologiques." *Population*, no. 3 (May–June 1988): 611–38.

Chodorow, Nancy. *The Reproduction of Mothering*. Berkeley: University of California Press, 1978.

Clatterbaugh, Kenneth. *Contemporary Perspectives on Masculinity*. Boulder, Colo.: Westview, 1990.

Coltrane, Scott. "Father-Child Relationships and the Status of Women: A Cross-Cultural Study." *American Journal of Sociology* 93 (1988): 1060–70.

Condorcet, Prudhomme. *Guyomar . . . paroles d'hommes (1790–1793)*. With an introduction by Elisabeth Badinter. Paris: POL, 1989.

Connell, Robert W. *Gender and Power*. Stanford, Calif.: Stanford University Press, 1987.

——. "Masculinity, Violence and War." In Kimmel and Messner, eds., *Men's Lives*, pp. 194–200.

——. "A Whole New World: Remaking Masculinity in the Context of the Environmental Movement." *Gender and Society* 14, no. 4 (December 1990): 452–78.

Connell, Robert W., Norm Radican, and Pip Martin. "The Changing Faces of Masculinity." In Kimmel and Messner, eds., *Men's Lives*, pp. 578–85.

Connell, Robert W., Tim Carrigan, and John Lee. "Toward a New Sociology of Masculinity." *Theory and Society* 5, no. 14 (Amsterdam: El-Sevrei, September 1985). Reprinted in Brod, ed., *The Making of Masculinities*, pp. 63–100.

Conway, Jill K., Susan C. Bourque, and Joan W. Scott, eds., *Gender, Politics and Power*. Ann Arbor: University of Michigan Press, 1987.

——. *Learning About Women*. Ann Arbor: University of Michigan Press, 1989.

Corneau, Guy. *Père manquant, fils manqué: Que sont les hommes devenus?* Quebec: Les editions de l'homme, 1989.

Daumas, Maurice. *Le syndrome des Grieux: La relation père-fils au XVIIIe siècle*, Paris: Seuil, 1990.

David, Deborah S. and Robert Brannon. *The Forty-Nine Percent Majority: The Male Sex Role*. New York: Addison-Wesley, 1976.

Dearborn, Mary. *The Happiest Man Alive: A Biography of Henry Miller*. New York: Simon and Schuster, 1991. In French: *Henry Miller: Biographie*. Belfond, 1991.

Delaisi de Parseval, Geneviève. *La Part du père*. Paris: Seuil, 1981.

——, ed. *Les Sexes de l'homme*. Paris: Seuil, 1985.

Delavenay, Emile. *D. H. Lawrence: L'Homme et la genèse de son oeuvre*. 2 vols. Paris: Librairie Klincksieck, 1969.

Delphy, Christine, ed. "Particularisme et universalisme." *Nouvelles questions féministes*, nos. 16–18 (1991).

D'Emilio, John and Estelle B. Freedman. *Intimate Matters: A History of Sexuality in America*. New York: Harper and Row, 1988.

Demos, John. *Past, Present and Personal: The Family and the Life Course in American History*. New York: Oxford University Press, 1986.

Dentan, Robert K. *The Semai: A Non-Violent People of Malaysia*. New York: Holt, Rinehart and Winston, 1979.

Devor, Holly. *Gender Blending: Confronting the Limits of Duality*. Bloomington: Indiana University Press, 1989.

Diamond, Milton. "Sexual Identity: Monozygotic Twins Reared in Discordant Sex Roles." *Archives of Sexual Behavior* 11, no. 2 (1982): 181–86.

Diderot, Denis. *Le Rêve de d'Alembert* (1769). In P. Vernière, ed., *Oeuvres philosophiques*. Paris: Editions Garnier, 1967.

——. *Suite de l'Entretien*. In P. Vernière, ed., *Oeuvres philosophiques*.

Dolto, Françoise. *Lorsque l'enfant paraît*. Vol. 2. Paris: Seuil, 1978.

Dor, Joël. *Le Père et sa fonction en psychanalyse*. Paris: Points Seuil, 1989.

Dover, K. Y. *Homosexualité grecque*. Paris: La Pensée Sauvage, 1982.

Dubbert, Joe. "Progressivism and the Masculinity Crisis." In Pleck and Pleck, eds., *The American Man*, pp. 303–19.

——. "Shaping the Ideal During the Masculine Century." In *A Man's Place: Masculinity in Transition*. Englewood Cliffs, N.J.: Prentice-Hall, 1979.

Duby, Georges. *Mâle Moyen Age*. Paris: Champs/Flammarion 1990.

Duby, Georges and Michelle Perrot, gen. eds. *Histoire des femmes*. Vol. 4, *The Nineteenth Century*. Paris: Plon, 1992.

Dumas, Didier. *La Sexualité masculine*. Paris: Albin Michel, 1990.

Dworkin, Andrea. *Pornography: Men Possessing Women*. London: Women's Press, 1981.

Edel, Leon. *Henry James: A Life*. Philadelphia: Lippincott, 1972.

Ehrenreich, Barbara. "A Feminist's View of the New Man." *New York Times Magazine*, May 20, 1984.

——. *The Hearts of Men: American Dreams and the Flight from Commitment*. New York: Doubleday/Anchor, 1983.

Ehrensaft, Diane. "Feminists Fight for Fathers." *Socialist Review*, no. 4 (1990): 57–80.

——. *Parenting Together*. Urbana: University of Illinois Press, 1987.

——. "When Women and Men Mother." *Socialist Review*, no. 49 (January–February 1980): 37–73.

Eisenstein, Hester. *Contemporary Feminist Thought*. London: Allen and Unwin, 1984.

Eisenstein, Hester and Alice Jardine, eds. *The Future of Difference*. New Brunswick, N.J.: Rutgers University Press, 1987.

Elliott, Mark L. "The Use of 'Impotence' and 'Frigidity': Why Has 'Impotence' Survived?" *Journal of Sex and Marital Therapy* 11, no. 1 (Spring 1985).

Erikson, Erik H. *Childhood and Society* (1950). 2d ed. New York: Norton, 1963.

——. *Identity: Youth and Crisis*. New York, Norton, 1968.

——. *Identity and the Life Cycle* (1959). New York: Norton, 1980.

Fagot, Beverly I. "Beyond the Reinforcement Principle: Another Step Toward Understanding Sex Roles." *Developmental Psychology* 21 (1985): 1097–1104.

——. "Consequences of Moderate Cross-Gender Behavior in Pre-School Children." *Child Development* 48 (September 1977): 902–7.

——. *Le Fait féminin: Qu'est-ce qu'une femme?* Edited by Evelyne Sullerot. Paris: Fayard, 1978.

——. "The Influence of Sex of Child on Parental Reactions to Toddler Children." *Child Development* 49 (June 1978): 459–65.

——. "Sex Differences in Toddlers' Behavior and Parental Reaction." *Developmental Psychology* 10 (1974): 554–58.

——. "Sex-related Stereotyping of Toddlers' Behaviors." *Developmental Psychology* 9 (1973).

Falconnet, G. and N. Lefaucheur. *La Fabrication des mâles*. Paris: Seuil, 1975.

Farrell, Michael P. "Friendship Between Men." In *Men's Changing*

Roles in the Family, a Special Issue of *Marriage and Family Review* 19, nos. 3–4 (Winter 1985–86): 163–97.

Farrell, Warren. *The Liberated Man*. New York: Random House, 1975.

Faure-Oppenheimer, Agnès. *Le Choix du sexe*. Paris: PUF, 1980.

Fausin, Bent, Steffen Kiselberg, and Niels Senius Clausen. "L'histoire des Hommes." In *Textes et images*. Copenhagen: Tidern Skifter, 1984.

Fausto-Sterling, Anne. *Myths of Gender: Biological Theories About Women and Men*. New York: Basic Books, 1985.

Feigen-Fasteau, Marc. *Le Robot mâle*. Paris: Denoël-Gonthier, 1980.

Fein, Robert A. "Research on Fathering: Social Policy and an Emergent Perspective." *Journal of Social Issues* 3–4, no. 1 (1978): 122–35.

Filene, Peter G. "Between a Rock and a Soft Place: A Century of American Manhood." *South Atlantic Quarterly* 84, no. 4 (Fall 1985): 339–55.

———. *Him/Her/Self: Sex Roles in Modern America* (1974). 2d ed. Baltimore and London: Johns Hopkins University Press, 1986.

———. "The Secrets of Men's History." In Brod, ed., *The Making of Masculinities*, pp. 103–9.

Fine, Gary Alan. "The Dirty Play of Little Boys." In Kimmel and Messner, eds., *Men's Lives*, pp. 171–79.

———. "Little League Baseball and Growing Up Male." In Lewis, ed., *Men in Difficult Times*, pp. 62–74.

Finkielkraut, Alain. "La nostalgie de l'épreuve." *Le Masculin* in *Le Genre humain*, no. 10 (June 1984): 57-63.

Finkielkraut, Alain and Pascal Bruckner. *Le Nouveau désordre amoureux* (1977). Paris: Points Seuil, 1979.

Flamant-Paparatti, Danielle. *Le Journal de Lucas*. Paris: Denoël-Gonthier, 1983.

Flem, Lydia. "Le stade du cowboy." *Le Masculin* in *Le Genre humain*, no. 10 (June 1984): 101–15.

Fogel, Gerald, ed. *The Psychology of Men*. New York: Basic Books, 1986.

Foucault, Michel. *The History of Sexuality*. Vol. 2, *The Use of Pleasure*. Translated by Robert Hurley. New York: Pantheon, 1985. In French: *L'Usage des plaisirs*. Paris: Gallimard, 1984.

———. *Le Souci de soi*. Paris: Gallimard, 1984.

———. *La Volonté de savoir*. Paris: Gallimard, 1976.

———, ed. *Herculine Barbin, dite Alexina B.* Paris: Gallimard, 1978.

Frain, John de. "Androgynous Parents Tell Who They Are and What They Need." *Family Coordinator* (April 1979): 237–44.

Freud, Sigmund. *Civilization and Its Discontents* (1929). Translated by Joan Rivière. London: Hogarth Press, 1961; New York: Norton,

1961. Vol. 21 in the *Standard Edition of the Complete Psychological Works* (hereafter, *SE*). 3d ed. 23 vols. Edited by James Strachey. Translated by James Strachey and others. London: Hogarth Press, 1953–66. In French: *Malaise dans la civilisation*. Paris: PUF, 1971.

———. *Five Lectures on Psychoanalysis* (1910), from lectures given at Clark University in Worcester, Mass., in 1909. *SE*, vol. 11. In French: *Les Cinq psychanalyses*. Paris: PUF, 1966.

———. *A General Introduction to Psychoanalysis*. New York: Boni and Liveright, 1920. In French: *Introduction à la psychanalyse*. Paris: Payot, 1970.

———. *Letters of Sigmund Freud*. New York: Basic Books, 1960. In French: *Correspondance (1873-1939)*. Paris: Gallimard, 1967.

———. *Un Souvenir d'enfance de Léonard de Vinci*. Paris: Gallimard, 1977. (*Leonardo da Vinci and a Memory of His Childhood*. Translated by Alan Tyson. *SE*, vol. 11. London: Hogarth Press, 1957.

———. *New Introductory Lectures on Psychoanalysis* (1933). New York: Norton, 1965. *SE*, vol. 22. In French: *Nouvelles conférences sur la psychanalyse*. Paris: Gallimard, 1971.

———. *Three Essays on the Theory of Sexuality*. *SE*, vol. 7. Translated by James Strachey. New York: Basic Books, 1963. In French: *Trois essais sur la théorie de la sexualité*. Paris: Gallimard.

———. *La Vie sexuelle*. Paris: PUF, 1970.

Friedman, Richard C. *Male Homosexuality: A Contemporary Psychoanalytic Perspective*. New Haven: Yale University Press, 1988.

Friedman, Robert M. and Leila Lerner, eds. "Toward a New Psychology of Men: Psychoanalytic and Social Perspectives." *Psychoanalytic Review* 73, no. 4 (Winter 1985).

Fuchs, Cynthia Epstein. *Deceptive Distinctions: Sex Gender and the Social Order*. New Haven: Yale University Press, 1988.

Gerlach-Nielsen, Merete. "Essai sur l'évolution du rôle masculin au Danemark, 1975–1985." Paper presented at the international colloquium of UNESCO (Athens, 1985). Published in part in *La Gazette des femmes* 8, no. 2 (Quebec, July–August 1986): 10–12.

Gillette, Douglas and Robert Moore. *King, Warrior, Magician, Lover: Rediscovering the Archetypes of the Masculine Nature*. San Francisco: Harper and Row, 1990.

Gilligan, Carol. *In a Different Voice*. Cambridge: Harvard University Press, 1982. In French: *Une si grand différence*. Paris: Flammarion, 1986.

Gilmore, David D. *Manhood in the Making: Cultural Concepts of Masculinity*. New Haven: Yale University Press, 1990.

Gleason, Philip. "Identifying Identity: A Semantic History." *Journal of American History* 69, no. 4 (March 1983): 910–31.

Godelier, Maurice. *La Production des grands hommes*. Paris: Fayard, 1982.

Goffman, E. *Stigma*. Englewood Cliffs: Prentice-Hall, 1963.

Goode, William J. "Why Men Resist?" In Kimmel and Messner, eds., *Men's Lives*, pp. 43–56.

Gorny, Violette. *Priorité aux enfants: Un nouveau pouvoir*. Paris: Hachette, 1991.

Green, Richard. "One Hundred Ten Feminine and Masculine Boys: Behavioral Contrast and Demographic Similarities." *Archives of Sexual Behavior* 5, no. 5 (September 1976).

———. *The "Sissy Boy Syndrome" and the Development of Homosexuality*. New Haven: Yale University Press, 1987.

Green, Richard et al. "Masculine or Feminine Gender Identity in Boys: Developmental Differences Between Two Diverse Family Groups." *Sex Roles* 12, nos. 11–12 (1985): 1155–62.

Green, Richard and Robert Stoller. "Treatment of Boyhood Transsexualism." *Archives of General Psychiatry* 26 (March 1972).

Greenson, Ralph. "Dis-Identifying from Mother: Its Special Importance for the Boy." *International Psycho-Analytic Journal* 49 (1968): 370–73.

———. "On Homosexuality and Gender Identity." *International Psycho-Analytic Journal* 45 (1964): 217–19.

———. "A Transvestite Boy and a Hypothesis." *International Psycho-Analytic Journal* 47 (1966): 396–403.

Groddeck, Georg. *Le Livre du ça* (1923). Paris: Tel/Gallimard, 1980.

Gronseth, E. "Work Sharing: A Norwegian Example." In Rhona Rapoport and Robert N. Rapoport, eds., *Working Couples*. St. Lucia: University of Queensland Press, 1978.

Gross, Alan E. "The Male Role and Heterosexual Behavior." *American Behavioral Scientist* 29, no. 5 (May–June 1986): 563–77.

Hahn, Pierre. *Nos Ancêtres les pervers: La Vie des homosexuels sous le Second Empire*. Paris: Olivier Orban, 1979.

Halperin, David M. *One Hundred Years of Homosexuality*. New York: Routledge, 1990.

Halsaa, Béatrice. "A Feminist Utopia." *Scandinavian Political Studies* 11, no. 4 (1988): 323–36.

Hantover, Jeffrey P. "The Boy Scouts and the Validation of Masculinity." *Journal of Social Issues* 34, no. 1 (1978): 184–95. Reprinted in Kimmel and Messner, eds., *Men's Lives*.

———. "The Social Construction of Masculine Anxiety." In Lewis, ed., *Men in Difficult Times*, pp. 87–98.

Harrison, James. "Warning: The Male Sex Role May be Dangerous to Your Health." *Journal of Social Issues* 34, no. 1 (1978): 65–86.

Hartley, Ruth. "Sex Role Pressures in the Socialization of the Male

Child." *Psychological Reports* 5 (1959): 458–68.

Heilbrun, Carolyn G. *Toward a Recognition of Androgyny*. New York: Harper/Colophon, 1973.

Herdt, Gilbert H. *Guardians of the Flutes*. New York: McGraw-Hill, 1981.

———, ed. *Rituals of Manhood: Male Initiation in Papua New Guinea*. Berkeley: University of California Press, 1982.

Herek, Gregory M. "On Heterosexual Masculinity." *American Behavioral Scientist* 29, no. 5 (May–June 1986): 563–77.

Herman, Imre. *L'Instinct filial*. Paris: Denoël, 1972.

Hirsch, Marianne and Evelyn Fox Keller, eds. *Conflicts in Feminism*. New York: Routledge, 1990.

Hite, Shere. *The Hite Report on Male Sexuality*. New York: Knopf, 1981. In French: *Le Rapport Hite sur les hommes*. Paris: Robert Laffont, 1983.

Hochschild, Arlie. *The Second Shift*. New York: Avon, 1989.

Hocquenheim, Guy. *Le Désir homosexuel*. Paris: Editions Universitaires, 1972.

Hofmann, Kurt. *Entretiens avec Thomas Bernhard*. Paris: La Table Ronde, 1990.

Hommes et du masculin, Des. BIEF. Lyons: Presses Universitaires de Lyons, 1992.

Hurtig, Marie-Claude and Marie-France Pichevin, eds. *La Difference des Sexes*. Paris: Tierce Sciences, 1986.

Institut national des statistiques et des études économiques (INSEE). *Données sociales*. Paris: INSEE, 1990.

———. *Les Femmes: Contours et caractécres*. Paris: INSEE, 1991.

Irigaray, Luce. *Je, Tu, Nous*. Paris: Grasset, 1990.

———. *Sexes et genres à travers les langues*. Paris: Grasset, 1990.

———. *Le Temps de la différence*. Paris: Livre de Poche, 1989.

Isay, Richard A. "Homosexuality in Homosexual and Heterosexual Men." In Fogel, ed., *The Psychology of Men*, pp. 277–99.

Jeffords, Susan. *The Remasculinization of America*. Bloomington: Indiana University Press, 1989.

Jeffreys, Sheila. *Anticlimax: A Feminist Perspective and the Sexual Revolution*. London: Women's Press, 1990.

Johnson, Miriam M. *Strong Mothers, Weak Wives*. Berkeley: University of California Press, 1988.

Johnson, Miriam M. and Jean Stockard. "The Social Origins of Male Dominance." *Sex Roles* 5, no. 2 (1979): 199–218.

Jonasdéttir, Anna G. "Does Sex Matter to Democracy." *Scandanavian Political Studies* 11, no. 4 (1988): 299–322.

Jost, Alfred. "Le développement sexual prénatal." In Fagot, *Le Fait féminin*, pp. 85–90.

Jourard, Sidney M. *The Transparent Self*. New York: Van Nostrand, 1971.

Jump, Teresa L. and Linda Haas. "Fathers in Transition: Dual-Career Fathers Participating in Child Care." In Kimmel, ed., *Changing Men*.

Kando, Thomas. "Males, Females and Transsexuals: A Comparative Study of Sexual Conservatism." *Journal of Homosexuality* 1, no. 1 (1974): 45–64.

Katz, Jonathan Ned. "The Invention of Heterosexuality." *Socialist Review* 1 (1990): 7–34.

Kaufman, Michael, ed. *Beyond Patriarchy*. Oxford: Oxford University Press, 1987.

Kessler, Suzanne J. "The Medical Construction of Gender: Case Management of Intersexed Infants." *Signs* 16, no. 1 (Fall 1990): 3–26.

Khan, Arnold. "The Power War: Male Response to Power Loss Under Equality." *Psychology of Women Quarterly* 8, no. 3 (Spring 1984): 234–47.

Kimball, Gayle. "Egalitarian Husbands." In Kimmel and Messner, eds., *Men's Lives*, pp. 550–58.

Kimmel, Michael S. "The Contemporary Crisis of Masculinity in Historical Perspective." In Brod, ed., *The Making of Masculinities*, pp. 121–53.

——."The Cult of Masculinity: American Social Character and the Legacy of the Cowboy." In Kaufman, ed., *Beyond Patriarchy*, pp. 234–49.

——. "Goodbye John Wayne." In Abbott, ed., *New Men, New Minds*, pp. 143–47.

——. "Hard Issues and Soft Spots: Counseling Men About Sexuality." In Kimmel and Messner, eds., *Men's Lives*.

——. "Men's Responses to Feminism at the Turn of the Century." *Gender and Society*, no. 1 (1987): 261–83.

——, ed. *American Behavioral Scientist* 29, no. 5 (May–June 1986): Special Issue on men.

——, ed. *Changing Men: New Directions in Research on Men and Masculinity*. Newbury Park, Calif.: Sage, 1987.

Kimmel, Michael S. and Jeffrey Fracher. "Counseling Men About Sexuality." In Kimmel and Messner, eds., *Men's Lives*.

Kimmel, Michael S. and Martin P. Levine. "Men and AIDS." In Kimmel and Messner, eds., *Men's Lives*, pp. 344–54.

Kimmel, Michael S. and Michael A. Messner, eds. *Men's Lives*. New York: Macmillan, 1989.

Kinsey, Alfred, et al. *Sexual Behavior in the Human Male*. Philadelphia: Saunders, 1948.

Kinsman, Gary. "Men Loving Men: The Challenge of Gay Liberation," In Kimmel and Messner, eds., *Men's Lives*.

Klein, Carole. *Mères et fils*. Paris: Robert Laffont, 1988.

Kleinberg, Seymour. "The New Masculinity of Gay Men, and Beyond." In Kimmel and Messner, eds., *Men's Lives*, pp. 101–14.

Kreisler, Léon. "Les intersexuels avec ambighuïté génitale." *La Psychiatrie de l'enfant* 13, no. 1 (1970): 5–127.

Lacan, Jacques. *Ecrits*. Paris: Seuil, 1966.

Lallemand, Suzanne. "Le b.a. ba Africain." *Pères et Fils* in *Autrement*, no. 61 (June 1984): 180–87

Lamb, Michael. "The Development of Mother-Infant and Father-Infant Attachments in the Second Year of Life." *Developmental Psychology*, no. 13 (1977): 637–48.

——. *The Role of the Father in Child Development*. New York: John Wiley, 1981.

——, ed. *The Father's Role: Applied Perspectives*. New York: John Wiley, 1986.

——, ed. *Non-Traditional Families: Parenting and Child Development*. Hillsdale, N.Y.: L. Erlbaum, 1982.

Lamb, Michael and Jamie Lamb. "The Nature and Importance of the Father-Infant Relationship." In *Fatherhood*, a Special Issue of *Family Coordinator* (October 1976): 379–84.

L'Androgyne. In *Cahiers de l'herméticisme*. Paris: Albin Michel, 1986.

Laqueur, Thomas. *Making Sex: Body and Gender from the Greeks to Freud*. Cambridge: Harvard University Press, 1990.

Latour, Sophie. "L'archétype de l'androgyne chez Léopold Ziegler." *L'Androgyne* in *Cahiers de l'herméticisme*, pp. 197–211.

Lee, John. *The Flying Boy: Healing the Wounded Man*. New Men's Press, 1987.

Lehne, Gregory. "Homophobia Among Men: Supporting and Defining the Male Role." In Kimmel and Messner, eds., *Men's Lives*, pp. 416–29.

Le Rider, Jacques. *Le Cas Otto Weininger*. Paris: PUF, 1982.

——. "Ludwig Wittgenstein et Otto Weininger." In *Wittgenstein et la critique du monde moderne*, pp. 43–65.

——. "Misère de la virilité à la belle époque." *Le Masculin* in *Le Genre humain*, no. 10 (June 1984): 117–37.

——. *Modernité viennoise et crises de l'identité*. Paris: PUF, 1990.

——. "Otto Weininger: Féminisme et virilité à Vienne." *L'Infini*, no. 4 (Fall 1983): 15–20.

——. "Thomas Bernhard: La misogynie d'un poète maudit." *Repères*, no. 4 (Lausanne, 1982).

——. *Wittgenstein et la critique du monde moderne*. Brussels: La Lettre volée, 1990.

Leridon, Henri and Catherine Villeneuve-Golkalp. "Enquête sur la situation des familles." In Institut national d'études démographiques (January 1988); table reprinted in *Population et sociétés*, no. 220 (January 1988).

Lessing, Theodor. *La Haine de soi: Le Refus d'être juif* (Berlin, 1930). Translated from the German. Kirchdorf: Berg International, 1990.

Lever, Maurice. *Les Bûchers de Sodome*. Paris: Fayard, 1985.

Levinson, Daniel J. *The Seasons of a Man's Life*. New York: Ballantine, 1978.

Levinson, Daniel J. et al. "Periods of Adult Development in Men: Ages 18–44." *Counseling Psychologist* 6 (1976): 21–25.

Levy, Robert I. "The Community Function of Tahitian Male Transvestism: A Hypothesis." *Anthropological Quarterly* 44, no. 1 (January 1971): 12–21.

———. *The Tahitians: Mind and Experience in the Society Islands*. Chicago: University of Chicago Press, 1973.

Lewis, Charles and Margaret O'Brien, eds. *Reassessing Fatherhood*. London and Newbury Park, Calif.: Sage, 1987.

Lewis, Robert A. "Emotional Intimacy Among Men." *Journal of Social Issues* 34, no. 1 (1978).

———, ed. *Men in Difficult Times*. Englewood Cliffs, N.J.: Prentice-Hall, 1981.

Lewis, Robert A. and Joseph H. Pleck, eds. *Men's Roles in the Family*, a Special Issue of *Family Coordinator* (October 1979).

Lewis, Robert A. and Marvin B. Sussman, eds. *Men's Changing Roles in the Family*, a Special Issue of *Marriage and Family Review* 9, nos. 3–4 (Winter 1985–86).

Lewis, Robert A. and Robert E. Salt. *Men in Families*. Newbury Park, Calif.: Sage, 1986.

Libis, Jean. "L'androgyne et le nocturne." *L'Androgyne* in *Cahiers de l'herméticisme*, pp. 11–26.

Lidz, Ruth and Theodore Lidz. "Male Menstruation : A Ritual Alternative to the Oedipal Transition." *International Journal of Psychoanalysis* 58, no. 17 (1977): 17–31.

Lionetti, Roberto. *Le Lait du Père*. Paris: Imago, 1988.

Lisak, David. "Sexual Aggression, Masculinity and Fathers." *Signs* 16, no. 2 (Winter 1991): 238–62.

Lloyd, Barbara B. and John Archer, eds. *Exploring Sex Differences*. London: Academic Press, 1976.

Loraux, Nicole. "Blessures de la virilité." *Le Masculin* in *Le Genre humain*, no. 10 (June 1984): 39–56.

———. *Les Expériences de Tirésias*. Paris: Gallimard, 1989.

Luria, Zella and Eleanor W. Herzog. "Sorting Gender Out in a Children's Museum." *Gender and Society* 5, no. 2 (June 1991): 224–32.

Lynn, Kenneth S. *Hemingway*. New York: Simon and Schuster, 1987; Paris: Payot, 1990.

Maccoby, Eleanor E. "Le sexe, catégorie sociale." *Actes de la recherche en sciences sociales*, no. 83 (June 1990): 16–26.

Maccoby, Eleanor E. and Carol N. Jacklin. "Gender Segregation in Childhood." In E. H. Reese, ed., *Advances in Child Development and Behavior* 20: 239–87. New York: Academic Press, 1987.

——. *The Psychology of Sex Differences*. 2 vols. Stanford, Calif: Stanford University Press, 1974.

Maccoby, Eleanor E., Margaret Ellis Snow, and Carol N. Jacklin. "Sex of Child: Differences in Father Child Interaction at One Year of Age." *Child Development* 54 (1983): 227–32

Madih, Louise Carus, Steven Foster, and Meredith Little, eds. *Betwixt and Between: Patterns of Masculine and Feminine Initiation*. La Salle, Ill.: Open Court, 1987.

Maffesoli, Michel. *Au Creux des apparences*. Paris: Plon, 1990.

Mahler, Margaret S. *Psychose infantile: Symbiose humaine et individuation*. Paris: Payot, 1982.

Mahler, Margaret S. and Kittly la Perrière. "Mother-Child Interaction During Separation-Individuation." *Psychoanalytic Quarterly* 34 , no. 4 (1965): 483–98.

Malson, Lucien. *Wolf Children and the Problem of Human Nature*. Translated by Edwin Fawcctt, Peter Ayrton, and Joan White. New York: Monthly Review Press, 1972.

Marignac, Thierry, ed. *Norman Mailer: Economie du machisme*. Paris: Du Rocher, 1990.

Marini, Marcelle. *Lacan*. Paris: Les dossiers Belfond, 1986.

Markstrom-Adams, Carol. "Androgyny and Its Relation to Adolescent Psycho-Social Well-Bcing: A Review of the Literature." *Sex Roles* 21, nos. 5–6 (September 1989): 325–40.

Masculin/Féminin. In *Actes de la recherche en sciences sociales* 1, no. 83 (June 1990) and 2, no. 84 (September 1990).

Maugue, Annelise. "L'Eve nouvelle et le vieil Adam: Identités sexuelles en crise." In Duby and Perrot, gen. eds., *Histoire des femmes* 4: 527–43.

——. *L'Identité masculine en crise au tournant de siècle*. Paris: Rivages-Histoire, 1987.

McIntosh, Mary. "The Homosexual Role." *Social Problems*, no. 16 (1968): 182–92.

McKee, Lorna and Margaret O'Brien, eds. *The Father Figure*. London: Tavistock Publications, 1982.

Mead, Margaret. *Male and Female*. New York: Morrow Quill Paperbacks, 1980. In French: *L'Un et l'autre sexe*. Paris: Denoël-Gonthier, 1966.

——. *Coming of Age in Samoa*. New York: Morrow Quill Paperbacks, 1973. In French: *Moeurs et sexualité en Océanie*. Paris: Plon, 1963.

Meslin, Michael. *L'Homme romain*. Paris: Editions Complexe, 1985.

Messner, Michael. "Ah, Ya Throw Like a Girl." In Abbott, ed., *New Men, New Minds*, pp. 40–42.

——. "Boyhood, Organized Sports, and the Construction of Masculinities." *Journal of Contemporary Ethnography* 18, no. 4 (January 1990): 416–44.

——. "The Life of a Man's Seasons: Male Identity in the Life Course of the Jock." In Kimmel, ed., *Changing Men*, pp. 53–67.

——. "The Meaning of Success: The Athletic Experience and the Development of Male Identity." In Brod, ed., *The Making of Masculinities*, pp. 193–209.

——. "Sports and the Politics of Inequality." In Kimmel and Messner, eds., *Men's Lives*, pp. 187–90.

Miller, Brian. "Gay Fathers and Their Children." *Men's Roles in the Family* in *Family Coordinator* (October 1979): 416–44.

——. "Lifestyles of Gay Husbands and Fathers." In Kimmel and Messner, eds., *Men's Lives*, pp. 559–67.

Mishima, Yukio. *Le Japon moderne et l'éthique du samouraï*. Paris: Gallimard, 1985.

Mishkind, Marc E., Judith Todin, Lisa Siberstein, and Ruth Striegel-Moore. "The Embodiment of Masculinity." In Kimmel, ed., *Changing Men*, pp. 37–52.

Mitscherlich, Margarete. *La Femme pacifique*. Paris: Des Femmes, 1988.

——. *La Fin des modèles*. Paris: Des Femmes, 1983.

Mitscherlich, Margarete and Helga Dierichs. *Des Hommes*. Paris: Des Femmes, 1983.

Mogensen, Gunnar Viby. *Time and Consumption in Denmark*. Valby: Dannmarks statistik, 1990.

Money, John. "Sexual Dimorphism and Homosexual Gender Identity." *Psychological Bulletin* 74, no. 6 (1970): 424–40.

Money, John and Anke A. Ehrhardt. *Man and Woman, Boy and Girl* (1972). Rev. ed. Baltimore: Johns Hopkins University Press, 1982.

Mongrédien, Georges. *Les Précieux et les précieuses*. Paris: Mercure de France, 1939.

Monneyron, Frédéric. "Esthéticisme et androgyne: Les fondements esthétiques de l'androgyne décadent." *L'Androgyne* in *Cahiers de l'herméticisme*, pp. 213–27.

Moreland, John. "Age and Change in the Adult Male Sex-Role." *Sex Roles* 6, no. 6 (1980). Reprinted in Kimmel and Messner, eds., *Men's Lives*, pp. 115–24.

Morin, Stephen F. and Ellen M. Garfinkle. "Male Homophobia." *Journal of Social Issues* 34, no. 1 (1978): 29–47

Morin, Stephen F. and Lonnie Nungesser. "Can Homophobia Be Cured?" In Lewis, ed., *Men in Difficult Times*, pp. 274–94.

Muccheille, Axex. *L'Identité*. Paris: PUF, 1986.

Munder-Ross, John. "Beyond the Phallic Illusion." In Fogel, ed., *The Psychology of Men*.

——. "Fathering: A Review of Some Psychoanalytic Contributions on Paternity." *International Journal of Psychoanalysis* 60 (1979): 317–26.

——. "The Riddle of Little Hans." In Cath, Gurwitt, and Gunsberg, eds., *Fathers and Their Families*, pp. 267–83.

——. "Towards Fatherhood: The Epigenesis of Paternal Identity During a Boy's First Decade." *International Review of Psychoanalysis* 4 (1977): 327–47.

Munroe, Robert and Ruth. "Psychological Interpretation of Male Initiation Rites: The Case of Male Pregnancy Symptoms." *Ethos* 1, no. 4 (Winter 1973): 490–98.

Nattiez, Jean-Jacques. *Wagner Androgyne*. Paris: Christian Bourgois, 1990.

Nungesser, Lonnie G. *Homosexual Acts: Actors and Identities*. New York: Praeger, 1983.

Nye, Robert A. "Sex Difference and Male Homosexuality in French Medical Discourse, 1830–1930." *Bulletin of the History of Medicine* 63 (1989): 32–51.

Olivier, Christiane. *Les Enfants de Jocaste*. Paris: Denoël-Gonthier, 1980.

——. "Pères empêchés." *Péres et fils* in *Autrement*, no. 61 (June 1984).

Osherson, Samuel. *Finding Our Fathers*. New York: Free Press, 1986.

Osherson, Samuel and Diana Dill. "Varying Work and Family Choices: Their Impact and Men's Work Satisfaction." *Journal of Marriage and the Family* (May 1983): 339–46.

Paul, Robert A. "Instinctive Aggression in Man: The Semai Case." *Journal of Psychological Anthropology* 1 (Winter 1978): 65–79.

Pawel, Ernest. *Franz Kafka; ou, Le cauchemar de la raison*. Paris: Seuil, 1988.

Pleck, Joseph H. "American Fatherhood: A Historical Perspective." *American Behavioral Scientist* 29, no. 1 (1985): 7–23.

——. "The Contemporary Man." In Kimmel and Messner, eds., *Men's Lives*.

——. "Man to Man: Is Brotherhood Possible?" In N. Glazer-Malbin, ed., *Old Family/New Family: Interpersonal Relationships*. New

York: Van Nostrand, 1975.

——. *The Myth of Masculinity*. Cambridge: MIT Press, 1981.

——. "Prisoners of Manliness." In Kimmel and Messner, eds., *Men's Lives*, pp. 129–38.

——, ed. "The Work-Family Role System." *Social Problems* 24 (April 1977): 417–27.

Pleck, Joseph H. and Elisabeth H. Pleck, eds. *The American Man*. Englewood Cliffs, N.J.: Prentice-Hall, 1980.

Pleck, Joseph H. and Janet Sayers, eds. *Men and Masculinity*. Englewood Cliffs, N.J.: Prentice-Hall, 1974.

Pleck, Joseph H. and Robert Brannon, eds. *Male Roles and the Male Experience*, a Special Issue of *Journal of Social Issues* 34, no. 1 (1978).

Plummer, Kenneth. *The Making of the Modern Homosexual*. London: Hutchinson, 1981.

Pollak, Michael. *Vienne, 1890*. Paris: Collective Archives, Gallimard-Julliard, 1984.

Pryor, Monique. *Tout ce qu'ils ont sur le coeur*. Paris: Robert Jauze, 1985.

Quiguer, Claude. *Femmes et machines de 1900: Lecture d'une obsession Modern Style*. Paris: Klincksieck, 1979.

Raphaël, Ray. *The Men from the Boys: Rites of Passage in Male America*. Lincoln: University of Nebraska Press, 1988.

Rapoport, Rhona and Robert N. with Siona Strelitz. *Fathers, Mothers and Society: Perspectives on Parenting*. New York: Vintage, 1980.

Raymond, Janice. *L'Empire transsexuel*. Paris: Seuil, 1981.

Research Group for Comparative Sociology, University of Helsinki. *Scandinavian Men and Women: A Welfare Comparison* (no. 28; 1980).

Reynaud, Emmanuel. *Les Femmes, la violence et l'armée*. Foundation pour les études de défense nationale, 1988.

——. *La Sainte virilité*. Paris: Syros, 1981.

Rich, Adrienne. "Compulsory Heterosexuality and Lesbian Existence." *Signs* 5 (Summer 1980): 631–60.

——. *Naître d'une femme*. Paris: Denoël-Gonthier, 1980.

——. *Of Woman Born*. New York: Norton, 1976.

Ricks, Shirley S. "Father-Infant Interactions: A Review of the Empirical Literature." *Family Relations* 34, no. 4 (October 1985): 505–11.

Risman, Barbara J. "Men Who Mother: Intimate Relationships from a Microstructural Perspective." *Gender and Society* 1, no. 1 (March 1987): 6–32.

Robinson, Bryan E. "Men Caring for the Young: An Androgynous Perspective." *Men's Roles in the Family* in *Family Coordinator*

(October 1979): 553–59.

Robinson, Bryan E. and Robert L. Barret. *The Developing Father.* New York: Guilford, 1986.

Rochlin, Gregory G. *The Masculine Dilemma.* Boston: Little, Brown, 1980.

Roiphe, Herman and Eleanor Galenson. *La Naissance de l'identité sexuelle.* Paris: PUF, 1987.

Ross, Hildy and Heather Taylor. "Do Boys Prefer Daddy or his Physical Style of Play?" *Sex Roles* 20, nos. 1–2 (1989): 23–33.

Rotundo, E. Anthony. "Boy Culture: Middle-Class Boyhood in Nineteenth-Century America." In Carnes and Griffen, eds., *Meanings for Manhood,* pp. 15–36.

——. "Patriarchs and Participants: A Historical Perspective on Fatherhood in the United States." In Kaufman, ed., *Beyond Patriarchy,* pp. 64–80.

Rousseau, Jean Jacques. *Emile* (1762). La Pléiade. Paris: Gallimard, 1969.

——. *Lettre à d'Alembert* (1758). Paris: Garnier-Flammarion, 1967.

Rubin, Lillian. *Intimate Strangers.* New York: Harper and Row, 1984. In French: *Des Etrangers intimes.* Paris: Robert Laffont, 1986.

Ruffié, Jacques. *Le Sexe et la mort.* Paris: Odile Jacob, 1986.

Sabo, Don. "Pigskin, Patriarchy and Pain." In Abbott, ed., *New Men, New Minds,* pp. 47–50.

Sanday, Peggy Reeves. *Female Power and Male Dominance.* New York: Cambridge University Press, 1981.

——. "Rape and the Silencing of the Feminine." In Tanaselli and Porter, eds., *Rape.* Oxford: Blackwell, 1986.

Sauer, Raymond J. "Absentee Father Syndrome." *Family Coordinator* (April 1979): 249–54.

Sayers, Janet. *Sexual Contradictions.* London: Tavistock, 1986.

Scott, Joan. "Genre: Une catégorie d'analyse historique." *Cahiers du Grig,* nos. 37–38 (Spring 1988): 125–53.

Scott, Joan and Mary Poovcy. "Feminism and Deconstruction." *Feminist Studies,* no. 14 (1988): 33–66.

Seavey, C. A., P. A. Katz, and S. R. Zalk. "Baby X: The Effect of Gender Labels on Adult Responses to Infants." *Sex Roles* 1 (1975): 103–10.

Sebbar, Leïla. *Le Pédophile et la maman.* Paris: Stock, 1980.

Segal, Lynne. *Slow Motion: Changing Masculinities, Changing Men.* London: Virago, 1990; New Brunswick, N.J.: Rutgers University Press, 1990.

Sergent, Bernard. *L'Homosexualité initiatique dans l'Europe ancienne.* Paris: Payot, 1986.

Sherrod, Drury. "The Bonds of Men: Problems and Possibilities in Close Male Relationships." In Brod., ed., *The Making of Masculinities*, pp. 213–39.

Sidel, Ruth. "But Where Are the Men?" In Kimmel and Messner, eds., *Men's Lives*, pp. 530–40.

Siderowicz, Laura S. and Lunney G. Sparks. "Baby X Revisited." *Sex Roles* 6, no. 1 (1980): 67–73.

Simoneau, Jean-Paul, ed. *Répertoire de la condition masculine*. Québec: Editions Saint-Martin, 1988.

Sipriot, Pierre. *Monntherlant sans masque*. Paris: Robert Laffont, 1990.

Sorensen, Thorkil and Preben Hertoft. "Male and Female Transsexualism: The Danish Experience with Thirty-seven Patients." *Archives of Sexual Behavior* 11, no. 2 (1982): 133–55.

Statistisk Arbok. Copenhagen: Norvège, 1990.

Stearns, Peter N. *Be a Man! Males in Modern Society*. 2d ed. New York: Holmes and Meier, 1990.

Stein, Peter J. and Steven Hoffman. "Sport and Male Role Strain." *Journal of Social Issues* 34, no. 1 (1978): 136–50.

Steinem, Gloria. "The Myth of the Masculine Mystique." In Pleck and Sayers, eds., *Men and Masculinity*, pp. 134–39.

Stoller, Robert. "The Bedrock of Masculinity and Femininity: Bisexuality." *Archives of General Psychiatry* 26 (March 1972): 207–12.

——. "Création d'une illusion: L'extrême fémininité chex les garçons." *Nouvelle revue de psychanalyse*, no. 4 (Fall 1971): 55–72.

——. "Faits et hypothèses: Un examen du concept freudien de bisexualité." *Nouvelle revue de psychanalyse*, no. 7 (Spring 1973): 135–55.

——. "Fémininité primaire." In *L'Excitation sexuelle*, pp. 59–82. Paris: Payot, 1984.

——. *Masculin ou féminin?* Paris: PUF, 1989.

——. *Recherches sur l'identité sexuelle*. Paris: Gallimard, 1978.

——. *Sex and Gender*. Vol. 2, *The Transsexual Experiment*. London: Hogarth Press, 1975.

——. "Transvestism in Women." *Archives of Sexual Behavior* 11, no. 2 (1989): 99–115.

Stoller, Robert and Gilbert H. Herdt. "The Development of Masculinity: A Cross-Cultural Contribution." *Journal of the American Psychoanalytic Association* 30 (1982): 29–59. Translated into French in Stoller, *Masculin ou féminin?* pp. 307–38.

Stoltenberg, John. "Other Men." In Abbott, ed., *New Men, New Minds*, pp. 122–29.

——. *Refusing to Be a Man*. Bloomington, Ill.: Meridian, 1990.

Tap, Pierre. *Masculin et féminin chez l'enfant*. Toulouse: Privat-Edisem, 1985.

Tavris, Carol. "Men and Women Report Their Views on Masculinity." *Psychology Today* (January 1977).

———. "Woman and Man." *Psychology Today* (March 1972).

Theweleit, Klaus. *Male Fantasies*. Vol. 1, *Women, Flood, Bodies, History*. Translated by Stephen Carway. Minneapolis: University of Minnesota Press, 1990.

Thomas, Chantal. *Thomas Bernhard*. Paris: Seuil, 1990.

Thompson, Cooper. "A New Vision of Masculinity." In Kimmel and Messner, eds., *Men's Lives*.

Thorne, Barry. "Girls and Boys Together . . . but Mostly Apart." In Kimmel and Messner, eds., *Men's Lives*, pp. 138–53.

Thuillier, Pierre. "L'homosexualité devant la psychiatrie." *La Sexualité* in *La Recherche* 20, no. 213 (September 1989): 1128–39.

Tiefer, Leonore. "In Pursuit of the Perfect Penis: The Medicalization of Male Sexuality." *American Behavioral Scientist* 29, no. 5 (June 1986): 579–99; reprinted in Kimmel, ed., *Changing Men*, pp. 165–84.

Tiger, Lionel. *Men in Groups*. New York: Random House, 1969.

Treadwell, Perry. "Biological Influences on Masculinity." In Brod., ed., *The Making of Masculinities*, pp. 259–85.

Types-paroles d'hommes: A propos des femmes, no. 5 (1983).

Types-paroles d'hommes: Masculin pluriel, no. 4 (May 1982).

Types-paroles d'hommes: Numéro mixte, no. 6 (1984).

Types-paroles d'hommes: Paternité, no. 1 (January 1981).

Types-paroles d'hommes: Plaisirs, nos. 2–3 (May 1981).

Tyson, Phyllis. "A Developmental Line of Gender Identity, Gender Role, and Choice of Love Object." *Journal of the American Psychoanalytic Association*, no. 30 (1982): 61–86.

Vidal-Naquet, Pierre. *Le Chasseur noir*. Paris: La Découverte-Maspero, 1983.

Vigier, Bernard and Jean-Yves Picard. "L'AMH: Hormone clé de la différenciation sexuelle?" *L'un et autre sexe* in *Science et vie*, no. 171 (June 1990): 22–31.

Walczak, Yvette. *He and She: Men in the Eighties*. New York: Routledge, 1988.

Weeks, Jeffrey. "Questions of Identity." In Caplan, ed., *The Cultural Construction of Sexuality*, pp. 31–51.

———. *Sex, Politics and Society*. 2d ed. London and New York: Longman Group, 1989.

———. *Sexuality and Its Discontents* (1985). London: Routledge and Kegan Paul, 1989.

Weininger, Otto. *Sexe et caractère* (1903). Translated from the German by Daniel Renaud, with a preface by Roland Jaccard. Paris: Editions L'Age d'Homme, 1989.

Whitam, Frederick L. "Culturally Invariable Properties of Male Homosexuality: Tentative Conclusions from Cross-Cultural Research." *Archives of Sexual Behavior* 12, no. 3 (1983): 207–26.

Wilson, Edward O. *On Human Nature.* Cambridge: Harvard University Press, 1978.

——. *Sociobiology: The New Synthesis.* Cambridge: Harvard University Press, 1975.

Winkler, John J. *The Constraints of Desire.* New York: Routledge, 1990.

Winnicott, D. W. *De la Pédiatrie à la psychanalyse.* Paris: Payot, 1978.

——. *L'Enfant et sa famille.* Paris: Payot, 1973.

——. *Processus de maturation chez l'enfant.* Paris: Payot, 1989.

——. *Women's Studies and Research on Women: Sex, Gender and Transvestism.* New Brunswick, N.J.: Rutgers University Press, 1989.

Yogman, Michaël. "La Présence du père." *Objectif Bébé* in *Autrement*, no. 72 (September 1985): 140–49.

——. "Observations on the Father-Infant Relationship." In Cath, Gurwitt, and Ross, eds., *Father and Child*, pp. 101–22.

Yorburg, Betty. *Sexual Identity: Sex Roles and Social Change.* New York: Wiley, 1974.

Yudkin, Marcia. "Transsexualism and Women: A Critical Perspective." *Feminist Studies* 4, no. 3 (October 1978): 97–106.

Zucker, K. J. "Cross-Gender Identified Children." In B. W. Steiner, ed., *Gender Disphonia: Development, Research, Management.* New York: Plenum, 1985.

Zuger, Bernard. "Early Effeminate Behavior in Boys: Outcome and Significance for Homosexuality." *Journal of Nervous and Mental Disease* 172, no. 2 (February 1984): 90–97.

INDEX OF NAMES CITED

INDEX OF NAMES CITED